Inventing the New

Historical Materialism Book Series

The Historical Materialism Book Series is a major publishing initiative of the radical left. The capitalist crisis of the twenty-first century has been met by a resurgence of interest in critical Marxist theory. At the same time, the publishing institutions committed to Marxism have contracted markedly since the high point of the 1970s. The Historical Materialism Book Series is dedicated to addressing this situation by making available important works of Marxist theory. The aim of the series is to publish important theoretical contributions as the basis for vigorous intellectual debate and exchange on the left.

The peer-reviewed series publishes original monographs, translated texts, and reprints of classics across the bounds of academic disciplinary agendas and across the divisions of the left. The series is particularly concerned to encourage the internationalization of Marxist debate and aims to translate significant studies from beyond the English-speaking world.

For a full list of titles in the Historical Materialism Book Series available in paperback from Haymarket Books, visit: www.haymarketbooks.org/ series_collections/1-historical-materialism.

Inventing the New

History and Politics in Jean-Paul Sartre

Luca Basso

Translated by
Dave Mesing

Haymarket Books
Chicago, IL

First published in 2023 by Brill Academic Publishers, The Netherlands
© 2023 Koninklijke Brill NV, Leiden, The Netherlands

Published in paperback in 2024 by
Haymarket Books
P.O. Box 180165
Chicago, IL 60618
773-583-7884
www.haymarketbooks.org

ISBN: 979-8-88890-332-2

Distributed to the trade in the US through Consortium Book Sales and
Distribution (www.cbsd.com) and internationally through Ingram
Publisher Services International (www.ingramcontent.com).

This book was published with the generous support of Lannan
Foundation, Wallace Action Fund, and the Marguerite Casey Foundation.

Special discounts are available for bulk purchases by organizations and
institutions. Please call 773-583-7884 or email info@haymarketbooks.org
for more information.

Cover art and design by David Mabb. Cover art is a detail of *Construct
72, after Kathleen Kersey (for Morris & Co.) Arbutus / Liubov Popova, textile
design 1923–24*, acrylic on wallpaper (2023).
Printed in the United States.

Library of Congress Cataloging-in-Publication data is available.

To Marine *in memoriam*

∵

Contents

Introduction

We know there is only one value for art, and even for truth: the 'first-hand,' the authentic newness of something said, and the 'unheard music' with which it is said. That's what Sartre was for us (for us twenty-year-olds during the Liberation). In those days, who except Sartre knew how to say anything new? Who taught us new ways to think? As brilliant and profound as the work of Merleau-Ponty was, it was professorial and depended in many respects on Sartre's work ... The new themes, a particular new style, a new and aggressive way of posing problems – these came from Sartre. In the disorder and hope of the Liberation, we discovered, we re-discovered everything: Kafka and the American novel, Husserl and Heidegger, incessant renegotiations with Marxism, enthusiasm for a *nouveau roman* ... It was all channeled through Sartre, not only because he was a philosopher and had a genius for totalization, but because he knew how to invent something new [*inventer le nouveau*].

GILLES DELEUZE, 'He Was my Teacher'

• • •

[N]egation is not pure destruction of some determination but a moment subordinated to the free production of a new [*nouveau*] *whole*. It is not the pure destruction of the marble through negation of its given form that will yield the statue ... The essential moment therefore is that of creation, that is, the moment of the imaginary, of invention [*invention*].

JEAN-PAUL SARTRE, *Notebooks for an Ethics*

• • •

[I]n certain circumstances, a group emerges 'hot' [*à chaud*] and acts where previously there were only gatherings and, through this ephemeral, superficial formation, everyone glimpses new, deeper, but yet to be created statutes [*statuts nouveaux*] (the Third Estate as a group from the standpoint of the nation, the class as a group in so far as it produces its apparatuses of unification, etc.) ... what is important is that this form constitutes itself in reality at certain moments of the historical experience and that it then forms itself as new [*neuve*]

... After the storming of the Bastille, Paris could never again be the
Paris of June 1789. New organisations [*nouvelles organisations*] arose
on the ruins of the old ... Joseph Le Bon ... said, from his prison, after
Thermidor, that no one – not even himself – could really understand
or judge events and actions which had occurred at *an other speed*.

JEAN-PAUL SARTRE, *Critique of Dialectical Reason*

∴

'Sartre knew how to invent something new', Gilles Deleuze writes in homage to
Sartre, whom he indicates, in a brief 1964 text, as his teacher, a claim that perhaps seems surprising.[1] *Inventing the New*, which provides the title for this book,
can be interpreted via a double reading, one relative to the overall representation of the philosopher in question, and the other concerning the nucleus of
the specific content of Sartre's political thought. Indeed, regarding the former,
Deleuze's point would seem to move completely against the grain of Sartre's
image in recent decades. Too often, as compared with an earlier, uncritical exaltation of Sartre, at least within a certain *milieu gauchiste*, what has followed
(which is also true for structuralism and so-called poststructuralism in its various senses) is an equally simplistic criticism and a substantial oblivion, as well
as a too rigid contrast between different figures within the French scene.

This book is not designed for the sake of provocation, to sustain the struc-
turalistic and antihumanistic character of Sartre's work, but rather to show that
determinate oppositions (such as that between humanism and antihumanism), which found their own *ratio existendi* in the 1960s and 1970s (as well as
in relation to a positioning both with respect to Marx and his internal trajectory and with respect to the political conjuncture), if hypostatised today, risk
leading into a *cul de sac*. It is not a matter of establishing a sort of posthum-
ous harmony among philosophers who polemicised with one another, such
as, for example, Sartre on one side and Althusser and Foucault on the other.
Neither is it a matter, with respect to a certain poststructuralist 'style', of counterposing, in equally acritical terms, the Sartrean approach to such a harmony.
Instead it must be kept in mind that, despite solutions which were radically
different in several cases, the philosophers working in the French context had
a field of problems that was in many ways common. And the very representa-

---

1   Deleuze 2004, p. 77.

tion of a subjectivist Sartre requires problematisation, above all if we examine the post-World War II situation. Such observations do not lead us to deny that there are problems present within the Sartrean horizon, from a theoretical as well as political perspective: the proof of this is that the second part of the *Critique of Dialectical Reason*, Sartre's most important political-philosophical work, remained incomplete and presents an unfinished character. Furthermore, his own function as an engaged intellectual, at times a bit 'priestly', led him in several cases to make choices, and to activate dialogues, which leave many doubts. The scope of this book thus does not consist in providing a resolved image, free of contradictions, but rather in highlighting the presence of the considerable and innovative elements of Sartre's political thought. From this perspective, a 'complexified' interpretation should also emerge here, but what should stand out here is not the old dialectical, historicist, and perhaps essentialist philosopher, but the fruitful tendencies which followed from his work.

The second variation of *Inventing the New* connects not to the role Sartre's philosophy plays, but rather to one of the most important political-theoretical nuclei in his work. At the centre of this discourse is the dynamic of revolution, in its capacity of questioning consolidated and apparently unmovable orders, through the destabilising *praxis* of the fused group. But this emphasis does not imply an undervaluation of the shadow areas, of the permanence of elements of seriality in a scenario not without chiaroscuro. In this direction, the book also includes writings which predate 1945, above all *Being and Nothingness*. Nevertheless, Sartre's postwar writings (primarily the period running from the early 1950s to the early 1970s) play the most prominent role. As he himself admitted, these works mark his strongest interest in history and politics. Without any ambition of exhaustiveness and by trying to make the various texts 'rotate' around the theoretical centre of gravity in the book, I have only made cursory reference to an important work of the latter period, *The Family Idiot*.

The red thread of the book is constructed through the relation between singularity, both of the subject and the political event with respect to one comprehensive schema, and the universality of history, on the basis of an attempt to grasp the meaning of the latter starting from the reference to *praxis*. This is not carried out by adopting a linear approach, but rather by moving in a spiral, in which what comes to be negated constantly comes to be reprised: it is a matter of an open relation, in which a complete synthesis is never reached. The first part of the book investigates the problem by beginning with what Sartre sees as the decisive moments of modernity, from a critical but also constitutive reference to Descartes on the freedom of the subject, passing through the eighteenth century, particularly Rousseau, and the epochal event of the French

Revolution, before finally arriving at Sartre's interaction (better understood with the passage of time) with Marx and Marxism, which is simultaneously marked by a criticism of certain of its limits and an attempt at its 'relaunching'. Moreover, the legacies of the French Revolution – and its slogans *liberté, egalité, fraternité* – are crucial along the path Sartre forged. One particularly open question, and even possible internal tension, concerns the relation between Sartre's strong valorisation of freedom starting with his earliest texts, on the one hand, and the key role fraternity plays in the *Critique of Dialectical Reason* for the fusional dimension of the acting in common of the group, on the other.

In the second part of the book, by developing the question of group institutionalisation, this problem is treated by starting from an analysis of 'the short twentieth century', and above all the Soviet Union as an incarnation of Marxism, which however also constitutes a deviation, or even a 'monster', in its ambivalent status with respect to the traditional Marxist schema. According to Sartre, transplanting Marxism in Russia meant establishing a particular incarnation, on the basis of an element of totalisation (which however is never a totality or fully accomplished outcome), with its double-face of unification and dispersion. Every *praxis* constitutes a totalisation insofar as it is configured as an overcoming in view of an end; such totalisation presents an ambiguous and never perfectly transparent character. However it may be, the serialisation underlying such a *praxis*-project also constitutes a disciplining of the propulsive force of the fused group. While many historical inquiries into the Soviet Union have taken place, Sartre's is perhaps the most extensive philosophical treatment, which has the merit of formulating a critique from a varied and complex perspective, characterised by a sort of historical prudence, irreducible to a simplistic reading of the situation following the Bolshevik Revolution. The critical approach, particularly after 1956, towards the Soviet Union, together with interest in the Cuban situation, and the ever-growing importance of anti-colonial struggles and a series of new experiences which will find their condensation in 1968, push Sartre to an always-increasing complexification of his political thought.

The stakes consist in grasping the relevance of the relation between the emancipative potentiality of subjects (on the basis of a sort of phenomenology of groups) and the overall historical horizon. Sartre's expression 'singular universal', in its apparently oxymoronic character, attempts to interpret this question by articulating a strict but also unstable relation between history and politics. What results is a representation that is anything but immediately subjectivist, since the subjects are 'quasi-objects' insofar as they are agents of events, and both the objectivity of the practico-inert and the collective, even with its reified character, constitute unavoidable elements. The attempt lies in rethinking subjectivation beyond the 'individual–collective' dualism, and in politically articulating the discourse by avoiding the risk, which is however partially present in Sartre, of a movementist distrust of any form of organisation. In this way what proves to be crucial (if arduous) is the problem of how to make the revolution last, of how to render its achievements effective, in such a way that the needs and capacities of subjects can be 'sedimented' in daily practices and institutional dynamics.

PART 1

Sartre: From Descartes to Marx

∵

The Invention Of Human Freedom: Descartes Beyond Descartes

1   Anthropology

The question of anthropology, with its simultaneously theoretical and political significance, provides an access point for understanding some of the distinctive characteristics of Sartre's work, particularly in the *Critique of Dialectical Reason*. On the one hand, Sartre insists over the course of his work on the centrality of anthropology as well as the fecundity of an encounter between philosophy and the human sciences. On the other hand, he outlines a perspective different to the various structuralist positions, however internally diversified they are. It is not by chance that Sartre is the target of severe criticism on the part of Lévi-Strauss:

> He who begins by steeping himself in the allegedly self-evident truths of introspection never emerges from them. Knowledge of men sometimes seems easier to those who allow themselves to be caught up in the snare of personal identity. But they thus shut the door on knowledge of man: written or unavowed 'confessions' form the basis of all ethnographic research. Sartre in fact becomes the prisoner of his Cogito: Descartes made it possible to attain universality, but conditionally on remaining psychological and individual; by sociologizing the Cogito, Sartre merely exchanges one prison for another.[1]

Here in the chapter 'History and Dialectic' in *The Savage Mind*, dedicated to refuting Sartre's approach in the *Critique of Dialectical Reason*, Lévi-Strauss polemicises with Sartre because of the relevance he attributes to consciousness. With respect to the Cartesian *cogito*, an 'individualistic' matrix, Sartre would sketch a sort of social *cogito*, limiting and dislocating the problem rather than resolving it. He thus remains within the 'prison' of personal identity, which Lévi-Strauss poses in strongly critical terms, invoking the priority of structures. As I will demonstrate in the following analysis, however, beyond the fact that

---

1   Lévi-Strauss 1966, p. 249.

Sartre himself indicates, at least in part, his debt to Descartes, Lévi-Strauss offers a reductive reading which is unable to grasp several key elements of Sartre's argument.

Althusser in turn sketches a 'theoretical antihumanism', and in doing so reserves some harsh references for Sartre and his humanism. He questions any form of anthropology, which he views as inevitably 'ideological':

> It is impossible to *know* anything about men except on the absolute pre-condition that the philosophical (theoretical) myth of man is reduced to ashes. So any thought that appeals to Marx for any kind of restoration of a theoretical anthropology or humanism is no more than ashes, *theoretically*. But in practice it could pile up a monument of pre-Marxist ideology that would weigh down on real history and threaten to lead it into blind alleys.[2]

For Althusser, Sartre embraces this 'philosophical myth of man', as he counts him polemically among the 'philosophers of consciousness (Politzer, Sartre, Merleau-Ponty)'.[3] Whether the aim is to completely get rid of anthropology (as in Althusser's case, as well as Foucault's)[4] or to understand it without starting from the *cogito* (as in Lévi-Strauss's case), one of the most immediate polemical references is to Sartre.

An interview with Sartre entitled 'Anthropology' contains a rather strict distinction between a 'philosophical' anthropology and anthropology as science:

> I maintain that the philosophical field is man [*homme*] himself ... But what does it mean that anthropology forcefully coincides with philosophy? ... [T]he man of anthropology is object, the man of philosophy is object-subject [*objet-sujet*].[5]

---

2 Althusser 2005, p. 196.

3 Althusser 2003, p. 54. On the relationship between the conceptions of Sartre and Althusser, see Rademacher 2002; Gaudeaux 2006, pp. 349–74: 'The difference between the Althusserian *intervention* and the Sartrean *commitment* resides in the "point-like" conception of will in the former, which is entirely unrelated to the continuity, linked to a projectual dimension, of the other' (p. 363); Silbertin-Blanc 2009; Basso 2017. More generally, see Poster 1975, especially pp. 340–60.

4 On Sartre and Foucault, see among others Richter 2011. For an overall account of Sartre's reception in structuralism and post-structuralism, see Weismüller 2004, pp. 365–406.

5 Sartre 1972b, pp. 83–4.

'The philosophical question is thus first and foremost: how to pass from quasi-object to subject-object'.[6] Insofar as it is philosophy, anthropology considers man in this way as the object of inquiry, but also as subject, not depriving him of the dimension of subjectivity – and thus of the possibility to change the present situation – even as it continues to recognise the existence of a series of 'objective' conditions.

Conversely, according to Sartre, anthropology as science examines man as an object, not grasping human subjectivity. On this front Sartre explicitly and critically references structuralism, which results in a domination of structures over man.[7] Maintaining this position does not mean, however, claiming that Sartrean anthropology is entirely antithetical to the development, however variegated, of so-called structuralism. Too often among the philosophers in question these operate as absolute oppositions, thereby stiffening categories such as humanism and antihumanism:

> As concerns the unconscious structure of language, we must admit that the presence of certain structures of language accounts for the unconscious. For me, Lacan has clarified the unconscious [*incoscient*] as a discourse that separates through language, or as the counter-purpose of speech, if you prefer to say it this way ... With that said – and to the extent that I agree with Lacan – it is necessary to conceptualise intentionality [*intentionnalité*] as fundamental. There is no mental process that is not intentional, but neither is there a mental process that is not entangled, deviated, betrayed by language.[8]

In this sense, Sartre's relation with Lacan must not be examined according to an idea of the total extraneity between their respective works. Despite appearances, there exist in Sartre points of contact with Lacan's theory of the unconscious as an authorless linguistic structure in which the subject is inserted without possessing a foundational character of discourse. The problematic of the 'barred subject' is also common to both: we are 'spoken' by language, rather than it being us who speaks language. In Sartre as well, subjectivity is articu-

---

6 Sartre 1972b, p. 88.
7 Sartre 1972b, pp. 86–7.
8 Sartre 1972b, p. 97. For a complex and eloquent interpretation of the relation between Lacan and Sartre, aimed at bringing out the relevance of this relation without 'squashing' one figure into the other, see Leguil 2012, p. 18: 'It is certainly not a question of comparing Lacan and Sartre by trying to make the philosopher of freedom a precursor to Lacan, nor Lacan a disciple of Sartre'. Sara Vassallo (2003) instead attempts to establish a Lacanian reading of Sartre.

lated on the basis of a critical perspective that confronts the Cartesian centrality of the I-consciousness. But there are also a number of dissenting points with
Lacan: for example, in Sartre language does not only carry a 'formal' function,
but also a practical, social function.

It is also necessary, however, to emphasise that several aspects of Sartre's
work recall Descartes, through the fundamental mediation of phenomenology,
in the early texts, but also in the postwar writings. In particular, the element
of consciousness as consciousness of something is crucial, and is based on a
strong valorisation of the dimension of intentionality in the Husserlian matrix. In any case, the thematic of anthropology has a key function for Sartre,
which surely outlines a different perspective from Lévi-Strauss's structuralism and Althusser's Marxism with structuralist veins. The question must be
interpreted on the basis of an extreme articulation of connections and references, insofar as one is not faced with a *sic et simpliciter* usage of philosophy
against the human sciences. After all, various parts of psychology, psychoanalysis (including Lacanian psychoanalysis) and anthropology as science all play
a significant role in Sartre's work. The most relevant aspect of the argument,
with its philosophical matrix, consists however in the attempt to grasp together
the objective and subjective dimension of anthropology, rather than only the
objective.

2   A Philosophy of Freedom

Starting with his earliest works on the imagination, and then more consistently
with *The Transcendence of the Ego* and still further in *Being and Nothingness*,
Sartre emphasises the centrality of man and his freedom. In these texts we find
a complex series of references and an intense confrontation with Descartes,
Hegel's *Phenomenology of Spirit*, Husserlian phenomenology and Heideggerian
philosophy. In particular, *Being and Nothingness* is presented as a constant *Auseinandersetzung* with *Being and Time*.[9] Already in *The Transcendence of the
Ego*, his traversal of Husserl had not pushed Sartre to grasp the centrality of the
I, but rather of consciousness insofar as it is an absolute and creative element,
equipped with a spontaneous character.[10] In that text, however, there is not yet

---

9   See Renaut 1993 who, with an entirely different perspective than the one I articulate here,
       inserts Sartre into the 'Heidegger generation' (pp. 27–70), while noting that 'by looking
       for the conditions to rescue the subject, Sartre oriented phenomenology in a direction
       diametrically opposed to what Heidegger wanted to give to it'.
10   Sartre 2004b, pp. 19–20. Cf. Moravia 2004, pp. 32–3.

a genuine theorisation of freedom. Instead, the reference to spontaneity plays a key role. Only in the years that follow will Sartre work out a strict connection between spontaneity and freedom. At the heart of the argument is a consciousness that is not solipsistic, but in relation with the world, and distinguished from intentionality. Surely in this regard Husserl's contribution is decisive, but with a distance taken from the 'solipsistic' risk of Husserl's thinking, which also plays an important function for Heidegger's 'being in the world'.

The influences and themes Sartre outlines there find their condensation in *Being and Nothingness*: it is enough to think of the element of consciousness (for itself) insofar as it is a transcendence of the phenomenon (in itself), and insofar as it is nothing, negation. In order to be that through which the nothing comes into the world, man must be free, but with the anxiety that derives from this freedom. Indeed, man tends to transcend himself, but such transcendence is the source of anxiety: 'To be free is to be condemned to be free'.[11] This dynamic of affirmation and negation, which consists in the fact that man tends towards presence but is instead absence, and therefore is at once affirmed and negated, can recall Camus's Sisyphus. Man is confronted with an incompleteness, with a lack of basis for support. The comparison with Dostoyevsky is intense in this regard, particularly the figure of Ivan Karamazov, who is a genuine point of departure for existentialism, as will emerge in *Existentialism is a Humanism*.[12] This state of things shows man in a position of both weakness and strength, since he can only count on himself – it is the atheist dimension of Sartrean existentialism. In this way, values do not exist objectively but rather are rooted in the single individual. Such a conception, however, does not have a static character, since man does not remain identical to himself, but is continuously open to change.

However, *Being and Nothingness* (which was to have a discussion of morality that in the end was not included in the text)[13] presents a final, much broader

---

11   Sartre 1992a, p. 129. On freedom, see: Philonenko 1981; Simont 1998, who emphasises the centrality of freedom, which however is not 'born in a virgin world, but one that is already split' (p. 116); Guigot 2007; Webber 2009, pp. 59–73. On the link between freedom and passion, see: Mészàros 1979, pp. 158–243. On the relation between freedom and necessity, see Howells 1988.

12   'Dostoyevsky once wrote: "if God does not exist, everything is permitted". This is the starting point of existentialism. Indeed, everything is permissible if God does not exist, and man is consequently abandoned, for he cannot find anything to rely on – neither within nor without'. Sartre 2007, pp. 28–9.

13   On the importance of the moral element of Sartre (which I will return to later on), see among others, Jeanson 1947; Münster 2007, particularly pp. 8–10; Scanzio 2000. Also, see the reformulation in Gorz 1977.

part, dedicated specifically to freedom, which further testifies to the enormous importance of the question. According to Sartre, man reveals himself to be constitutively free, never being fully 'crushed', or determined from the outside or even the inside.

> Descartes following the Stoics has given a name to this possibility which human reality has to secrete a nothingness which isolates it – it is *freedom* ... [F]reedom is not a faculty of the human soul to be envisaged and described in isolation ... Thus freedom as the requisite condition for the nihilation of nothingness is not a property which belongs among others to the essence of the human being.[14]

Here the Stoic matrix of this conception is highlighted, prior to the Cartesian, which makes freedom the key element of the entire reflection: 'The free project is fundamental, for it is my being'.[15] Freedom appears strongly connected to the dimension of choice, in contrast to necessity: Sartre holds further that there is a risk of 'necessitarianism' in Leibniz's contrasting vision of freedom.[16]

Concerning the latter notion, the reference to the project is crucial – to the 'possible', the transcendence of the 'present state of things', in the tension towards a 'beyond' with respect to this state. Such a horizon reveals an emancipatory potential, but also a series of internal limits. Indeed, action belongs to a free, not a necessary subject: the free man, as 'for itself', constitutes a nothing with respect to a world that appears incomprehensible. This perspective would seem to put any transformative hypotheses in crisis, since according to such hypotheses there arises a substantial solitude of man as the prey of anxiety.[17] However, man takes the form of a useless passion: the very thematic of passion is pervaded by the element of the absurd. Concerning the latter, the confront-

---

14 Sartre 1992a, pp. 24–5.
15 Sartre 1992a, p. 479.
16 Sartre 1992a, p. 469.
17 Cf. Murdoch 1987. Murdoch emphasises the centrality of the individual in Sartre, but also its profound isolation. In her view freedom is configured as chance, and the subject, pressed between what is morally unacceptable and what is impossible, can do nothing but rebel: it would thus be a matter of an act aiming at failure. From a much different perspective (which does not make any reference, even in a marginal way, to the *Critique of Dialectical Reason*) than the one I adopt here, Murdoch maintains that the hypothesis of a social and political articulation of Sartre's work is extremely problematic.

ation with Camus's *The Stranger*, with which Sartre is simultaneously critical and in harmony, is intense: 'since man's dominant characteristic is "being-in-the-world" the absurd is, in the end, an inseparable part of the human condition'.[18] *Being and Nothingness* concludes precisely with an articulation of this position:

> Every human reality is a passion in that it projects losing itself so as to found being and by the same stroke to constitute the In-itself which escapes contingency by being its own foundation, the *Ens causa sui*, which religions call God. Thus the passion of man is the reverse of that of Christ, for man loses himself as man in order that God may be born. But the idea of God is contradictory and we lose ourselves in vain. Man is a useless passion.[19]

Man's freedom, 'a useless passion', can be understood even more clearly if we examine Sartre's literary works – his novels, short stories, and plays. Throughout the book I concentrate on Sartre's works that are, so to speak, 'philosophical' in a narrow sense, but it cannot be forgotten that Sartre was at the same time a philosopher, writer, playwright, and literary critic. If the texts of literary criticism (one thinks, for example, of *What is Literature?*) are arranged clearly in a theoretical outline, the literary writings also present an immediate philosophical significance, for better and for worse (in the latter case, due to their rather didactic character), since the protagonists express theses embodying definite positions. These are 'situation novels', populated by consciousnesses that are partly lucid and partly obscure. In particular, *Nausea* in some ways constitutes the literary *pendant*, so to speak, of *Being and Nothingness*: the two texts can be interpreted together. From *Nausea*, with its protagonist Roquentin, there emerges clearly the image of a man aware of the weight of his own existence. The very title of the text vividly expresses such a diagnosis of the human

---

18   Sartre 1955, p. 26. Regarding the concept of the absurd, see the critique in Haug 1976, particularly pp. xvi ff., according to which there is present an apologetic pessimism concerning the bourgeois scenario which in no way can be intertwined with Marxism. For reasons that will emerge over the course of this book, I find such an approach to be extremely reductive and rigid. Holz (1951) also criticises Sartre starting from Hegelian-Marxist premises. See also Schaff 1965, who, on the basis of a naively humanistic approach that cannot be shared, argues that the Sartrean attempt to politically valorise existentialism is inadequate. More recently, see Dahlmann 2013. For a comparison between Sartre and Camus from a different perspective than the one I take here, see Neudeck 1975.

19   Sartre 1992a, p. 615.

condition within the 'absurdity of the world'.[20] Man appears as distinguished from the dimension of contingency:

> The essential thing is contingency [*contingence*] ... To exist is simply *to be there*; those who exist let themselves be *encountered*, but you can never *deduce* anything from them ... All is free, this park, this city, and myself.[21]

It follows that the role of human existence is central: 'Existence [*existence*] everywhere, infinitely, in excess, for ever and everywhere; existence which is limited only by existence ... So many existences missed, obstinately begun again and again missed ... existence is a fullness which man can never abandon'.[22] The short stories in *The Wall* also echo such a position.

In a much less direct way, the theatrical works *The Flies*, a remake of Aeschylus's *The Libation Bearers*,[23] and *No Exit* fit into this same problematic. In particular, in *The Flies* Orestes embodies the drama of freedom, the freedom of to take revenge in an atrocious way, to such a degree that Sartre writes in an accompanying note:

> Finally he will have to kill, to take his crime on his back and pass to the other side of the river. Freedom, in fact, is not an abstract power of passing over the human condition: it is the most absurd and inexorable

---

20 Sartre 2013b, p. 130. Cf. Paci 1988, who, starting from an approach with a reciprocal interaction between phenomenology and existentialism, emphasises the 'nihilistic' character of Sartrean existentialism: 'Sartre, without knowing it, is the other face of Kant. If there is freedom every choice is made into nothing, and no choice has reason or a foundation; consequently, on the level of the finite every human act is negative' (p. 41); Rovatti 1969, pp. 95–6, according to whom *Nausea* is 'the mode of being of the alienation in the thing'; Jeanson 1947, who highlights the problematic character of existence within the ontology of freedom; Fergnani, pp. 19–61, esp. pp. 41–2, who polemicises with Jeanson's approach: the latter, understanding consciousness only as degraded consciousness, underestimates the critical scope in Sartre's notion of experience; Contat, 2009, pp. 39–62; O'Donohoe 2013; Cabestan 2015, pp. 95–153.

21 Sartre 2013b, p. 131.

22 Sartre 2013b, p. 133.

23 Sartre 1976a, pp. 47–124. On *The Flies*, see Vertraeten 1972, pp. 28–9: '[I]f *The Flies* are the expression of *Being and Nothingness*, these *can* perfectly "crystallise" the encounter with others ... However, in my view, *The Flies* go further than the properly philosophical problematic of alterity. Indeed, the war, as a material and cultural context in which this theatrical work is inscribed, forces a radicalisation of the problematic'; see also Carney 2007, pp. 92–101.

of endeavors. Orestes will advance on his own path, without justifications, without excuses, without delays, alone. As a hero.[24]

In outlining the problem of freedom, the war as well as the Resistance played a decisive function for Sartre, producing several significant changes, in particular an attribution of increasing significance to the historical and social dimension. From the writings examined so far there surely emerges a certain abstract character of analysis: we are faced with a sketch not so much of a human nature, but rather of a condition that contains the risk of an invariance. But the setting of *Being and Nothingness* is irreducible to such a static scenario, since the argument is placed into history, and particularly the capitalist order, as the relevance of the concept of alienation, with its clear Marxian, or rather Hegelo-Marxian, ancestry also testifies.

The concept of situation is crucial for grasping the non-abstractly ahistorical character of *Being and Nothingness*. It also allows us to further clarify the dimension of freedom. Man is free but 'in situation', understanding by this the set of elements that condition humans within a definite context.

> Since the situation is illuminated by ends which are themselves projected only in terms of the *being-there*, which they illuminate, it is presented as eminently *concrete* ... Just as the situation is neither objective or subjective, so it can be considered neither as the free result of a freedom not as the ensemble of the constraints to which I am subject; it stems from the illumination of the constraint by freedom which gives to it its meaning as constraint. Among brute existents there can be no connection; it is freedom which founds the connections by grouping the existents into instrumental-complexes; and it is freedom which projects the *reason* for the connections – that is, its end ... Thus freedom enchains itself in the world as a free project toward ends. The For-itself is a temporalization. This means that it is not but that it 'makes itself'.[25]

The situation embodies the (albeit unstable) connection point between individual, singular existence and the historical horizon in its universality. Such reference appears crucial and must be understood neither in a subjectivist nor an objectivist sense, but rather in relation to the key element of freedom and its link with the dynamic of the project: as will become clear later on, the sketch

---

24   The passage is recalled in Contat and Rybalka 1970, p. 88.
25   Sartre 1992a, pp. 550–1.

of the 'singular universal', in its apparently oxymoronic character, is inscribed within the *conatus* in question. Lévi-Strauss's critique, which we examined at the outset of the chapter, remains simplistic, since Sartre's position, even while it contains a series of limits and unresolved problems, is irreducible to a Cartesian subjectivism, and the element of the situation plays a decisive role in this regard. A literary and theoretical manifesto such as *What is Literature?* insists precisely on the 'in situation' character of literature. The strict link between freedom and situation emerges in this context: 'Being situated is an essential and necessary characteristic of freedom. To describe the situation is not to cast aspersions on freedom'.[26] In this way, the situation is not conceptualised in contrast to freedom, as if identified *sic et simpliciter* with objectivity, but instead remains connected to man's project, and therefore also to his freedom, although on the basis of a circumscription of its feasibility.

If we must draw up a balance sheet on Sartre's work until *Being and Nothingness*, it can surely be defined as a 'philosophy of freedom'. The notion of freedom, as project but also as the checkmate of man, can even be considered as the foundation of his entire thinking. In Sartre there exists the risk of arriving at a conception founded on a sort of absoluteness of individual freedom, with the possibility of choosing, but also with the anxiety that this choosing brings. From a political perspective, however, such a position does not contain a liberal character (rather, Sartre's criticism of liberalism was always firm). Despite the relevance of the notions 'we'[27] and 'relation',[28] Sartre seems to undervalue the impact of the external environment, of objectivity, of the conditions in which individuals find themselves working, and the 'disciplining' structures of society. Moreover, the reference to a collective dimension also turns out to not really be outlined: there is sometimes instead a sense that such a dimension is conceived as a summation of individuals with the full freedom of choice.

Such a position has lent support to numerous critics, obviously including those writing from a Catholic position for its atheistic character, but also from Marxists for the abstract and insufficiently social and historical articulation of this approach. However, it was Sartre himself who remarked that the war and the Resistance gave rise to an increasingly attentive consideration of the social and historical: this was not an expression of self-critique, but rather an attempt to recalibrate the discourse. After all, Sartre always held that his permanent

---

26   Sartre 1988, p. 133.
27   Sartre 1992a, pp. 246–7.
28   Sartre 1992a, pp. 361–2.

activity was 'thinking against himself'.[29] Sartre did not deny his 'philosophy of freedom' during the postwar period, then, but his thinking would take on an increasingly stronger political connotation, examining subjectivity not in an absolute way but in its relation with others. And yet, both *Being and Nothingness*, – above all in its final part – and *The Birds*, with the drama of Orestes, already contain a non-solipsistic idea of freedom.

3   Humanism and Intersubjectivity: Towards the *Critique of Dialectical Reason*

Emphasising the relevance of the experience of the war and the Resistance for the rearticulation of Sartre's discourse does not entail supposing that we are faced with two 'Sartres', one before the war and one after, between which there is a break. Rather, such emphasis helps demonstrate that Sartre's theoretical-political work in a strict sense substantially begins after World War II. From this point in my analysis forward, I will examine Sartre's postwar writings almost exclusively, with particular reference to the *Critique of Dialectical Reason*, while occasionally recalling these earlier texts.

> It is certain that there was a change in my notion of freedom. I always remained faithful to the notion of freedom, but I recognize the factors that can change the results with any individual ... I think, in conclusion, that the consciousness of being free, in 1940 or 1942, was the guarantee itself, the intuitive guarantee of freedom. Now, it seems to me that this fact certainly implied freedom, but it does not exhaust it, because true freedom is not grasped. It is, actually, an escape [*échappement*] to certain conditions of history, which is given in several cases, tat however cannot but be in a relation to certain circumstances ... [30] [In *Being and Nothingness*] I tried to give several general ideas on the existence of man, without taking into account the fact that this existence is always historically situated [*située*] and defined starting from this situation [*situation*] ... I always thought that morals existed. But this can only exist in concrete situations, therefore assumes man really engaged [*engagé*] in a world in order to then see what freedom becomes in this world.[31]

29   Beauvoir 1985.
30   Sartre 1977, pp. 75–6.
31   Sartre 1977, pp. 97–8.

In this way, it is not a matter of questioning the centrality of freedom, but rather showing, first, the objective, historical conditions to individual freedom, and second, the relationship with other individuals, the social dimension of the discourse.

The notion of freedom continually returns in Sartre's most important political text, the *Critique of Dialectical Reason*, but also in his writings that are not directly political, such as *La liberté cartésienne* (1946), for example. It seems necessary to recall the idea that the Stoics and Descartes comprise decisive sources for Sartre on freedom. However, the latter constitutes a genuine obsession for French philosophers. According to Sartre, Descartes represents the philosophy of freedom, which marks the French spirit and the origin of modern thought:

> Descartes, who is above all a metaphysician, takes things in the other direction: his originary experience is not that of freedom that creates 'ex nihilo', but first of all that of autonomous thought that with its own forces discovers intelligible relations among essences which already exist. It is for this reason that for us French people, who have lived Cartesian freedom for three centuries, implicitly understand by 'free will' the exercise of an independent *thought* rather than the production of a creative act; and that, in addition, our philosophers assimilate freedom to the act of judgment, as Alain does.[32]

Freedom emerges not in the sense of a creation from nothing, but as the autonomy of thought, as an act of judgment. Sartre insists on the character of 'invention'[33] in Descartes's method: we find in him 'a magnificent humanistic affirmation':[34]

> [F]reedom does not at all come from man insofar as he is, as a plenum, in a world without gaps [*lacune*], but on the contrary insofar as he is not, insofar as he is finite, limited ... Descartes sways without interruption between the identification of freedom with negativity or the negation of being – what would coincide with the freedom of indifference – and the conception of free will as simple negation of the negation. In a word, he failed to conceive negativity as productive.[35]

---

32 Sartre 1947, pp. 314–15.
33 Sartre 1947, pp. 320–1.
34 Sartre 1947, p. 321.
35 Sartre 1947, pp. 327–8.

Despite the limit that Sartre points out, thus attempting to call into question the theological substrate of his thinking, Descartes's contribution proves fundamental, and also contains political reflections which cannot be underestimated:

> Two centuries of crises will be necessary – crises of Faith, crises of Sciences – because man recovers the creative freedom that Descartes placed in God and because we finally came to suspect this truth, the essential basis of humanism: man is the being whose appearance makes a world exist. But we will not completely rebuke Descartes for giving to God what belongs to us, but rather admire him for laying the foundations of democracy in an authoritarian epoch, for following the implications of the idea of *autonomy* all the way through, and for having understood, well before the Heidegger of *Vom Wesen des Grundes* [English translation: *The Essence of Reasons* – TN] that the unique foundation of being is freedom.[36]

> A man cannot be more of a man than others, because freedom is infinite in each man in the same way. In this sense no one more than Descartes demonstrated the link between the spirit of science and the spirit of democracy, because universal suffrage can be established on nothing other than this universally shared faculty of saying 'no' and 'yes'.[37]

The attempt is to unhinge Descartes's theological framework, which presupposes (or at least tries to demonstrate) the existence of God, insofar as it is the foundation of the freedom of man. The practical destruction of the element of transcendence places responsibility entirely on man, with his force and his weakness, his capacities together with his 'nausea'. In a certain sense, Feuerbachian humanism, distinguished by a radical critique of teleology, could be reactivated here (*homo homini deus est*), but one that is deprived of every 'Promethianism'. If Descartes grasped the centrality of the man-freedom complex and interpreted freedom or autonomy above all as freedom of judgment, such a position concerns all individuals. In this way, there does not exist a man who is freer than others, insofar as everyone is endowed with freedom. The epistemological foundations of such a conception appear compatible with a democratic practice, such as that articulated by the French Revolution ('one

---

36   Sartre 1947, pp. 334–45.
37   Sartre 1947, p. 319.

head, one vote') onward. In this regard Descartes was a precursor, albeit with a series of difficulties, which also derive from the limits of the context and epoch in which he moved.

However, the question of existentialist humanism needs to be explored. The reference is to the famous text *Existentialism is a Humanism* (1946), a transcription and rearticulation of a well-attended lecture. Sartre gave his approval for the publication of the text and the discussion which followed the lecture, but in many ways later regretted this choice. As is well known, Heidegger's harsh criticism would arrive soon after its publication.[38] This conference arose out of a number of needs, among them that of 'popularising' Sartre's existentialism, but even more that of bringing out its *engaged* character, and thus its possible political application. In particular, Sartre wanted to mend the rift that had arisen between himself and Marxists, who accused him of disengagement, abstraction, and conformity with bourgeois ideology. It is enough to recall, for example, his friend Paul Nizan, with whom he had dealt with for a long time, as well as figures with different positions such as Pierre Naville, Henri Lefebvre, and Gyorgy Lukàcs. But such an attempt created more problems than it resolved, producing further misunderstandings.

Although the text in question has an occasional character, which presents various limits, several elements remain particularly interesting. The first aspect to consider is that it is necessary to reason in terms that are articulated through the concept of humanism, problematising them, but also avoiding some caricatured interpretations which are provided in order to criticise them. In fact, Sartre tries to work out a differentiation between two modalities of humanism. The first, against which he polemicises, appears founded on a sort of 'cult of humanity' as an absolute end, a conception that can lead directly to fascism.[39] In later texts such as the *Critique of Dialectical Reason*, Sartre critically demarcates himself from such bourgeois humanism:

> Bourgeois humanism [*humanisme bourgeois*], as a serial ideology [*idéologie sérielle*], is solidified ideological violence. As such, it is a stereotyped determination of everyone by the other ... So, in the name of the great civilising task of *modern man* (the man of culture, the humanist who has studied the 'humanities') and in order to defend the cultural wealth of this limited humanity, it is necessary vigilantly to oppress new barbarians (the proletarians).[40]

---

38   Cf. Heidegger 2008.
39   Sartre 2007, pp. 52–3.
40   Sartre 2004a, pp. 753–4.

Such bourgeois humanism, while having a universalistic appearance, actually presents a clear anti-proletarian character. The vivid criticism of this modality of humanism allows for a complication of the image, which has become almost a caricature, of an 'all-around' Sartrean humanism, without the necessity of determining the distinctive signs. It is not a matter of maintaining, in a spirit of provocation, the thesis of a Sartrean antihumanism, but neither should Sartre's argument be 'caged' within a one-dimensional and abstract humanism, as in the interpretation provided by someone such as Althusser, for example.[41]

Counterposed to bourgeois humanism, Sartre's existentialist humanism starts from the consideration that man is constantly in the making, proving to be 'always outside of himself'.[42] Here a dynamic conception emerges, one open to the dimension of action, and thus capable of bringing the subjectivity of man into play.[43] In his presentation in the journal *Les Temps modernes*, Sartre remarks that such a conception of human freedom, insofar as it is full of responsibility, presents a potentially emancipative character:

> In this way we consider man: a total man. Totally engaged and totally free. It is this free man however who needs to be *freed* by widening his possibilities of choice. In certain situations there is no place other than an alternative, in which one of the terms of death. We must make sure that man can, in every circumstance, choose life.[44]

---

41   Cf. Rancière 2011, esp. pp. 18–20. Here Rancière, who elsewhere strongly criticises Sartre, provides an articulate reading of humanism, with its political implications, by also distancing himself from Althusser: 'In Sartre, the whole problematic of "men" making history is bound up with a perfectly clear set of political problems' (p. 18). 'Sartre's theses have also had quite precise political effects. During the Algerian War, for example, they were behinds the propaganda in favour of insubordination and behind the establishment of a network of direct support to the FLN. In May 68, they legitimized support for the student uprisings. After May 68, they were implicated in the alliance Sartre forged with Maoist militants, in the editorship of *La Cause du peuple*, in the Lens tribunal, in the establishment of new forms of interaction between intellectuals and the popular masses and in the creation of a new daily paper (*Libération*). Are not all of these political practices right under our noses? And do they not attest to some sort of convergence between Sartre's theoretical questions and the questions the Cultural Revolution raised? This is what has to be discussed if we want to have a conversation about the political effects of Sartre's thought [on humanism]' (p. 19).

42   Sartre 2007, p. 52.

43   Ibid.

44   Sartre 1988, p. 265.

In *The Communists and Peace* Sartre provides a political articulation of the question, on the basis of a critique of every typology of abstract humanism, with the object of begetting a concrete, real humanism firmly anchored to human needs.[45] In such valorisations of human capacities and needs, understood not ahistorically but rather within a social context, the reference to Marx, in particular his earliest writings, is strong.

As a doctrine of action which poses as its own basis the priority of existence over essence, existentialism insists upon the man–freedom complex. Man is not defined in abstract, unchangeable, 'essentialistic' terms, but rather by starting from his self-making,[46] according to a phenomenological attention for the concreteness of his action. Moreover, freedom involves an assumption of responsibility,[47] which also entails an 'inventing of man [*inventer l'homme*]'.[48] Once again, the character of commitment (and certainly not that of quietism[49]) emerges in Sartrean existentialism. Sartre identifies the Cartesian *cogito ergo sum* as a point of departure, understanding this not according to an individualistic modality, but on the basis of a dynamic intersubjectivity:

> [T]he man who becomes aware of himself directly in the *cogito* also perceives all others, and he does so as the condition of his own existence. He realizes that he cannot be anything ... unless others acknowledge him as such ... The other is essential to my existence, as well as to the knowledge I have of myself ... We are thus immediately thrust into a world that we may call 'intersubjectivity' [*inter-subjectivité*]. It is in this world that man decides what he is and what others are.[50]

The attempt consists in avoiding any solipsism of the I, which was partially present in Descartes, and remains a partially unresolved problem in Husserl's phenomenology as well. In this way, the emphasis on the centrality of consciousness does not lead to an individualistic vision: 'the other is essential to my existence'. The crucial nature of the element of intersubjectivity emerges as distinct from every unrelated conception of subjectivity. Here we find a continuous exchange between the individual and universal dimensions: 'every

---

45   Sartre 1968a, pp. 200–1.
46   Cf. Sartre 2007, p. 22.
47   Sartre 2007, pp. 24, 25, 27, 29, 34.
48   Sartre 2007, p. 29. Translation modified.
49   Sartre 2007, p. 36.
50   Sartre 2007, pp. 41–2.

project, however individual, has a universal value'.[51] 'We will freedom for free-dom's sake through our individual circumstances. And in thus willing freedom, we discover that it depends entirely on the freedom of others, and that the free-dom of others depends on our own'.[52] Intersubjectivity comes to play a key role in the understanding of human existence as free, but not freedom individualist-ically understood. With the passage of time, such an intersubjective dimension increasingly becomes more relevant to the path Sartre charts, 'complexifiying' the framework outlined earlier in his thinking.

From this viewpoint, it is necessary to recall a point raised in the previous section: *Being and Nothingness* should have contained a final part on morality, which was not carried out. Such a need remained, in some ways, a desideratum, insofar as Sartre never worked out a genuine 'systematisation' of this question. It should be noted, however, that in the postwar period he tried to fill the void left in this regard by *Being and Nothingness*. In particular, *Notebooks for an Ethics* (1947–1948) and *Truth and Existence* (1948), writings published posthum-ously, specifically constitute an attempt to devise a morality, although Sartre had doubts about this, such that they were not published. The *Notebooks*, a collection of notes, are arranged as a genuine 'repository' of observations on morality, conceived not in unpolitical terms, but rather as a 'theory of action. But action remains abstract if it is not labor and struggle.'[53] Such morality foun-ded on real action is rooted in the existence of a man that 'is not a reflection [*riflet*], but transcendence and invention [*invention*]',[54] in the attempt to go beyond the 'present state of things': 'surpassing [*dépassement*] that concrete situation [*situation*], invention starting from that situation'.[55] The element of negation in Sartre is connected to such a dynamic of continuous creation.[56] The central role that the concept of freedom has in such a practice of tran-scending the given, in such 'inventing the new',[57] is clear: 'a freedom is not a

---

51   Sartre 2007, p. 42.

52   Sartre 2007, p. 48.

53   Sartre 1992b, p. 17. Translation modified.

54   Sartre 1992b, p. 74.

55   Sartre 1992b, p. 313. Translation modified.

56   Cf. the passage I cited as an epigraph to the introduction: Sartre 1992b, p. 464, as well as p. 539.

57   For an interpretation of the concept of freedom starting from Sartre's *Notebooks* on the basis of an *Auseinandersetzung* with Heidegger's perspective, see Nancy 1993, pp. 96–105: 'Freedom here is not "the foundation of foundation" ... but is the foundation *in default* of foundation ... Thus freedom finds itself again endowed with an essence (the project) and with an aseity (the decision to assume itself) which operates, within its own limits, as a foundation whose foundation (which is apparently found in subjectivity) we would not question' (pp. 97–8). The order of the world actually denies the absoluteness of subjectiv-

faculty of surpassing, it is the surpassing itself. If surpassing no longer occurs, freedom disappears'.[58] This freedom is not articulated in individualistic terms, but rather according to a relation constituted with things and others, that is not conceived in an unconfrontational way, as the relevance of alienation makes clear. The moral characterisation of this discourse comes to be configured in historical and political terms, rather than beginning from an abstract assumption of human nature.

The text *Truth and Existence*, immediately following the *Notebooks*, in many ways constitutes a sort of continuation and deepening of the scenario in the prior text. Here Sartre interprets truth as a disclosure and gift to the other, but, differently than Heidegger, begins not from Being, but rather on the basis of an intersubjective articulation of discourse: 'the total truth is a concrete reality because it is the development of the manifestation across *all* of human history and the manifestation is the manifestation of *everything*'.[59] 'The foundation of truth is freedom',[60] with its creative and expansive character, since freedom, 'far from slipping into *a priori* categories (whether or not of identity), is conscious of itself as free of any presuppositions and capable of inventing [*inventer*] any kind of hypotheses starting from a given'.[61] Such freedom, as a tension towards the "new", remains connected to the element of historialisation, which it configures as an encounter between history and project:

> It is evident that historialization [*historialisation*] is the objective surpassing [*dépassement*] of the age and that, on the other hand, historicity [*historicité*] is pure expression of the age ... Therefore we must make ourselves historical against a mystifying history, that is, historialize ourselves against historicity ... It is not by attempting to transcend our age towards the eternal or towards a future of which we have no grasp that we will escape from historicity; on the contrary, it is by accepting to surpass ourselves only in and through this age, and by seeking in the age itself the concrete ends that we intend to propose ourselves.[62]

---

ity: 'Sartre's "finite" is a pure and simple hindrance to being infinite ... Sartrean freedom ... is the final name of this unhappiness of consciousness ... Sartre's man is not "possessed" by freedom: he is forced by it into the "free" knowledge of his infinite deprivation of Sartrean freedom' (pp. 98–9).

58 Sartre 1992b, p. 330.
59 Sartre 1992c, p. 7.
60 Sartre 1992c, p. 13.
61 Sartre 1992c, p. 16.
62 Sartre 1992c, pp. 79–80. Translation modified.

Within this scenario, to some extent owing to Heideggerian origins, the differentiation between historialisation and historicity, and the valorisation of the former, linked to the 'for itself', against the latter, 'pure expression of the age', brings out the tension towards a 'beyond' with respect to the 'present state of things', beginning however from an assumption full of one's own historical conditioning. I will return to the importance (and re-articulation) of the category of *historialisation* later in the book.

For the purposes of deepening this conception of freedom, for which in Sartre's postwar work the social and political dimension becomes increasingly clear, the novel series 'The Roads to Freedom' is particularly important. This series contains *The Age of Reason* (1945), The *Reprieve* (1945), and *Troubled Sleep* (1948). Mathieu, a professor of philosophy, reaches the 'age of reason', discovers life and goes beyond juvenile rejection, André Gidé's gratuitousness of memory, and egocentrism, and tries to frame its vicissitudes within a social and political horizon. In *Troubled Sleep* he carries out a free gesture, an attempt at resistance: he shoots at Nazis, risking his life.[63] This is an isolated action, which does not articulate a collective position, but the theme of 'own'-'other' becomes more relevant than in the writings of the 1930s. Starting with *Troubled Sleep*, Mathieu, the lone man, is contrasted with Brunet, the militant. Moreover, in various political writings (such as, for example, in the 'Portrait of the Adventurer'),[64] Sartre focuses on the figure of the militant. The short, unfinished novel *Strange Friendship* [*Drôle d'amitié*] (1949) fits into this context, as Brunet submits his own subjectivity to the 'collective' embodied by the Communist Party, but is interned in a German prison camp in World War II, and becomes profoundly disillusioned after the Molotov-Ribbentrop Pact.[65] Within the story, in which there are several parts of Sartre's friendship with Nizan, what emerges is an increasing search for a social and political articulation of discourse, and at the same time the disorientation regarding the failure of the attempt conducted previously.

An analogous kind of thinking can be developed by looking at the theatrical texts which immediately followed the war. There we find a 'theatre of situations', whose characters directly personify determinate ideas.[66] Particularly significant are *The Devil and the Good Lord* (1951), with its protagonist Goetz,

---

63   Sartre 1973b.
64   Sartre 2013c, pp. 198–209.
65   Sartre 1981, pp. 1461–534.
66   For a philosophical and political reading of the theatre grounded in the complex of Sartre's work, Verstraeten (1972, p. 223) remains decisive: 'The logic of this theatrical work was not ... idealist, but materialist and dialectical'. Such a conception of the theatre is founded on

a mercenary leader,[67] but even more so *Dirty Hands* (1948),[68] whose protagonist Hugo is a young bourgeois who wants to perform a radical action (which will eventually be a political homicide) capable of bringing him to the proletariat. On the one hand, the social and political embroilment appears increasingly intense, with the attempt, to use the title of the text, of 'dirtying the hands'. On the other hand, however, we witness the action's extreme solitude, and a difficulty to really achieve a collective articulation of the discourse: this second aspect drew harsh criticism from French communists. In this way the intersubjective dimension becomes increasingly more relevant, but very often takes the form of a *conatus*, or even an internal tension, rather than a concrete realisation. However, with the reference to the Resistance Sartre remarks that the action of a single person can take on a disruptive political nature:

> One word was sufficient enough to provoke ten, or one hundred arrests. Is this total responsibility, in total solitude, not the unveiling itself of our freedom? In this way, in the shadow and in blood, a republic, the strongest of republics, constitutes itself. Each of its citizens knows that they owe themselves to everyone and that they can only count on themselves: each of them realize in the most total abandonment their own historical role and their own responsibility. Each of them, against the oppressors, begins to be freely, irredeemably themselves. And choosing alone in their freedom, they choose the freedom of everyone [*liberté de tous*].[69]

We have arrived at Sartre's reflection in the *Critique of Dialectical Reason*, wherein the relation between one's own freedom and the freedom of everyone, with its political relevance, becomes crucial. In *Search for a Method*, which is in some ways an introduction to the *Critique of Dialectical Reason*, there emerges the centrality of the free man, with his project, rooted in a situation but capable of going beyond it, and the presence of objective conditions, which cannot be left aside:

---

the element of freedom: 'Freedom is the dialectical itself as the movement of the *reciprocal* surpassing of man through man and world'.

67   Sartre 1960a, pp. 1–150.

68   Sartre 1976a, pp. 125–242. On this text, see Contat 2008, pp. 543–57: 'the adventurer is Hugo, who is irrecuperable and in the end wants himself to be. Compared to him is Hoederer. A militant? Rather, the living synthesis of the adventurer and the militant. We thus understand that Sartre's problem is to get out of solitude by fully safeguarding it as the first condition of freedom' (p. 547).

69   Sartre 1977, pp. 73–4.

Man defines himself by his project [*projet*]. This material being perpetually goes beyond the condition which is made for him; he reveals and
determines his situation by transcending it in order to objectify himself
– by work, action, or gesture ... This immediate relation [*relation*] with
the Other than oneself, beyond the given and constituted elements, this
perpetual production of oneself by work and *praxis*, is our peculiar structure. It is neither a will nor a need nor a passion, but our needs – like our
passions or like the most abstract of our thoughts – participate in this
structure ... This is what we call existence [*existence*], and by this we do
not mean a stable substance which rests in itself, but rather a perpetual
disequilibrium, a wrenching away from itself with all its body. As this
impulse toward objectification assumes various forms according to the
individual, as it projects us across a field of possibilities, some of which
we realize to the exclusion of others, we call it also choice or freedom
[*choix ou liberté*].[70]

However, *Search for a Method* is sustained by the attempt to keep existentialism and Marxism together.[71] Within this search, the dimension of anthropology
is key for both the former[72] and the latter. In particular, Sartre's reformulation
of Marxism advances directly from the recognition of the centrality of man:
'Marxism will degenerate into a nonhuman anthropology [*anthropologie inhu-
maine*] if it does not reintegrate man into itself as its foundation'.[73] The contributions of philosophy, but also the human sciences (anthropology, psychology, psychoanalysis) cannot but remain central in Sartre's approach: 'without
living men, there is no history'.[74] Such a perspective presents an extreme attention for man, in the concreteness of his lived experience, on the basis of an
interweaving of phenomenology and existentialism, and an articulation of a
different argument than Lévi-Strauss's structuralist approach. In this regard,
the dimension of biography plays a strategic role (we can think of the study on
Flaubert[75] but also Baudelaire), since man must be scrutinised throughout his
entire life, rather than limited to the moment he begins to work. In a Freudian

---

70   Sartre 1963, pp. 150–1.
71   Sartre 1963, p. 71.
72   Cf. Sartre 1963, p. 168: 'In choosing as the object of our study, within the ontological sphere,
      that privileged existence which is man (privileged *for us*), it is evident that existentialism
      poses to itself the question of its fundamental relations with those disciplines which are
      grouped under the general heading of *anthropology*'.
73   Sartre 1963, p. 179.
74   Sartre 1963, p. 132.
75   Cf. Barnes 1981.

way, Sartre valorises childhood, rebuking Marxists for undervaluing its importance.[76] 'Thus the comprehension of existence is presented as the human foundation of Marxist anthropology'.[77] The latter, if understood in this sense, would
allow the concept of existentialism to be rendered useless: 'From the day that
Marxist thought will have taken on the human dimension (that is, the existential project) as the foundation of anthropological Knowledge, existentialism
will no longer have any reason for being. Absorbed, surpassed and conserved by
the totalizing movement of philosophy, it will cease to be a particular inquiry
and will become the foundation of all inquiry'.[78] Existentialism would 'dissolve'
into Marxism, into a Marxism however that is radically rethought, precisely by
starting with the needs of existentialism.

Such an articulation should not be taken in essentialistic terms, however, in
the sense of an unchangeable idea of human nature: 'It would be impossible
to find a "human nature" which is common to the Murians, for example, and
to the historical man of our contemporary societies'.[79] It is thus not a matter
of identifying a historical invariant, as if there existed an unchanging human
nucleus within the course of time. Starting in this way, Sartre indicates his
own position as 'a structural, historical anthropology',[80] providing a definition
which may sound surprising, especially in terms of the adjective 'structural',
given the polemic of structuralists, in particular Lévi-Strauss, against Sartre.
For Sartre the 'structural' dimension is clearly not identified with a structuralist
approach in that sense, referring instead to those 'practical sets' into which man
is inserted and from which he cannot be apart. Man must be interpreted not
in the abstract, as if there existed a human nature unlinked from the specific
conditions of his given existence, but rather on the basis of a full assumption
of his historicity. The nucleus of existential discourse consists precisely in the
emphasis upon *existence* over essence, as testified to by its distance from any
abstract delineation of the human being: the very modality with which Sartre
interprets humanism, which is not without its own internal limits, eschews any
ahistoric conceptualisation not connected to a specific *praxis*.

Moreover, in the *Critique of Dialectic Reason*, the aspects of structural, historical anthropology return: 'Man exists for man only in given circumstances

---

76   On Sartre's relation with Freud, see among others: Zervos 2009, pp. 54–121 who instead
      interprets Sartre's position in terms which are very different than the approach I take here,
      insofar as Sartre's distance from Marxism is emphasised; Mayer 2006.
77   Sartre 1963, p. 176.
78   Sartre 1963, p. 181.
79   Sartre 1963, pp. 169–70.
80   Sartre 1963, p. 169.

and social conditions, so every human relation [*relation*] is historical'.[81] We find a dialectic between freedom and necessity, on the basis of an interaction between individual and society: 'this new dialectic, in which freedom and necessity are now one, is not a new incarnation of the transcendental dialectic: it is a human construction whose sole agents are individual men as free activities. For this reason, in order to distinguish it from constituent dialectics, we shall refer to it as the constituted dialectic'.[82] In any case, in the *Critique of Dialectical Reason* the entire treatment of the 'fused group' is permeated by the reference to freedom, and the interrelation between 'me' and the 'other'.[83] Observing the centrality of freedom also means bringing out the relevance of the *cogito ergo sum*, understanding such an element not as connected to creation but rather to the *cogito*, which unites all men. In Descartes, a Descartes who lived in an epoch and context that were still authoritarian, Sartre sees a nexus operative between science and democracy, which begins precisely from the universality of the *cogito*. The Cartesian vision presents various limits, however, which Sartre tried to remedy with recourse to Husserlian phenomenology, albeit on the basis of a thorough reformulation of the latter: beyond putting the theological presuppositions of the discourse into question, it aims to avoid the risk of solipsism present in Descartes. For Sartre, freedom cannot assume an individualistic character, but instead presents at its own base a continuous exchange between 'me' and the 'other': Descartes beyond Descartes.

---

81   Sartre 2004a, pp. 97–8.
82   Sartre 2004a, p. 342.
83   Sartre 1991a, p. 402.

'Fused Group' And *Fraternité*: Between Rousseau And The French Revolution

1   The Practico-Inert: Objectivity and Alienation

I have so far maintained that Sartre's notion of freedom, with its subjective potentialities and its connection to the question of humanism, is crucial for the trajectory of his thought, while also emphasising that Sartre increasingly interprets this notion by placing it into a well-defined historical and social context, especially within his postwar writings. He contends first that the dimension of subjectivity cannot be considered as an absolute, or as separate from objective conditions, and second that one's own freedom cannot be separated from the freedom of others, and that in this way freedom avoids an individualist connotation. I will now focus more extensively on the first point concerning freedom and the sphere of objectivity.

In Sartre's postwar writings, objectivity plays an increasingly important function. In particular, a key term for framing the problem in the *Critique of Dialectical Reason* is the practico-inert, which denotes all that is in the way of man, all of that into which he is 'thrown' and therefore whatever is not directly produced by his action. 'Practico-' indicates the outcome of a movement of transformation, while 'inert' highlights the fact that *praxis* is grafted onto an objective and material background. In some ways we see with the concept a sort of 'translation' of the idea of 'spectral objectivity' Marx analyses in *Capital*. But, as will become clear in what follows, there are also differences between Sartre and Marx. We find a strict nexus between freedom and situation: individuals are not considered abstractly, but rather as inserted into a determinate context. At the heart of the argument is the idea of the 'primacy of material conditions' with respect to the action of individuals. Such an objective dimension cannot be negated *sic et simpliciter*, nor immediately surpassed by a 'Promethean' subjectivity:

> Thus the very *praxis* of individuals or groups is altered in so far as it ceases to be the free organisation of the practical field and becomes the re-organisation of one sector of inert materiality in accordance with the exigencies of another sector of materiality. *Invention*, even before it is made, may in certain circumstances be an exigency of the *practico-inert*

> *Being* ... In the eighteenth century, the first steam pump, which was made
> in England, inscribed itself within a tradition of effort and research which
> was itself crystalised in material objects.[1]

The connection between the practico-inert and materiality, and therefore objectivity, is strict. However, action is rooted in need, which pushes the subject
to enter into contact with the dimension of objectivity:

> *The entire historical dialectic rests on individual praxis in so far as it is*
> *already dialectical,* that is to say, to the extent that action is itself the
> negating transcendence of contradiction, the determination of a present
> totalisation in the name of a future totality, and the real effective work-
> ing of matter ... Everything is to be explained through *need*; need is the
> first totalising relation between the material being, man, and the mater-
> ial ensemble of which he is part.[2]

Although there is ambiguity present on this question, and there are other passages in Sartre which also seem to move in a different direction, the *Critique*
tends to interpret need not according to a naturalisation, as if it constituted an
originary element, but rather starting from an emphasis on its historical conditioning.

Based on a 'regressive method', Sartre's point of departure presents an individual, and not collective, character, rooting itself in the practice of a single
man. Numerous critics of such an approach begin precisely from the idea that
in Sartre the presupposed 'individual' infects the entire argument, creating difficulties for Sartre's articulation of the collective dimension in his account. But
Sartre, in the first part of the *Critique*, adopts a method that is in several respects
analogous to that which Marx outlines in the *1857 Introduction*, consisting in
the passage 'from the abstract to the concrete', according to a logical movement that does not correspond with the real historical movement. In this sense,
beginning the exposition with individual action does not necessarily imply the
choice of bringing every element back to the individual dimension. Within the
dynamic outlined, labour plays a role of mediation, since man, working upon
matter through labour, becomes quasi-object, inertia:

---

1 Sartre 2004a, pp. 191–2. Translation modified.
2 Sartre 2004a, p. 80.

Matter ... is governed by laws of exteriority. If it is true that matter effects
an initial union between men, this can only be so to the extent that it
has passively received the seal of that unity ... This synthesis, therefore,
represents the material condition of historicity. At the same time, it is
what might be called the passive motor of History. ... [T]his univocal relation *in our History* in a particular and contingent form since the whole
of human development, at least up until now, has been a bitter struggle
against *scarcity* ... [A]fter thousands of years of History, three quarters
of the world's population are undernourished. Thus, in spite of its contingency, scarcity is a very basic human relation, both to Nature and to
men.[3] ... [E]veryone has the experience of the practico-inert in his work
and in his public life (and, to a lesser degree, in his private life) and that it
is, in fact, characteristic of our everyday life. We also saw that it remained
abstract because this inert bond of sociality does not explain the group, as
an organised plurality, but that this universe of passive-activity was still,
for particular individuals (depending on their function, their class, etc.) a
field which they could not leave.[4]

The practico-inert is configured as a central element of our everyday life. We
should note the widespread relevance that the concept of everyday life had
throughout French thought in the 1960s and 1970s. But the practico-inert characterises everyday life phenomenologically rather than in response to the Lefe-
bvrian *conatus* of its transformation. Above all, it concerns public life, the social
dimension, the labour sphere, all within a definite context, on the basis of the
action of situated individuals who are not considered abstractly. It can legit-
imately be asked whether Sartre's thought concerns all societies within history, or a specific analysis of capitalism. There exists indeed an ambivalence,
or perhaps an ambiguity, in this regard. On the one hand, a sort of historical
invariance seems to be operative, for which this dynamic could be useful for
all epochs, in discontinuity with the Marxist focus on historical determination. But on the other, in the last instance Sartre's reasoning remains focused
on capitalism in its specific difference with pre-capitalist forms. Moreover, as
I emphasised in chapter one, already in *Being and Nothingness*, the scenario,
while containing a complex analysis of the human condition, found its full
realisation within capitalism, as the relevance assumed by the concept of alienation (even if there is some ambivalence), rooted in the labour dynamics of

3   Sartre 2004a, pp. 122–3.
4   Sartre 2004a, p. 336.

the modern world, testifies. The difficulty also consists in the fact that Sartre does not perform a detailed analysis of labour conditions, presenting a rather general, and at times generic, reading of them.

The reference to the relation between man and nature, and the mediation played here by labour, gives rise to the centrality of the element of intersubjectivity: '*human labor*, the original *praxis* by which man produces and reproduces his life, is *entirely* dialectical: its possibility and its permanent necessity rest upon the relation of interiority which unites the organism with the environment and upon the deep contradiction between the inorganic and organic orders, both of which are present in everyone'.[5] Labour responds to the need to overcome *rareté*, that is, scarcity or rarity:

> [Labor] is *primarily the organism* which reduces itself to a controlled inertia so as to act upon inertia and satisfy itself as need ... Thus the human labour of the individual, and, consequently, of the group, is conditioned in its aim, and therefore in its movement, by man's fundamental project, for himself or for the group, of transcending scarcity, not only as the threat of death ... But for *precisely this reason* scarcity [*rareté*] will, without ceasing to be the fundamental relation, come to qualify the group or the individual who struggle against it by *making themselves scarce so as to destroy it*.[6]

Such a process must be interpreted by focusing not only on the 'inert' but also the 'pratico-', with its character of invention. Often such a situation, particularly within labour dynamics, proves to be anything but peaceful, due to *rareté*, which comes to determine a clash between individuals. *Rareté* constitutes a key notion in the *Critique*, which however presents some ambiguities: in particular, the risk consists in conceptualising it as an originary given, on the basis of a sort of naturalisation. Despite the real incongruities, it must be noted that such a category, while substantially extraneous to the Marxist framework, connects to the importance of material needs and living conditions for individuals within a society, such as capitalism, characterised by anything but an abundance of resources for all.

In such a situation we witness an 'inert relation of sociality': the practico-inert, which is not an element capable of encapsulating that which unites individuals, as opposed to the 'present state of things'. Seriality, which is strongly

---

5 Sartre 2004a, p. 90. For an analysis of the relation between praxis and inertia as part of a re-articulation of the question of materialism, see Caeymaex 2005a.

6 Sartre 2004a, pp. 136–7.

connected to the practico-inert, does not activate a commonality among individuals. Seriality holds individuals together, either where they are randomly found in the same place (a bus stop, for example) or in a more 'structured' relation (such as an office), without them truly acting in common. We thus find a mere summation of unrelated individuality: 'the serial individual's serial thought expires in the practico-inert field and implicitly concerns common individuals as instruments, and inorganic instruments as living functions, as absolutely equivalent'.[7] Seriality does not mean equality, with its emancipatory and destabilising character, but mere equivalence, on the basis of the subjection of individuals to a determinate arrangement. However, it is necessary to specify that series and group should not be interpreted in terms of a linear and static succession, but instead according to more complex coordinates:

> [S]eriality defines the field which we have called the *practico-inert* ...
> There is actually no *a priori* ground for supposing that seriality is an
> earlier statute than the group, although it is true that the group consti-
> tutes itself in and against it. Not only do we always find groups and gath-
> erings together, but also, *only* dialectical investigation and experience will
> enable us to determine whether the seriality in question is an immediate
> gathering or whether it is constituted by old groups which have been seri-
> alised.[8]

There exists a strict relation among the practico-inert, seriality, and the collective, but this complex must be understood not as temporally anterior to the dimension of the group. Instead, it is necessary to keep all of the dynamics present at once. With respect to Sartre's prewar writings, there emerges more consideration of 'objective' material conditions: the idea of an immediately emancipative subjectivity must therefore be put into question. At the same time, however, objectivity is subjected to a strong criticism, taking the form, in the last instance, of alienation:[9]

---

7   Sartre 2004a, p. 566.
8   Sartre 2004a, p. 678.
9   On the theme of alienation: Chiodi's work (1973 [1965]) has had a primary role for the recep-
    tion of this question in Italy (particularly pp. 119–50). For him, differently than the perspective
    I articulate here, Sartre's approach is irreconcilable with the Marxian approach. Fergnani
    (1978, esp. pp. 185–97) rightly emphasises: 'Contrary to the opinion of several critics – Chiodi
    above all ... – it is not true that the French philosopher has avoided the particular character
    of alienation examined by Marx' (p. 187). Alienation is not fully identified with objectivation,
    and is not presented as a permanent dimension: 'Disalienation is ... presented as a tendency
    and objective limit that no actual historical-empirical person can claim to be adequate in

It would be quite wrong to interpret me as saying that man is free in all situations, as the Stoics claimed. I mean the exact opposite: all men are slaves in so far as their life unfolds in the practico-inert field and in so far as this field is always conditioned by scarcity [*rareté*]. In modern society, in effect, the alienation [*aliénation*] of the exploited and that of the exploiters are inseparable; in other societies, the relation between master and slave – though very different from what Hegel described – also presupposes a reciprocal conditioning in alienation.[10]

The importance of freedom is not negated but circumscribed to the specific situation, delimiting the margins of feasibility. The practico-inert plays a crucial role in this respect. As such, it would be difficult to envisage a scenario of liberation: the humanistic charge of Sartre's discourse also can find itself in difficulty within such an approach.

The notion of alienation, first of all, refers to modern, capitalist society, with its structural relation between exploiters and exploited, without excluding reference to earlier societies. By further starting from a confrontation, in many ways in critical terms, with Hegel and several French readers of Hegel, Sartre seems to produce an equivalence between objectivation and alienation, or better, he conceives the latter on the basis of the former. On this point his solution appears closer to Hegel than Marx, who differentiated precisely between the two terms. Undoubtedly in the *Critique of Dialectical Reason*, objectivation assumes a greater relevance than in Sartre's earlier writings, but it is conceived as absolute alterity, as negativity and, in this sense, as the foundation of alienation. Alienation, in fact, is configured as the rule of objectivation within a determinate society, since materiality, connected to the tools of labour, conditions human relations.

The ambivalence I referenced earlier also returns concerning alienation. On the one hand, the discourse is situated in a specific context, while on the other, it presents a transhistorical connotation:

> Alienation [*aliénation*] as a real and strict process within the system arises in and through *alterity* as infinite recurrence: it concretises the abstract structure in an entirely concrete historical movement; but the dispersive skeleton, as a relation of fleeting impotence amongst the workers them-

---

a full sense' (p. 198). Cf. Carney 2007, pp. 77–91, who interprets such a concept, from *Transcendence of the Ego* onwards, as a critique of every type of essentialist foundation; see also Fischbach 2011.

10   Sartre 2004a, p. 332.

selves, is a necessary part of this concretisation. Industrialisation produces its own proletariat; it drains it from the countryside, and regulates its birthrate. But, here as elsewhere, a statute of impotence is produced, through the serialisation of the proletarians.[11]

Despite a certain generality to the approach, the primary reference is to the modern, capitalist world, with strong Marxist antecedents. Sartre articulates an "anti-workerist" position: factory labour does not constitute a realisation of man, but rather his *de-realisation*. Behind such a critique of exploitation in the factory, the element of alienation returns in an overwhelming fashion. From one angle, however, with respect to Marx or Marxism – and I will return to this point more fully in the next chapter – there emerges an aspect of discontinuity, or at least problematisation. Indeed, Sartre also emphasises what in his view is often neglected, or is a sort of 'first order' alienation, founded on the fact that one's own action becomes *other*.

Sartre insists on the relevance of the "human" dimension of the discourse:

> [A]ny philosophy which subordinates the human to what is Other than man, whether it be an existentialist or Marxist idealism, has hatred of man as both its basis and its consequence: History has proved this in both cases. There is a choice: either man is primarily himself, or he is primarily Other than himself. Choosing the second doctrine simply makes one a victim and accomplice of real alienation [*aliénation réelle*].[12]

If the human dimension is negated, we impotently witness the omni-pervasiveness of alienation. The distance of this position from some structuralist positions, as well as in part the Althusserian position, is clear. Sartre warns against the risk that unilateral emphasis on structures ends up in a functionalist conception, in which subjective action remains barred or only possible in interstices, without receiving a theoretical expression. Sartre's approach sometimes presents the opposite risk of undervaluing the external environment of the individual. In a sense, it could be claimed that Althusser is too Durkheimian and Sartre is not Durkheimian enough. Whatever the case may be, for Sartre no element can be reduced to either the natural or the social: individual *praxis*, despite its difficulties and contradictions, plays a crucial function, contrary to what is maintained by a certain dogmatic Marxism. This element is laden with

11   Sartre 2004a, p. 679.
12   Sartre 2004a, p. 181.

the conviction of the possibility (and not *necessity*) of a process of transformation which leads beyond the 'present state of things', and of alienation which
distinguishes it: 'the experience of alienation is not an instantaneous intuition
... but a process which temporalises itself and which the "ways of the world" can
always interrupt, either provisionally or definitively, from outside and within
by the intervening transformation of the conditions of the experience'.[13] The
entire problematic of alienation is addressed starting from objectivation, with
its estranging character. It concerns a world of dispersion, of impotence: the
existentialist echoes here are clear.

From our discussion so far, what has continuously emerged in Sartre's critique of seriality, and therefore objectivity, is the theme of alienation. In a serial
scenario, individuals constitute a 'collective', a 'discrete multiplicity', that is, 'the
most obvious, immediate, and superficial gatherings of the practical field', 'inorganic social beings':[14]

> [W]e are concerned here with a plurality of isolations [*pluralité de
> solitudes*]: these people do not care about or speak to each other and, in
> general, they do not look at one another; they exist side by side along-
> side a bus stop. ... [T]he intensity of isolation, as a relation of exteri-
> ority between the members of a temporary and contingent gathering,
> expresses *the degree of massification* of the social ensemble, in so far as
> it is produced on the basis of given conditions. At this level, reciprocal
> isolations, as the negation of reciprocity, signify the integration of indi-
> viduals into one society ... as in Proust's 'Every person is very much along'.
> Finally, in our example, isolation becomes, for and through everyone, for
> him and for others, the real, social product of cities.[15]

The isolation of the individual and the sociality of the collective represent two
sides of the same coin. In the next chapter I will return to this question, and
also consider it in relation to the Marxian approach. Sartre certainly takes up
various aspects of the latter, on the basis however of a different conceptual
structure and with particular attention to the psychological and anthropological dimension of the problem. Further, the interpenetration of sociality and
isolation emerges with particular force in the city. Here we cannot help but
notice affinities between Sartre's formulation and those of figures alluded to
earlier such as Henri Lefebvre and Michel de Certeau:

---

13   Sartre 2004a, p. 338.
14   Sartre 2004a, p. 252.
15   Sartre 2004a, pp. 256–7.

[T]he collective is defined *by its being*, that is to say, in so far as all *praxis* is constituted by its being as mere *exis*; it is a material, inorganic object in the practico-inert field in so far as a discrete multiplicity of active individuals is being produced in it under the sign of the Other [*multiplicité discrète d'individus agissants*], as a *real unity within Being* ... In order to understand the collective one must understand that this material object realises the unity of interpenetration of individuals as beings-in-the-world-outside-themselves to the extent that it structures their relations as practical organisms in accordance with the new rule of *series*. Let us now illustrate these notions by a superficial everyday example. Take a grouping of people in the Place Saint-Germain. They are waiting for a bus at a bus stop in front of the church.[16]

In the series the individuals remain connected in random or formal rather than 'substantial' terms, on the basis of an extreme atomisation and a monotonous repetitiveness of everyday acts. 'Organic isolation, suffered isolation, lived isolation, isolation as a mode of behaviour, isolation as a social statute of the individual, isolation as the exteriority of groups conditioning the exteriority of individuals, isolation as the reciprocity of isolations [*réciprocité d'isolements*] in a society which creates *masses*'.[17] The group responds precisely to the need of overcoming such serial logic. But, as emphasised earlier, this does not mean that the group emerges as a linear historical succession.[18] The question is articulated in more complex terms than a timeline of phases which reflects a continuous shuffling between the elements. Rather, from a logical point of view the series must be examined first in order to conceptualise its overcoming – and its conservation – in the group. It is important to keep in mind that the first part of the *Critique* is supported by a method analogous to that in Marx's *1857 Introduction*, in which the exposition begins with the 'abstract' in order to arrive at the 'concrete'.[19] In a Hegelian way, we can insist on the logical character of such a process, but, in a manner out of step with Hegel, by highlighting the non-homogeneity between the logical dimension and the historical dimension, and between thought and reality. In that sense, for Sartre the series has priority on the logical level, but maintaining such a position does not mean holding that there is a historical succession. In any case, the overcoming of the 'present state of things', of the serial horizon, is also possible because man does not only

16   Sartre 2004a, pp. 255–6.
17   Sartre 2004a, p. 258.
18   Sartre 2004a, p. 18.
19   Sartre 2004a, p. 19.

possess a 'nature-dialectic', but also a 'culture-dialectic',[20] which can push beyond materiality, and therefore beyond the practico-inert. While different than
in Hegel, in Sartre a dialectical reason remains operative, one which rejects the
dualistic logic of analytic, positivistic reason, incapable of grasping interpenetration, but not on the basis of an immediate identification between nature
and culture.

2   Acting in Common: the Storming of the Bastille

The group arises from the collective, but is constituted as its negation,[21] and
therefore as the negation of serial logic,[22] seeking to give rise to a free interaction among individuals.

> [W]e must emphasise that groups [*groupe*] (both as practical organ-
> isations, directly established by human *praxis*, and as present, concrete
> undertakings) can arise only on the foundation of a collective which,
> however, they do not eliminate (at least not entirely) and, conversely, that
> in so far as, whatever its aim, it necessarily acts through the medium of
> the practico-inert field, it must itself, as a free organisation [*organisation
> libre*] of individuals with a common aim, produce *its collective structure*,
> that is to say, *exploit its inertia for practice* ... [T]he group is defined by its
> undertaking and by the constant movement of integration which tends to
> turn it into pure *praxis* by trying to eliminate all forms of inertia from it.[23]

Such a union has as its basis a common need or danger against which determinate 'countermeasures' are activated:

> [T]he group constitutes itself on the basis of a need or common danger
> and defines itself by the common objective which determines its com-
> mon *praxis*. Yet neither common need, nor common *praxis*, nor com-
> mon objectives can define a community [*communauté*] unless it makes
> itself into a community by feeling individual need as common need, and
> by projecting itself, in the internal unification of a common integration,
> towards objectives which it produces as common.[24]

---

20   Sartre 2004a, p. 341.
21   Sartre 2004a, p. 21.
22   Sartre 2004a, p. 22.
23   Sartre 2004a, pp. 254–5.
24   Sartre 2004a, p. 350.

Need or danger constitute a sort of 'fuse', but these elements are not sufficient to give rise to a genuine community, understood as having an expansive character, such as what Marx and Engels called 'real community' in *The German Ideology*.[25] This dimension, however, is not counterposed to individual freedom as a foundation and point of departure for the argument: Sartre's entire approach tries to highlight the co-implication between 'own' and 'others'.

There are traces of Rousseau here which have received little consideration from scholars of Sartre.[26] Occasionally, Sartre scholars reference the autobiographical dimension of Rousseau's argument: it is enough to think of Rousseau's *Confessions* and Sartre's *The Words*. If we also recall the more strictly political texts, several other points of contact can be identified which are very important. The emphasis on solidarity, on an 'organic' link between individuals, with Rousseauian heritage, is more relevant within the *Critique of Dialectical Reason* than what emerges explicitly (Rousseau is cited, but not often). In this sense, Rousseau's concept of the general will can be recalled, in its irreducibility to a 'summation' of wills and its 'qualitative' characterisation, based on a 'fusional' manner. The Rousseauian gap between the will of all, understood as a mere addition of particular wills, and the general will, in its going beyond such a horizon, operates in Sartre as the gap between series and group. The latter surpasses a scenario founded on the juxtaposition of unrelated individualities, coming to arrange itself in qualitative terms and in that sense reactivating several aspects of the general will. Beyond Sartre's own dialectic of isolation and community, there is another chord from the Genevan thinker which rings out.[27] Indeed, if Rousseau's directly political texts interact with works such as *Émile* and *Julie, or the New Heloise*, an internal tension emerges. On the one hand, there is a 'constructivist' element present, which moves toward a full realisation of individuals as a result of the social contract, while on the other, there is a strong awareness of the constitutive limits of politics, starting from the idea

---

25   Cf. Marx 1978, p. 197: 'Only in community [*Gemeinschaft*] [with others has each] individual the means of cultivating his gifts in all directions; only in the community, therefore, is personal freedom possible ... In the real community [*wirkliche Gemeinschaft*] the individuals obtain their freedom [*Freiheit*] in and through their association [*Assoziation*]'.

26   On Sartre's relation with Rousseau, see Lapissade 1961, esp. p. 517, where it is maintained that Rousseau, through Hegel and Marx, constitutes the true inspiration of Sartre's political theory; Chiodi 1965, esp. pp. 93–100, which strongly reappraises Lapissade's judgment but still emphasises the importance, for the sake of understanding the relation between series and group, of Rousseau's distinction between the will of all and the general will; Jameson 1971; Goldschmidt 1983, p. 782; Knee 1987; Darnell and Rohatyn 1992.

27   On Rousseau, some studies which are particularly relevant in this direction include Polin 1971; Baczko 1974; Baczko 1999, esp. pp. 165–83; Starobinski 1971.

that freedom, in the last instance, 'is found in no form of government: it is the heart of the free man'.[28] So it sometimes seems that such freedom can be added to a condition of solitude or isolation, such as for example in the community of Clarens in *Julia, or the New Heloise,* which is far from the 'corrupt' Paris, being based on the desperate search for authenticity, that authenticity which historical development has rendered increasingly inaccessible to us. The 'enigma' of Rousseau consists in being a thinker of the 'social contract' man in *On the Social Contract* and, at the same time, in isolating the *moi* from society – a thinker between sociality and solitude, with an (unfulfilled) desire for transparency. Without downplaying notable differences between the two philosophers (for example, the presence in Sartre of a critique of contractualism), the tension indicated in Rousseau remains operative to some degree within Sartre's reflection in the *Critique.*

To return to a specific treatment of the latter, through the common action of the group individuals experiment with the possibility of genuinely influencing reality on the basis of an intersubjective relation:

> [R]eciprocity [*réciprocité*] is always concrete. It cannot be based on a universal abstract bond, like Christian 'charity'; nor on an *a priori* willingness to treat the human person, in myself and in the Other, as an absolute end; nor on a purely contemplative intuition revealing 'Humanity' to everyone as the essence of his fellows. It is the individual's *praxis,* as the realisation of his project, which determines his bonds of reciprocity with everyone. And the quality of being a *man* does not exist as such: *this* particular gardener recognises in *this* particular road-mender a concrete project, which is expressed in his behaviour and which others have *already recognised* by the very task which they have set him.[29]

We thus do not find an abstractly humanistic vision, which outlines an ahistoric concept of Humanity, since the recognition remains materialised in a specific, concrete *praxis,* in which one's own needs and the needs of others encounter (and clash with) one another. In the scenario sketched here, the individualistic character of Sartre's earlier texts is, if not eliminated, at least weakened: reference is not made to a political individualism, to a form of liberalism, but rather to an ontological conception centred on the single man and his freedom. In the *Critique of Dialectical Reason,* the element 'others' becomes

---

28   Rousseau 1979, p. 473.
29   Sartre 2004, pp. 109–10.

central for the very political constitution of 'me', so that the latter cannot be understood independently from the relations that maintain it. In this sense, an element of intersubjectivity remains operative, or to borrow from Simondon, an element of 'transindividuality'. Sartre does not use this term, but it is useful for grasping the way that he poses the problem:

> [I]n their mutual *recognition* [*reconnaissance*] each of them discloses and respects the project of the Other, as also existing outside his own project ... Thus the mutual relation is haunted by its unity as if it were an inadequacy of being transforming its original structure. This *disquiet* of reciprocity, in its turn, is intelligible as the moment in which the dialectic of each experiences the dialectic of the Other as a limitation on the project of totalisation, imposed in and by the very attempt at synthesis. For this reason, it is always possible for reciprocity to collapse into its terms as a false, crushing totality. And this can be positive as well as negative. A collective undertaking [*enterprise commune*] can become a kind of infernal impulsion when each insists on continuing it out of consideration for the Other. Apprentice boxers are often dominated *by their fight* ... [30]

Reciprocity is connected to a 'common enterprise', and therefore to a dimension that cannot end up as reducible to a single individual. But this process also demonstrates a darker side, that the community can come to be configured as 'a kind of infernal impulsion' on the basis of a merely destructive stubbornness.

> [T]he necessity of the group is not present *a priori* in a gathering ... Thus the group would function as a hyper-organism in relation to individual organisms ... But it would be a mistake to reduce the organicist illusion to the role of a reactionary theory ... the constitution of a group (on the basis, of course, of real, material conditions) as an ensemble of solidarities [*ensemble de solidarités*] has the dialectical consequence of making it the negation of the rest of the social field, and, as a result, of occasioning, in this field in so far as it is defined as non-grouped, the conditions for an antagonistic grouping [*groupement antagoniste*] ... the non-grouped, on the outside, behave towards the group by positing it through their very *praxis* as an *organic totality*.[31]

---

30   Sartre 2004, pp. 115–16.
31   Sartre 2004a, pp. 345–6.

The organic link between individuals, even with its risks, is not realised in abstraction, but rather starting from a common action aimed at questioning the 'present state of things'. It is only in *praxis* that that 'fusional' element so valorised by Sartre is realised: within the 'fused group'[32] a genuine coincidence between the individual and common dimensions seems to be verified. Here I think Rousseau's thought provides an extremely relevant reference point (even if Sartre is not explicit). In Rousseau, community takes on the traits indicated here in numerous ways. We should however continually keep in mind the instability of the fused group: such 'fusionality' is never given once and for all, but remains connected to the contingency of action. The French Revolution is decisive as an example of the meaning of this idea: it is a true paradigm through which the entire first part of the *Critique of Dialectical Reason* can be interpreted.

It is noteworthy that in the numerous studies on the French Revolution, Sartre's name almost never appears, and thus his contribution to the understanding of this historical event is almost completely ignored. Sartre's sources on the French Revolution are varied, from Georges Lefebvre to Jean Jaurès, who is mentioned several times.[33] Sartre carries out a complex and multi-layered analysis of the Revolution and its internal dynamics, from its initial, germinal moment, passing through the Terror, in order to arrive at the Thermidor, but also at the consequences of such a process in the nineteenth century. He begins by portraying the situation immediately prior to the storming of the Bastille:

> [S]ome incidents ... resulted in a new wave of serial, defensive violence [*violence sérielle*], and arsenals were looted ... It was a collective enterprise [*conduite collective*] ... the unity of impotence (inertia) had, *by sheer weight of numbers*, transformed itself into a massive force [*force massive*] ... In so far as everyone wanted to defend himself against the dragoons ... the result, *in the field of praxis*, was that *the people of Paris armed themselves against the king* ... The violent contradiction between the militia

---

32   Sartre 2004a, p. 390. On the fused group, cf. Simont 1998, p. 159: 'in the fused group it could be said: "I am the Other"'. 'In such intensive quantity of fusion, the parts no longer precede the whole, but the articulated totalisation of the integration of each part always precedes from itself at the same time as it does not cease coming to itself and totalising itself in each one' (p. 161).

33   Regarding Sartre's analysis of the French Revolution and specific references to the historiographical debate, see Jameson 1971, p. 257, who emphasises the fact that in the Critique, the French Revolution constitutes a 'paradigm of group behavior': Mazauric 2010; Ducange 2011; Rizk 2006; Rizk 2014, esp. pp. 236–44; Rametta 2009.

and the people, occurring within the people, produced the possibility of an internal Unity as the negation of the external unity.[34]

As Sartre had already incisively underscored in *Search for a Method*, a fundamental 'spring' of the Revolution was fear, an element underestimated by various Marxist approaches:

> Lefebvre has irrefutably established that after 1789, fear was the dominating passion [*passion*] of the revolutionary populace (which does not exclude heroism – quite the contrary) and that all these days of the popular offensive ... are fundamentally *defensive* days ... *Today* this simple fact escapes Marxist analysis. The idealist voluntarism of the Stalinists can conceive only of an *offensive* action; it attributes negative sentiments to the class whose power is declining and to this class alone.[35]

It is interesting to examine Sartre's text *Mai-juin 1789* in order to see a further elaboration on the months immediately prior to the revolutionary outbreak. He wrote the work in the 1950s, but it was only published posthumously in 2008. In the text, the disruptive nature of the process being activated is clear, founded on the substitution of Enlightenment reason for tradition.[36] At the centre of the argument is the strategy with which the Estates-General, starting in May 1789, addressed the situation facing them. The two main phases, which are the object of Sartre's text, are the following. The first begins with the convocation of the Estates-General and ends with the intervention of the King at the end of May. The second concerns the action of the Third Estate, which in June began to take the initiative, breaking with the preceding inertia. A rationalist and universalist *conatus* emerges: the Parisian people as a concrete reality is configured precisely as universality, but endowed with a fictitious character by remaining founded on an abstraction such as the national will.[37] In a way that is analogous to the Marxian 'real abstraction' in the *1857 Introduction*, there emerge universal stakes, whose fictitious dimension is not synonymous with irreality, but on the

---

34   Sartre 2004a, pp. 354–6.
35   Sartre 1963, pp. 127–8.
36   Cf. Sartre 2008b, esp. p. 72. Also cf. Bourgault's commentary in Ibid., pp. 5–17.
37   Cf. Ibid., p. 62, p. 76. Also cf. Barot's commentary, in which the stakes of the universal in 1789 are underlined. It is a matter of a fictive universality, but such a fiction remains 'charged' with reality, as with abstraction in Marx: '[T]he universal as necessary fiction however contains an *efficacy* ... The 'national people' of 1789 is a contradictory fiction of this type ... crystalisisation-fetishisation ... The constitution of the national Assembly in May–June 1789 is a process of this type' (p. 78).

contrary present themselves as laden with material effects. Such an approach also remains crucial for understanding the part of the *Critique of Dialectical Reason* dedicated to the French Revolution.

In the *Critique*, Sartre highlights the fact that a dynamic of rebellion developed: the inertia became massified on the basis of a numerical 'weight'. To borrow from Engels (who is often criticised by Sartre, even on the basis of an ungenerous contrast to Marx), quantity becomes quality, such that the people become constituent power.[38]

> [T]he crowd [*foule*] felt that it had been *tricked* ... There was nothing magical in this new reaction: it merely expressed the reinteriorisation of a reciprocity. From this moment on, there is something which is neither group nor series, but what Malraux, in *Days of Hope*, called the Apocalypse – that is to say, the dissolution of the series into a fused group [*groupe en fusion*] ... in the Apocalypse, though seriality still exists at least as a process which is about to disappear, and although it always may reappear, synthetic unity is always here. Or, to put the same point in another way, throughout a city, at every moment, in each partial process, the part is entirely involved and the movement of the city is fulfilled [*achèvement*] and signified in it ... The city was a fused group.[39]

In such an Apocalypse we find an attempt to surpass serial logic. In the fused group, with its disruptive action, with its capacity to overcome barriers, it seems that the individual and common dimensions are immediately identified with one another, within a situation and a specific logic.

The question of topology (city, neighbourhood ...) is crucial.[40] Whether or not he was aware, Michel de Certeau incorporates (or at least arrives at results which are not very dissimilar) such topological attention into his analysis of the of students' *prise de parole* in 1968, with its destabilising charge.[41] Sartre references the neighbourhood of Sant'Antonio, in the shadow of the Bastille, whose conquest will be the fruit of the activity of the fused group:

---

38   For a reading that is simultaneously harmonious with and critical of Sartre's itinerary in the *Critique* in terms of the revolutionary dynamic, in which fused groups are presented as 'constituent power in the subjective sense', see Negri 1999, p. 296.

39   Sartre 2004a, pp. 357–8.

40   Despite the apparent distance between the two, a comparison between Sartre and Lefebvre (1968a) on this question would be quite interesting.

41   See de Certeau 1997, pp. 1–76.

I run with all the others; I shout: 'Stop!'; everybody stops. Someone else shouts, 'Let's go!' or, 'To the left! To the right! To the Bastille!' And everyone moves off ... But the order is not *obeyed*. Who would obey? And whom? It is simply the common *praxis* [*praxis commune*] becoming, in some third party, regulatory of itself in me and in all the other third parties, in the movement of a totalisation which totalises me and everyone else ... The words circulate from mouth to mouth, it might be said, like a coin from hand to hand. And, in fact, the discourse is a sound-object, a materiality.[42]

A real integration is produced in such a situation, not on the basis of a logic of obedience or faith to an order, but starting from an action that gathers the individuals. Freedom and equality reciprocally invoke one another: each and all, laden with passion, led towards the Bastille according to a sort of revolutionary 'contagion'.

The element of intersubjectivity materialises vividly in the storming of the Bastille. Everyone appears, at the same time, sovereign and subject. Again, even if he is not cited, it is difficult not to think of Rousseau. The reference is not only to the *Discourse on the Origin of Inequality*, with its radical critique of inequality, but also to *On the Social Contract*, with its 'constructivism'. The latter represents a distinctive feature of every revolution: differently from the medieval right to resistance, which seems to restore, to reaffirm an order threatened by a specific unjust monarch, the revolution is configured as a genuine *tabula rasa*, as a destruction of the present state of things and construction of something radically new with respect to the past.[43] In other words, it is a matter of 'inventing the new'. At the same time – and here the reference to the practico-inert is key – every revolutionary development inevitably feels the effects of the present situation and its specific limits. This element will return in a particularly significant way with Sartre's analysis of the Russian Revolution and the Soviet Union which followed it.

[I]n certain circumstances, a group emerges 'hot' [*groupe à chaud*] and acts where previously there were only gatherings and, through this eph-

---

42   Sartre 2004a, pp. 379–80.
43   See Jameson 1971, pp. 259–60: '[T]he scandal of the revolutionary event for academic his-
      tioriography lies in the radically new type of event which it offers to historical narration ...
      [E]verything – all gestures and thoughts, routines, decisions, private life as well as public
      life – is henceforth drawn into relationship with the revolutionary process, reorganized
      around it'. On the category of revolution from a 'compositional' lens, see Koselleck 2004,
      pp. 43–57.

emeral, superficial formation, everyone glimpses new, deeper, but yet to be created statutes [*statuts nouveaux*] (the Third Estate as a group from the standpoint of the nation, the class as a group in so far as it produces its apparatuses of unification, etc.). Sieyès question about the Third Estate, which was *nothing* (and therefore a pure multiplicity of inertia, since it existed as nothing) but could be *everything* (that is to say – as certain people then thought, including Sieyès himself, by an abstraction from which, as a liberal bourgeois, he soon recovered – the nation, as a totality perpetually reshaping itself, the nation as permanent revolution) shows clearly how *through the troubles of 1788–9 and the groups which formed* sporadically (which up until that time were called *riots*) the bourgeois even more than the worker in the cities (though work was *really* done by the workers) glimpsed the transition from an ossified, cold world to an Apocalypse ... But it was France that they discovered through the storming of the Bastille ... what is important is that this form constitutes itself in reality at certain moments of the historical experience and that it then forms itself as new [*neuve*].[44]

The 'hot' group creates a completely different reality than the scenario in the past. Earlier I mentioned Rousseau's relevance for understanding Sartre's argument. It is not a matter of mechanically taking up Rousseau's schema (again it is enough to think, for example, of the contractualist dimension, which is constitutive in *On the Social Contract*, and largely absent in Sartre),[45] but rather of grasping the centrality of the *j'accuse* originated by Rousseau's observation that 'man is born free and everywhere is in chains',[46] as well as the centrality of the attempt to build a radically new community.

Sartre's direct reference, however, is to Sieyès, a 'bourgeois liberal' capable of accurately interpreting the reality of the Third Estate which is nothing but can become everything. Sieyès's interpretation finds its basis in a logic of cleansing. In his view, the other two estates were passive outgrowths which disgraced France, and thus the aim was to give rise to a new construction entirely centered on the Third Estate.[47] From this viewpoint, it is necessary to keep in mind the Marxian thematisation of the proletariat, which takes up this logic and carries it to its most radical consequences: starting from and then going

---

44   Sartre 2004a, pp. 382–3.
45   On Sartre's relationship with social contract theory, see Guigot 2001, pp. 350–71.
46   Rousseau 2002, p. 156.
47   Cf. Sieyès 1993 [1789], pp. 207–98. On Sieyès, among others see Bastid 1970; Bredin 1988; Scuccimarra 2002.

beyond the Third Estate.[48] Within such a process we find a liquidation of the serial dimension and the full arrival of the fused group. Later I will examine the limits of Sieyès's argument, but here it is necessary to reaffirm the crucial character of the grammar of the 'new' in the *Critique of Dialectical Reason*: 'new states', 'new form'.

> The reality of the *praxis* of a (fused) group depends on the liquidation (either simultaneous or subject to temporal dislocations which can be ignored) of the serial, both in everyone and by everyone in everyone, and its replacement by community [*communauté*] ... *through* the individual invention of common action [*invention individuelle de l'action commune*] as the sole means of reaching the common objective, in fact, that the historian demonstrates and evaluates the urgency, the imperious clarity, and the totalising force of the *objective*[49] ... In so far as the group is ... a common *praxis*, the community of *praxis* is still expressed in the appearance of a group as the interiorisation of multiplicity and the reorganisation of human relations ... From the outset, in fact, we can understand that the group is a directed process ... after the storming of the Bastille, Paris could never again be the Paris of June 1789. New organisations [*nouvelles organisations*] arose on the ruins of the old ... In this sense, a group defines its own temporality [*temporalité*], that is to say, its practical speed and the speed with which the future comes to it ... Joseph Le Bon ... said, from his prison, after the Thermidor, that no one – not even himself – could really understand or judge events and actions which had occurred at *an other speed*.[50] ... The action of the group is necessarily new [*neuve*] in so far as the group is a new reality and its result an absolute novelty [*nouveauté*]. *The people have taken the Bastille.*[51]

The fused group is rooted in a situation, on the basis of a directed process, of an action that is also a passion, in which the individual and common dimensions seem to perfectly coincide. This dynamic presents a forceful temporality. One of the distinctive signs of the revolution consists precisely in the character of radical acceleration that it impresses upon the course of events, giving rise to 'an absolute novelty', a harbinger of 'new organisations'. Sartre's

---

48   Among numerous passages, particularly important on this question with regard to a comparison between the Third Estate and the proletariat is Marx 1978, pp. 53–65.
49   Sartre 2004a, p. 387. Translation modified.
50   Sartre 2004a, pp. 389–90.
51   Sartre 2004a, p. 389.

expression 'the individual invention of common action' is particularly important for understanding the scenario. Such *praxis* of the fused group also leads
to violence, but Sartre does not criticise this element, insofar as 'this common freedom [*liberté commune*] gets its violence not only from the violent
negation which occasioned it, but also from the realm of necessity, which it
transcended'.[52] While he subjects it to critique from another point of view,
Sartre admits this violence in relation to the revolutionary ferments. In the
Critique of Dialectical Reason such a notion comes to play a decisive function,
almost forming a sort of condition of politics: the entire work could be interpreted starting from it. Sartre takes an ambivalent position in this regard. On
the one hand, and in continuity with his work prior to the *Critique*, particularly in *Being and Nothingness*, violence is considered an evil from the point of
view of the Other. On the other hand, violence is expected, in the sense of the
counter-violence of the oppressed against the oppressor. In 1789 the counter-
violence belongs to the revolutionaries against the dominant classes, who were
defenders of the Ancien Régime. Later I will highlight the relevance of such
an element in relation to Sartre's anticolonial critique, particularly with reference to the Algerian situation (above all, in the Preface to *The Wretched of the
Earth*).

To return to the French scenario in 1789, the masses converge within the
space of the neighbourhood, in the place where the insurrection happens.
The space is so to speak transformed into time: the material availability of the
neighbourhood impresses onto the situation a temporalisation marked by the
lived experience of the subjects who form the 'fused group'. And not just any
fused group, but rather that specific fused group in that determinate conjuncture. We see here an analysis that is, in many ways, a phenomenology of the
experience of the subjects, who are in turn destined to become 'quasi-objects',

---

52   Sartre 2004a, p. 406. Translation modified. For a different position than what is outlined
      here on violence, see Münster 2007, especially pp. 51–106. Münster comments in critical
      terms on the difference between Camus's (as well as Arendt's) categorical rejection and
      the Sartrean position, which, while not accepting 'offensive' violence, explicitly admits the
      right of the oppressed to use force; Verstraeten 1972, which insists on the crucial nature of
      the question of violence for understanding Sartre's ethics and politics; Verstraeten 2008,
      p. 116: 'All of the "violence" of the *Critique* resides in this ambivalence of need: *negation and
      negation of the negation or affirmation ... Thus violence is structurally constitutive of dialect-
      ical ontology*'; Guigot 2001, pp. 27–190 (here p. 125): 'violence is not an effect of sociality,
      but the ontic configuration of *rareté* and its ontological modality of representation. *Pos-
      itive violence is rareté in action in fraternity and terror*. Insofar as they are "brother", the
      Other always constitutes a risk'; Guigot 2007, pp. 179–227, and on the French Revolution
      in particular: pp. 190–200; Gaudeaux 2005.

products of the event that they triggered themselves. Against an established common practice, Sartre (at least in the *Critique of Dialectical Reason*) does not articulate a subjectivist position, since the subjects are 'acted on' by the event, on the basis of through a continuous exchange between subjectivity and objectivation, starting not from an abstract schema but from the immanence of *praxis*.

> [T]he essential characteristic of the fused group is the sudden resurrection of freedom ... against the common danger [*danger commun*], freedom frees itself from alienation [*aliénation*] and affirms itself as common efficacity. Now, it is precisely this characteristic of freedom which produces in each third party the perception of the Other (the former Other) as *the same*: freedom is both my individuality and my ubiquity ... This has nothing to do with the radical transformation [*transformation*] of freedom as individual *praxis*, since the statute of this freedom is to live the very totality of the group as a practical dimension to be realised in and by its singularity [*singularité*]. But it is true that there is a new relation between freedoms here, since in every totalisation of the group, the freedoms acknowledge themselves to be *the same*.[53]

In this formulation there emerges both a point of continuity and a point of discontinuity with the works up to *Being and Nothingness*. The continuity consists in the recognition of the crucial nature of the concept of freedom, with its complex, Stoic, Cartesian, but, even more so Enlightenment, roots.[54] Freedom is interpreted as liberation, on the basis of an expansive dynamic, which involves a multiplicity of subjects. But, with respect to Sartre's early texts, freedom is circumscribed and rearticulated, bearing in mind that the practico-inert does not disappear completely: a dark 'undercurrent' persists.

In order to grasp the overall sense of the argument, it is necessary to specify that Sartre examines this process on the basis of a regressive method (analytic, structural), thus beginning the exposition with individual *praxis* and only then arriving at the common dimension. Sartre could be accused of thinking by starting from the individual and conceiving common action on the basis of a constitutive reference to individual workings, without thoroughly understanding the 'complexification' present in the collective dimension. If this objection

---

53   Sartre 2004a, pp. 401–2. Translation modified.
54   Here see Jean Starobinski's magisterial essay (2006).

brings out a real difficulty of the argument, the relevance of the method must not be forgotten.[55] In this regard the comparison between Sartre's approach and that of Marx in the *1857 Introduction* is productive, as Marx begins with the more abstract and simpler element in order to then arrive at more concrete and complex structures. Moreover, the choice to begin *Capital* with the commodity is inscribed in this context.[56]

> It would be instructive to examine how such a relatively homogenous group ... creates its differentiations in action, on the basis of objective structures, by investigating the various stages of the taking of the Bastille, under the guidance of Flammermont and Lefebvre, but such an examination would take too long. In any case, this differentiation originates in the fact that the whole group is always *here* in the *praxis* of *this* third party, and that *for this third party* it is also over there, that is to say, *here* yet in the *praxis* of another third party ... But in a fused group, a mere means to common security [*salut commun*], these differentiations, however advanced they may be, do not survive action [*action*] ... this new state of the group (which manifests itself historically in every revolutionary situation) is defined by new characteristics, conditioned by new circumstances [*circumstances neuves*].[57]

Taking up Lefebvre's (as well as Flammerment's) analysis, Sartre highlights the dynamic produced by the common *praxis* of the fused group, with its continuous invention of the new ('new characteristics, conditioned by new circumstances'). In addition to the French Revolution, of course the reference to Rousseau here seems crucial, even if it is not explicit. It must not be forgotten that in French Marxism, a confrontation with the Genevan thinker was constant.[58] More specifically, it seems to me that there are two main elements of possible interaction with Rousseau. The first, already noted above, consists in the construction of a radically new horizon with respect to the past, starting from a critique of the 'present state of things'. However, this invokes not only Rousseau, but various *philosophes*, with their foundation myths and more or less utopian outlines of a new City.[59]

---

55   Cf. Sartre 1963, p. 148.

56   Cf. Marx 1990, pp. 125 ff.

57   Sartre 2004a, pp. 411–13.

58   On the relation between French Marxism and Rousseau, see most recently Dardot and Laval 2012, esp. pp. 685–89. In Italy, the connection between Rousseau and Marx was particularly researched and valorised by Della Volpe 1964.

59   Cf. Baczko 1999, esp. pp. 245–60.

There exists at least one other reason for the reference to Rousseau: the identification of the crucial nature of the common dimension and the 'fusional' characteristic of the group. Sartre takes up the Rousseauian (and later revolutionary) conception, so to speak of *égaliberté*,[60] consisting in the recognition of the point of departure in free and equal individuals, a condition of thinkability of the general will itself. In Rousseau's logic the common dimension does not constitute a negation of individual action, even if a series of internal difficulties exists in this regard. Rousseau's attention to the common dimension cannot be neglected, as well as his 'fusional' characterisation of individuals' action: such an element emerges in *On the Social Contract*, with the relevance of the general will and the legislator as a figure capable of instilling virtue in the hearts of the citizens on the basis of a full identification with the life of the community,[61] and, perhaps even more strictly, in texts such as *Julie, or the New Heloise*, in which the emphasis on the fusion of the individual in the community holds up the entire argument.[62] Such a valorisation of the common dimension leads Sartre, if not to put in question, at least to 'complicate,' to problematise his early assumption, in many ways absolute, of the crucial nature of freedom. At the same time, the emphasis on the 'fusional' element does not appear without difficulty: in particular, there is the risk of questioning any aspect of differentiation. It is important to keep in mind that the community in question is outlined not in the abstract, on the basis of an organicist model, but starting from the event, from the destabilising action of the storming of the Bastille. Without doubt Alain Badiou's political thought, with the decisive function played by the element of the *event*, despite the differences in their respective articulations, is strongly indebted to Sartre's approach.[63]

---

60   Cf. Balibar 2014.
61   Cf. Rousseau 2002, p. 191: 'To these three kinds of laws is added a fourth, the most important of all, which is engraved neither on marble nor on bronze, but in the hearts of citizens; a law which creates the real constitution of the State ... I speak of manners, customs, and above all of opinion'.
62   Cf. Rousseau 1997.
63   Regarding his confrontation as well as his debt to Sartre's conception, see the considerations in Badiou 2011: '[M]y notion of the event could find its genesis, especially being the absolute Sartrean that I am, in the description of the fused group, and particularly all of the episodes of the French Revolution Sartre interprets in this sense. Already my friend Emmanuel Terray maintained that the fundamental orientation of *Being and Event* remained faithful to Sartre' (p. 248).

3 The Dynamic of Fraternity

Sartre's entire philosophico-political trajectory is distinguished by fidelity to the three 'slogans' of the French Revolution: *liberté, égalité,* and *fraternité.* It would be excessive to examine the question of freedom in Sartre further. Regarding the second element, for Sartre it became clear how in the French Revolution a *conatus* unfolded towards the equality of men, united by an action (the storming of the Bastille) which precisely appears to question the existing hierarchies. For an even fuller examination of this thematic, Sartre's posthumously published work *Liberté-Égalité* is of great interest. Here Sartre, carrying out an analysis of the French Revolution, insists less upon freedom, interpreted originally as a constitutive element of the nobility, than upon equality, insofar as it is a distinctive mark of the bourgeoisie at the time, in its disruptive character with respect to the past.[64] But in the *Critique of Dialectical Reason* and the writings which followed it, Sartre particularly emphasises *fraternité,* in several respects the 'forgotten' slogan of the French Revolution, as it is less relevant to the dominant line inaugurated by Sieyès's *What is the Third Estate?.* It is unnecessary to dwell on the fact that the 1791 constitution found its basis in the concepts of freedom, as an overcoming of the estates' logic in the *Ancien Régime* and its bourgeois connotation, and equality, albeit in a juridical rather than social sense. In this regard the Jacobins would carry out a partial shift in terrain, trying to give equality a social meaning. Later, in *On the Jewish Question,* Marx's polemic against social inequality (starting with the justification of private property) and the purely monadic idea of freedom would be incisive.[65] The immanent critiques made by those (for example, women and colonised

---

64 Cf. Sartre 2008a. Cfr. De Coorebyter 2010, who focuses on the concepts of freedom and equality, also by means of Sieyès, showing how Sartre's foundation presents different characteristics with respect to the Marxist approach: the modality itself with which ideology is conceived does not correspond to Marx's approach. Indeed, for Sartre, bourgeois ideology, in itself, is not a mystification. With regard to equality, Sartre demonstrates its centrality in the dynamic of the Revolution, but at the same time emphasises that it verifies social inequalities, as emerges from the recognition of the right to property (in part. pp. 30–1). In this regard some of Marx's considerations, starting with *On the Jewish Question,* can be reactivated. According to De Coorebyter, the originality of Sartre's reading consists in the fact that the distinctive mark of the bourgeoisie (which is a mercantile and not industrial bourgeoisie, as it will become in the nineteenth century) is not constituted by freedom, but equality: indeed, freedom was rather the prerogative of the nobility (pp. 40–1). 'The third part of *Liberté-Égalité* develops the hypothesis that the bourgeois claim on equality consists not in claiming participation in the rights or privileges of several for everyone, but in the lowering of the superior caste to the level of the inferior caste' (p. 42).

65 Cf. Marx 1978, pp. 26–52.

people) who assumed but then radicalised the principles of the French Revolution, thereby bringing out internal problems, should also not be forgotten here. In this way, the internal limits of equality (and freedom) are clarified. Freedom and equality, even with their contradictions, played a decisive role in the French Revolution. At the same time, it is undeniable that such elements, in the historical development which followed them, represented, albeit in a differentiated way, the basis of the European constitutions.

The history of *fraternité* is much more complex, peripheral, and thwarted, insofar as this element emerged in the dominant thread of the French Revolution, culminating in the 1791 constitution, and even more so in the Terror. Its fortunes in the nineteenth century were also not linear. In particular, in 1848, *fraternité*, which was embraced also by workers' constituencies, remained the object of a harsh polemic from Marx, who remarks that such an idyllic concept conceals the presence of a 'prosaic' laceration into classes.[66] There are also traces of the concept in the workers' movement, but surely the 'slogans' of equality, in the first place, as well as freedom, played a more decisive role. In the *Critique of Dialectical Reason* Sartre sets out his own reflection precisely by beginning with a strong valorisation of fraternity. Resuming the argument outlined about the fused group-common *praxis* complex, with the French Revolution, the existing particularistic arrangements were dismissed and replaced with a new collective subject, the sovereign nation, in the form of representation ('one head, one vote'), as Sieyès had vividly theorised.

In order to grasp Sartre's notion of *fraternité*, the element of a pledge is crucial:

> All [of a pledge's] derivative forms ... derive their meaning from this basic form of pledge [*serment originel*]. But we must be careful not to confuse this with a *social contract* [*contrat social*]. We are not trying to describe the basis of particular societies – which, as we shall see, would be absurd; we are trying to explain the necessary transition from an immediate form of group which is in danger of dissolution to another form, which is reflexive but permanent. A pledge is a *practical invention* [*invention pratique*]. It cannot be presented as a possibility *for the individual*, unless it is assumed that the possibility is social [*social*] and that it appears only on the basis of groups which are already bound by a pledge ... [T]he act of making a pledge cannot be anything but common: the order is "Let us swear".[67]

---

66   Marx 1964, especially pp. 44–5.

67   Sartre 2004a, pp. 419–21. Translation modified. Cf. Sartre 2004, p. 443: 'Through the pledge, the group secures an ontological statute which will mitigate the dangers of differentiation.

Sartre rightly notes the irreducibility of the 'practical invention' of the pledge
to the social contract. However, it is necessary to emphasise that the 'constructivism' of the revolutionary pledge remains compatible with the contractualist
approach. 'The pledge is not a subjective or merely verbal determination: it is
a real modification of the group by my regulatory action ... my pledge becomes
my surety for myself in that it is me offering myself, in every third party, as everyone's guarantee of not relapsing'.[68] After the storming of the Bastille, which
united the individual and common dimensions, and attributed the same purpose to everyone, it was necessary to avoid the individual return to a purely
individual acting. Within such a dynamic the group becomes a sort of end in
itself, and thus gives rise to an organisation. Every individual holds their own
'mediated reciprocity' with the other individual no longer in the immanence of
action, but from the solemnity of the act of the pledge. In the twentieth century,
an example of the group pledge is the soviets.

The brother is the other that with me has spoken the pledge to reciprocal
fidelity, which involves neither I nor you, but what Sartre calls the 'third party'.
Only in the measure in which each is witness to the other as a 'third party' can
the latter act as an element formed neither by an I or a you, but a multiplicity
of 'third parties'. Each member of the group constitutes a 'third party' for all
of the others, and in this way each other represents a 'third party' for themselves: 'In the context of this new task, every third party as such will seek in
himself the dissolution into free common activity [*libre activité commune*] ...
At this moment, he is sovereign, that is to say, he becomes, through the change
of *praxis*, the organiser of common praxis'.[69] Fraternity activates a community
that is eccentric to the sovereign nation. It can be asked how much such a vision
owes to Rousseau's approach, and the element of the general will, in its irreducibility to the will of everyone or the will of the majority, and its attempt to
'capture' the *moi commun*. Within such a framework, the risk consists in the fact
that the individual dimension can remain 'sunk within' the common dimen-

---

As I have already said, this pledge is not necessarily a real operation or an explicit decision
... So, whether or not a pledge was really made, the organisation of the group becomes the
immediate objective'.

68   Sartre 2004a, p. 422. Cf: Sartre 2004, pp. 427–8: 'A pledge necessarily involves ... (1) the
characteristics of an order ... (2) the characteristic of a manipulation of myself ... the real
moment of the common action [*action commune*] is contained in the order "Let us swear"'.

69   Sartre 2004a, p. 370. Cf. Jameson 1971, p. 253, who remarks on the relevance of the 'third
party' (which is also presented as an implicit critique of the binary dimension of structuralism): 'The group needs to interiorize its unity in some more basic way, and this is done
by the interiorization of the formerly external third party. Now each member of the group
becomes a third to all the rest, and this is to be understood not statically but dynamically'.

sion: it is a matter of the 'fusional' character of the group. But this question can also be articulated in other terms, insisting on its antiessentialist valence, and thus on the constitutive reference to an action capable of putting 'the present state of things' into question: in 'common praxis', indeed, 'each' and 'all' converge.

The emphasis on fraternity gives an account of the fact that 'common being' does not mean mere identity, on the basis of a logic of uniformity:

> [T]his fraternity [*fraternité*] is not based, as is sometimes stupidly supposed, on physical resemblance expressing some deep identity of natures ... We are brothers in so far as, following the creative act of the pledge, *we are our own sons*, our common invention [*invention commune*] ... fraternity is the real bond between common individuals [*lien réel des individus communs*]. In so far as everyone lives *his being* and that of the Other (whether in simply being there, close to the Other, or in the resemblance-solidarity of black rebels, or of whites on the defensive) in the form of untranscendable reciprocal obligations. Indeed: the colour of their skin, taken as a pure, reciprocal obligation by the black rebels of San Domingo, and, at the same time, as everyone's material, inert guarantee against the possibility of alienation [*aliénation*], the colour of their skin being taken, in and by everyone, not as a universal physiological characteristic, but as a historical characteristic based on the *past unity* of a free *promotion* – this is fraternity, that is to say the fundamental, practical structure of all the reciprocal relations between the members of a group.[70]

The concept of the 'common individual',[71] the outcome of the fused group, gives rise to the irreducibility of this idea to any form of atomism. With the pledge, as a practical invention, we become brothers on the basis of a series of reciprocal obligations which, instead of being imposed duties, are activated by that real co-implication between 'own' and 'other' that is repeatedly invoked. In Santo Domingo fraternity passes through the element of the skin not in physical terms but in historical ones, starting from the common attempt to go-beyond alienation.

---

70   Sartre 2004a, pp. 437–8. Translation modified.
71   Sartre 2004a, p. 449: 'At the level of the fused group, the common individual [*individu commun*] appeared to us as an organic individual in so far as he interiorised the multiplicity of the third parties and united it through his *praxis* ... The *common* characteristic of the individual ... becomes everyone's juridical power [*pouvoir juridique*] over organic individuality in himself and in every third party'.

Fraternity maintains an open relation with the other two 'slogans' of the French Revolution – freedom, always conceived by Sartre as an unrenounceable point of departure – and equality. With regard to the latter, again the situation in Santo Domingo is emblematic: it is a struggle for equality understood not only as mere uniformity. Further, Sartre outlines an 'egalitarian fraternity',[72] which testifies to the interweaving of fraternity and equality. Fraternity moreover constitutes a 'bridge' between freedom and equality, insofar as they are connected through a deep, substantial link, and not a purely rational one. The interaction between 'own' and 'other' is heard by each and all. Beyond the specific use of the notion of *fraternité*, a comparison with Rousseau again proves meaningful, in his figure of the legislator capable of instilling the general will in the hearts of citizens. For Rousseau there exist 'laws' that are more important than positive laws: these are customs, connected to the virtue of citizens.[73]

Following the reasoning within the internal dynamic of the French Revolution, the group, which begins as a means, becomes an end, in order to prevent individuals from returning to a purely individual praxis. The pledge maintains that reciprocity among individuals that earlier was spontaneously present among individuals who shared a common action in the storming of the Bastille. After the revolution, what proves to be necessary is an organisation that can render the constitutive elements effective.[74] If violence was carried out against the outside during the insurrection, with the passage of time it became interiorised within the group. 'The fundamental reinvention [*réinvention*], within the pledge, is the project of substituting a real fear, produced by the group itself, for the retreating external fear, whose very distance is deceptive. And we have already encountered this fear ... it is called Terror'.[75] This discourse is in several respects situated in continuity with the Hobbesian approach, since it brings out the 'political nature' of fear in its internal dynamic. Indeed, it is a matter of a fear that is no longer external, but internal to the group, and that thus materialises itself in the Terror.

In the development of the French Revolution, fraternity is maintained among the individuals of the group at the price of an increasing terror – the 'Fraternity-Terror'.

---

72   Sartre 2004a, p. 466.

73   Cf. note 61, page 24 above.

74   Cf. Sartre 2004a, pp. 446–7: 'Organisation, then, is both the discovery of practical exigencies in the object and a distribution of tasks amongst individuals on the basis of this dialectical discovery ... Voluntarism and opportunism are characterised, in the organisation, as the action of the group on its members ... The group defines, directs, controls, and constantly corrects the common praxis'.

75   Sartre 2004a, p. 430. Translation modified.

I am a brother in violence to all my neighbours: and it is clear that anyone who shunned this fraternity would be suspect ... The invention [*invention*] of the Terror as a counter-violence engendered by the group itself and applied by common individuals to every particular agent (in so far as he contains a threat of seriality) is, therefore, a use of common force [*force commune*], hitherto used against the enemy, in order to reshape the group itself ... And this possibility that fraternity with a given person may suddenly change, through the betrayal of the brother, into lynching and extermination, is given in fraternity itself as its source and limit.[76]

Fraternity is conserved, but in a violently forced way, in looking for internal enemies in a climate of continuous suspicion. The group no longer remains conditioned by a common action, but rather comes to take on an increasingly absolute and self-referential valence. We could ask if there is operative in Sartre the Hegelian idea that the Terror had present at its basis a 'fury of disappearing', according to an abstract, intellectualist logic.[77] Sartre's critique actually presents coordinates that are largely different, aiming rather at bringing out the dynamic of fraternity, and at exposing the alienating character (versus the vitality of the fused group) of the organisation, and after this, the institution. In terms of the relation between movement and organisation, in fact, Sartre articulates a position that is incompatible with the Hegelian one.

In the purged Convention, the 'collective' [*collectif*] manifested from below the impossibility of the group being a subject [*sujet*] (contrary to what Durkheim believed) and its degree of reality was directly proportional to this very impossibility. It is on this account that it had its own structures, laws and rigidity ... However, in so far as everyone attempts to realise the group as a unified praxis, and in so far as he reveals the other-reality of the community [*communauté*] as an unpredictable serial deviation ... he must strive to liquidate the Other as a factor of dispersive inertia.[78]

In distinction from Durkheim and his primacy of the 'social', Sartre strongly valorises the individual *conatus*, conceiving of it in discord not with the common dimension, but with the serialising hypostatisation of the latter accomplished by the organisation. In this way the group, becoming an end in

---

76 Sartre 2004a, pp. 439–40. Translation modified.
77 Cfr. Hegel 1977, p. 355 ff.
78 Sartre 2004a, p. 595.

itself, risks 'strangling' individual praxis into a collective praxis configured as the negation of the Other.

> [T]here is no Platonic Idea of Terror, but only different Terrors and if the historian wishes to identify characteristics which are common to him, he will have to do it *a posteriori*, on the basis of careful considerations ... The Terror of 1789 to 1794 is inseparable from the Revolution itself and has meaning only within a totalising reconstruction effected by historians ... I am not attempting to set out the essential relations, even reduced to the utmost simplicity, which might constitute *an essence* [*essence*] *of Terror*: there is no such essence. I only wish to describe certain conditions ... which are necessarily realised by the being-in-the-group of a common individual when Terror occurs as a historical development in specific circumstances [*circonstances définies*]. The plurality [*pluralité*] of Terrors even during the revolutionary Terror (1789 to 1794) seems to me so obvious that I have chosen for my example a limited and induced terror.[79]

The distance from Hegel's approach is also clear from the fact that Sartre's aim does not consist in comprehending the essence of the Jacobin terror. Moreover, Sartre adopts the term 'Terror' in the *Critique of Dialectical Reason* not only in reference to Jacobinism, but insofar as it is a distinctive feature of the Revolution, of everyone following the logic of the pledge.[80] At the root of his argument stands not so much a critique of the Terror as an analysis of the dynamic of fraternity at the moment in which it passes from an organism to an organisation, and then from an organisation to an institution. However, it is again necessary to keep in mind the regressive method of the first part of the *Critique*, analogous to Marx's *1857 Introduction*, departing from the abstract, from the 'simple': the development thus should not be developed in terms of temporal succession.

With the institution we see a further element of the organised moment. Through the latter, the group, having become a genuine end for its members, has preserved fraternity among its members at the price of an increasing regime of terror. But the organised group comes to find itself in a checkmate position, unable to really give rise to a 'hyperorganic unity'. On the one hand it poses individual freedoms to its own base, while on the other it considers them an obstacle to its own development. In this way the organisation comes to be an institution, which tries to resolve the problem.

---

79   Sartre 2004a, p. 597 n. 73. Translation modified.
80   On the terror, see Guigot 2001, p. 121: 'For Sartre there are ... various Terrors, which the historian can only totalise with prudence'.

The group reacts to this permanent danger, appearing at the level or organisation, with new practices: it produces itself in the form of an *institutionalised group* [*groupe institutionnalisé*]; which means that 'organs', functions and powers are transformed into institutions; that, in the framework of institutions, the community tries to acquire a new type of unity by institutionalising sovereignty, and that the common individual transforms himself into an institutional individual [*individu institutionnel*].[81]

The discourse here is quite general, and in order to establish a historical articulation, it is necessary to refer to the development within the Revolution up through the Thermidor and to the emergence of Napoleon Bonaparte, and the subsequent events in the nineteenth century which led to the reinforcement of the French state, with its structures of discipline. Within this scenario the expansive dimension proper to common action is disempowered. The fused group, from the phase of its 'heroic' constitution (the storming of the Bastille), reaches a situation in which direct participation in the event ceases, and in this way a 'cooling down' is produced, which risks a return to seriality on new grounds. The subject is liquidated, in the name of the superior interest of the group and the triumph of the logic of control. We no longer find a unity truly satisfying for its components singularly considered: individuals feel unified only through something outside of them. The purge of those who do not wish to be united to the order is the consequence of the development.

Sovereignty is inscribed within this process: it is enough to think of Sieyès's reflection on this front, in which the expansive character of constituent power is 'caged' in the constituted power of the state-form. In this way the neutralisation of every conflictual dynamic and the formation of a new totalisation are confirmed, but at the price of the elimination of every prospect of social integration.

> [T]he institution [*institution*] can actually appear only at a particular moment in the involution of the group, and as an exact index of its disintegration ... The institutional moment, in the group, corresponds to what might be called the systematic self-domestication of man by man ... In so far as the ossification of the ossified *praxis* which is the institution is due to our own impotence, it constitutes for each and for all a precise index of *reification* [*réification*] ... [T]he common individual tries to become a

---

81   Sartre 2004a, p. 591.

thing which is held against other things by the unity of a seal; the model for the institutional group is *the forged tool*. And everyone is implicated as such in institutionality. But on the other hand this is also because they are its victims *even before they are born.*[82]

According to Sartre, the logic of the institution risks producing a genuine disintegration of the group, on the basis of an objectivising, alienating, and serialising perspective. Later I will draw out some elements which complicate the schema noted here, which will enable a reading of the institution as not unilaterally destructive.

Individuals remain united by something, the state, which however appears entirely external to them. Indeed, the institution refers back to authority,[83] and authority to sovereignty,[84] embodied in the state. '[T]he sovereign reigns through and over the impotence of all; their living practical union would make his function useless, and indeed impossible to perform'.[85] If the sovereign institution had arisen to avoid the crushing of the group, the outcome is instead constituted precisely in this way, and thus by an increasing individual atomisation, the other face of seriality. On the basis of a circularity (always keeping in mind the categorial dimension of the first part of the *Critique*, and not 'bending' the discourse into terms of temporal succession), the risk consists in the return to the series: in this perspective, Sartre subjects the state-element to a strong critique. In this way *fraternité* tends to completely dissolve, since no other link seems to exist to the state-form other than an external one (or it remains entirely 'caged' within a disciplinary system). Although Sieyès is cited, more or less positively (the idea of the Third Estate, which is nothing and must become everything), a strict distance from his perspective emerges. For him, revolutionary discourse, with the formation of the Assembly and then the emanation of the constitution, becomes a representative discourse, and thus an institutional discourse. In Sieyès the constituent tension of the Third Estate is 'enclosed' within a constitutional and political structure, and the revolutionary *conatus* is

---

82   Sartre 2004a, pp. 605–6.
83   Cf. Sartre 2004a, p. 607: 'The institutional system as an exteriority of inertia necessarily refers to authority [autorité] as its reinteriorisation; and *authority*, as a power [*pouvoir*] over all powers and over all third parties through these powers, is itself established by the system as an institutional guarantee of institutions'.
84   Cf. Sartre 2004a, p. 207: 'The foundation of authority is ... sovereignty [*souveraineté*], in so far as, after the stage of the fused group, it is the quasi-sovereignty of the regulatory third party'.
85   Sartre 2004a, p. 628.

mostly neutralised.[86] In many ways the exponents of the Terror tried, instead, to re-open the revolutionary 'fuse' through a permanent mobilisation.

Two possible limits or risks to Sartre's account are the following. The first is a too strict antithesis between the 'positivity' of the movement, linked to the common action (materialised in the storming of the Bastille) of the fused group, and the 'negativity' of any form of organisation, or even more so, institution, which inevitably leads to a process of ossification, with oppressive effects for the individual. At times it seems that the radical critique of the state-form, and more generally, that the law should not be fully charged with an imminent crossing of spheres, is consolidated into a too immediate 'anti-juridicism' endowed with an absoluteness that creates difficulty for a political articulation of the group in the aftermath of the revolutionary event. Sartre's approach presents an *anarchisant* risk, so to speak, finding at its root a strong valorisation of the individual dimension (which coheres with what happened in Sartre's earlier itinerary). I will return to this question extensively in the second part of the book when I turn to Sartre's analysis of the passage from the Bolshevik Revolution to the Soviet Union.

It is necessary to re-emphasise the paradigmatic character of the French Revolution for Sartre's thought. Indeed, the French Revolution, in many respects the 'mother' of all revolutions, constitutes an 'inventing the new'. The identification of the French Revolution as *exemplum* problematises the idea of the full inscription of the first part of the *Critique* onto a categorial level. This event, in its immanence, decisively shines a light onto all of the notions which are unpacked and cannot be understood abstractly or absent from the historical dimension. Common praxis, with its character of acceleration, is aimed at creating new modes of life, new relations among individuals, as the concrete experience of the French Revolution vividly displayed. It is necessary to add an additional consideration here, which complicates the argument. Undoubtedly, even if through the reference to the historical event of the French Revolution, we find ourselves facing a strong valorisation of the expansive dimension of the fused group. But maintaining such a thesis does not mean assuming that Sartre's gaze is exclusively centered on the revolutionary subject-revolutionary event complex. Indeed, the practico-inert plays a decisive function, and never disappears, just as seriality is not configured simply as an element prior to the group. This aspect gives rise to the existence of 'undiscovered areas' within the revolutionary process. Moreover, for Sartre, the Terror does not represent only a specific phase, but remains constitutive of the entire French Revolution. The

---

86   Cf. Negri 1999, especially pp. 212–20.

purge, which we saw operative within the organisation and the institution, was present right from the beginning: Sieyès's own *What is the Third Estate?* is pervaded by such logic against the other two privileged and unproductive estates.

To this problematisation we can add one more, relative to the notion of the group. Sartre's original attempt, even starting from an analysis of the French Revolution, consists in giving an account of the complexity of social stratification. The group allows such plurality to be grasped, as it is open to different developments, which are not always predictable: it is irreducible to specific genetic and functional determinations of socio-economic nature, even though it is related to these elements. We see a sort of phenomenology of groups, of the sets of individuals gathered by an action, within specific conditions however, and never fully lacking serial aspects. Such a notion, which also contains its several limits (for example, sometimes a certain genericity), presents the merit of trying to catch a multiplicity of situations and subjects, even with their chiaroscural character, not always in a revolutionary dynamic. In this sense it is necessary to deepen the relation between the concepts of group and class, a question that will require a confrontation with Marx and Marxism.

The *Novum* Of Communism Between Freedom And Equality: Marx

1   The Confrontation with Marx and Marxism

Sartre's relation with Marx and Marxism is extremely complex. This book's entire argument could actually focus on this problematic, on which there exists a full-fledged literature.[1] Moreover, throughout this work I make continuous reference to Marx and Marxism: there are numerous explicit or implicit references in the preceding chapters, particularly chapter two. Investigating this problem means locating an element that is central for the very understanding of Sartre's theoretico-political itinerary. In this regard, however, it is necessary to make a qualification. As Sartre himself points out in various places (and particularly in *Search for a Method*, one particularly important text for deepening these problematics), already in the 1920s he had begun to read Marxist works with passion, from *The German Ideology* to *Capital*, but there is no doubt that a stronger interest arose starting with the war and the Resistance. In this sense, there are deep traces of Marx earlier than this period, and especially in *Being and Nothingness* (one thinks of the question of alienation), but it is above all in the postwar period that Sartre carries out a genuine *Auseinandersetzung* with Marx and Marxism.

I examine this problem in its complexity, with its lights and its shadows, without wanting either to reduce Sartre to Marxism or to emphasise the distance in positive or negative terms. There emerge points of both continuity and discontinuity, but these must be interpreted in a complementary way, in relation to Sartre's theoretical trajectory and his political positioning when he was in turn confronted with the specific events of the time. One limit in several treatments (one thinks, for example, in Italy, of that of Pietro Chiodi)[2]

---

1   On the relation between Sartre and Marxism, there are a number of interpretations. See Gorz 1967; Desan 1965, who tends to emphasise the irreconcilability between Sartre's perspective, in the last instance founded on individual praxis, and the Marxian perspective; Hartmann 1966; Fetscher 1988; Jameson 1971; Poster 1975, pp. 265–305; Schwartz 1976; Jay 1984, pp. 331–60; Dobson 1993, esp. pp. 180–8; Aronson 1995, pp. 34–44; Coombes 2008; Basso 2019.

2   Chiodi's work (1973 [1965]) has had a primary role for the reception of this question in Italy. While he makes several important observations, he interprets both Sartre and Marxism static-

consists in stiffening both Sartre's treatment and the Marxist approach, while outlining a framework that is too unitary. It is clear that, assuming a position such as that of Chiodi, one can only arrive at the idea of an extreme distance (one beyond interest of a continuous comparison) of Sartre from Marxism, interpreting such a perspective either in a critical mode, as an abstract, anti-materialist vision (on the basis of an 'orthodox' Marxist approach), or on the contrary, as a productive extraneity with respect to Marxism and its limits. The entire path I trace here is aimed at avoiding this type of approach, instead trying to engage Sartre's relation with Marx and Marxism in dynamic terms on the one hand, and on the other, trying to establish an overall representation of this relation.

The problem cannot be examined abstractly but must instead be connected to the historical and political events of the postwar period, and to Sartre's *engagement* within them. Maintaining this thesis does not mean that there exists no 'red thread' of this reflection, consisting in the attempt to establish a structural connection between existentialism and Marxism.[3] In 'Materialism and Revolution' (1946), written in the immediate aftermath of the war, we find a critical confrontation with the Marxism of the time, which according to Sartre is characterised by a dualism between the 'practical' element of revolutionary action and the 'theoretical' element, in simplistic terms, of materialism. Substantially, however, Marxism is thoroughly criticised in this text, in the sense that Sartre here interprets it as founded only upon a practical dimension, and as incapable of arriving at a rigorous and complex discursive articulation. However, it is important to clarify that Sartre's polemical objective is not represented by Marx, but by Marxism, or a certain way of understanding Marxism, based on the aforementioned divergence. Sartre's thought also moves in the direction of a problematisation of materialism, in order to understand whether

---

ally, and in this way only an absolute incommunicability can result between the two horizons. According to Chiodi, the entire framework of the *Critique of Dialectical Reason* is incompatible with the Marxian approach: for example, the way in which concepts such as alienation and class are sketched, for him, is anti-Marxist. Fergnani (1978, esp. pp. 11–12) outlines some critical and accurate observations. For an approach that is different from Chiodi, but also very far from the perspective I outline here, see Barale 1981, particularly chapter two (pp. 79–112), which is significantly titled 'For an Imaginary Marxism', as well as Barale 1977, especially pp. 150–320. For an overall summary of the Italian debate, see also Valentini 1959.

3   On the relation between Marxism and existentialism, there are a number of interpretations: Murdoch 1987; Barnes 1974, pp. 98–129; Cera 1972, esp. pp. 137–54; Lawler 1976; Archard 1980; Flynn 1984, for whom there emerges in Sartre a 'revisionist' Marxism (p. xiii), with Sartre being 'a libertarian socialist' (p. 198): 'What Sartre's theory lacks most basically ... is an ontology of relations' (p. 206); Flynn 2011; Flynn 2014.

and to what degree it is philosophically adequate and convincing, and not only functional for political action. 'In a word, what is necessary is a theoretical philosophy which shows that the reality of man is action [*action*] and that acting on the universe is one and the same with understanding the universe as it is. To put it in other terms, action is the unveiling of reality *at the same time* as a modification of this reality'.[4] Here we see a reprisal, which is also a reformulation, of the question of the Marxian link between theory and praxis. The emphasis on the necessity of such a link does not imply a subsumption of theory to praxis, or an abdication of the truthful character of philosophy. In this sense, the element of materialism must not be uncritically assumed as 'myth'. It is necessary to observe that, in this phase, the Sartrean idea of a 'Marxist' philosophy of praxis constitutes only a *conatus* and not an actual realisation. Indeed, in 'Materialism and Revolution' the *pars costruens* is not really developed and risks reproducing, without particular innovations, the conceptual schema of *Being and Nothingness*, with a difficulty in providing a political articulation of the argument.

In the early 1950s Sartre further develops these questions by examining them in connection with historical and political events, with reference to both the French situation and to international dynamics (one thinks, first of all, of Indochina and Korea). After a period of militancy in the *Rassemblement démocratique révolutionnaire* (RDF), Sartre increasingly drew near to the PCF, becoming a sort of fellow traveler, and, just like various leftist intellectuals of the time, considered the USSR as in some ways a model, at least in its oppositional function confronting the bourgeois, capitalist world. To examine Sartre's situation in the 1950s, it is necessary to keep in mind that two tomes of *Situations* (VI and VII) are dedicated precisely to the 'Problèmes du marxisme'. A significant text in this regard, published in installments in *Les Tempes modernes* between 1952 and 1954, is *The Communists and Peace*. We must be very attentive when evaluating this text: too often it is immediately criticised, without appreciating its ambivalences and fruitful aspects, in addition to the limits and problems that remain open. Merleau-Ponty's critique in *Adventures of the Dialectic* remains emblematic in this regard, where Sartre is reprimanded as an 'ultrabolshevik'.[5] Sartre later takes a distance from his own thesis in *The Communists and Peace*. There are surely aspects in this text that link to Sartre's positioning in these early years of the 1950s, in which his drawing nearer to the PCF was particularly marked. For this reason, he launches a harsh polemic

---

4   Sartre 1946, p. 352.
5   Merleau-Ponty 1955.

towards those intellectuals who did not make specific stands and who, despite giving a progressive appearance, in fact provided a legitimation of bourgeois rule.

Within the text, the object of analysis of such *engagement* remains strongly connected to the role of the party. Beyond the polemics against this or that specific claim, the 'heart' of the critique on the part of various intellectuals, within so-called 'Western Marxism', in confronting Sartre resides precisely in the fact that, in *The Communists and Peace*, he assigns a decisive role to the party. The hypothesis of a discrepancy between class and party is not really contemplated (or, if it is contemplated, it is subjected to a strong critique), as if the former could find its unity, its 'sedimentation', its true political actualisation, only in the latter. In this sense, a solution such as Luxemburg's is partially rejected. Class, without the presence of the party, is pure mass, exteriority, dispersion: we could maintain, adopting Sartre's terminology in *Being and Nothingness*, that, in order to become 'for itself', to carry out a transcendence of the 'in itself', the function of the party reveals itself as necessary. The relation between the single worker and the party is outlined on the basis of a supremacy of the latter over the former:

> [T]he worker, transformed by the organization into a subject [*sujet*], finds his practical reality beginning with his metamorphosis; whatever he thinks or does, it begins with his *transformation*; and the latter, in its turn, takes place in the actual framework of the Party's policy. His freedom [*liberté*], which is simply his power to transcend the given situation – in short, to act – manifests itself then within this given reality which is the organization; he forms his opinions on the context of the principles which the Party gives to him ... In a word, the party is his freedom.[6] Without the C.P., the French proletariat would not have an empirical history.[7]

With regard to the long-standing question of the relation between spontaneity and organisation in the history of Marxism, the risk is on the one hand maintaining that the latter can be easily evaded, not really posing the problem of the political articulation of the argument, and on the other hand conceiving the single worker and the class as totally 'resolved' in the party, without a real 'gap', and therefore on the basis of a complete subordination to the party. Surely Sartre's attitude in *The Communists and Peace* tends towards a strong accentu-

---

6 Sartre 1968, pp. 130–1. Translation modified.
7 Sartre 1968, p. 134.

ation of the role of the party, through which the freedom of the worker and the class which belongs to it would become concrete: it follows that any form of spontaneism is strongly criticised.

In 'Portrait of the Adventurer', Sartre outlines an analogous position:

> When [the militant] entered the Party, the goal metamorphosed itself under his eyes: he understood that his demands would only be realized by the creation of a socialist society. And he metamorphosed himself at the same time as the goal: in him and through him the Party pursued the realization of that absolute goal. The singularity [*singularité*] acknowledged in him was the singular will to make that realization come true.[8]

The relevance of the party and thus the class–party nexus also emerges in the extremely polemical *Response to Claude Lefort*:

> I see that the leaders are nothing without the masses, but the working class has coherence and power only in so far as it has confidence in the leaders ... The Party cannot be distinguished from the masses except insofar as it is their union ... The Party shapes the social framework of working class memory.[9]

It is not a matter of negating the subjectivity of the masses, but of constantly keeping open the relation between them and the party, which can render them effectual, transforming their passions into political actions.

Such a position appears difficult to reconcile with the strong valorisation, on the part of the 'early' Sartre, of the freedom of man, of the *conatus* towards individual singularity. However, even in the *Critique of Dialectical Reason* there unfolds a critique of collectives which tend to 'strangle' the propulsive force of single individuals and their action. In terms of the more specific and directly political question of the relation between spontaneity and organisation, in the *Critique of Dialectical Reason*, but even more in the texts which follow it, Sartre's 'pendulum' appears to have swung to the side of the movement. Or better yet, the very dynamic of the group is conceived in such a way as to suggest that, with the organisation and even more with the institution, one loses the propulsive force of the 'germinal phase' and risks arriving in a situation of disciplined and disciplining, which results in a new seriality. However, Sartre's valorisation of

---

8   Sartre 2013c, p. 202. Translation modified.
9   Sartre 1968, pp. 272–3.

1968 led to a strongly critical approach regarding the serialising character of the organisation. Here the risk Sartre takes appears opposed to that present in *The Communists and Peace*.

Sartre's position outlined in this work and other texts of the early 1950s will quickly come to be profoundly rearticulated. Whether or not we agree with him (and from various perspectives, we probably do not, without for this reason maintaining that Sartre is fully convincing in these years), with respect to Merleau-Ponty's critique of Sartre's 'ultrabolshevism', it is important to note that such a polemic can acquire a determinate meaning in relation to the text in question, and to the other short writings from these years, but not to Sartre's entire political reflection. I will not focus here on the complex reasons, philosophical and political, underlying the progressive distancing between Sartre and Merleau-Ponty, but instead limit myself to emphasising that the phase where Sartre features as an object of analysis is concentrated between *Humanism and Terror* (1947) and *Adventures of the Dialectic* (1955). *Humanism and Terror*, albeit with a growing set of problematisations and doubts, keeps open a relation with Marx, on the basis of a sort of 'Marxism of waiting', a critique of liberalism, and an approach in many ways harmonious with the 'subjective' valorisation of the proletariat in Lukács's *History and Class Consciousness*. Merleau-Ponty contrasts this 'Marxism of waiting' with a 'scholastic' Marxism, arguing that Marxism should be articulated through a critical and open dialectic, on the basis of a continuous 'exchange' between interiority and exteriority.[10] Merleau-Ponty's polemic regarding the Moscow Trials does not imply an acceptance of Koestler's theses and did not anticipate the diagnosis of an end of Marxism. There is no doubt that Sartre resented the approach of *Humanism and Terror* intensely, as well as the fact that, by his own admission, in the immediate postwar period he recognised that Merleau-Ponty was more 'internal' than him with regard to determinate theoretico-political and directly political questions. But, subsequently, *Adventure of the Dialectic* marks a radical departure from Marxism, not on the basis of a programmatic anti-communism, but a 'noncommunism' which questions the very possibility of a Marxist dialectic, even though formulated in critical and open terms. Much later he will return to the question of the relation with Sartre, but, anyway, Merleau-Ponty came to assume a strongly critical approach towards his own theses in *Humanism and Terror*, or at least closed the possibility of such a dialectic, which in this text was still open, although not without ambivalences and doubts: this need also explains the verbose character of the text, the obsessive

10   Merleau-Ponty 1969.

necessity of clarifying, which is also a self-clarification. In any case, the position Merleau-Ponty takes towards Sartre regarding his 'ultrabolshevism', and a reading of Marxism that was in his view voluntaristic and moralisitc, and not really materialist, appears – however much a series of problematic elements in Sartre's reasoning emerge – rather virulent, and in many ways ungenerous.

As I emphasised earlier, it is necessary to outline an argument about Sartre's early 1950s work that is more complex than the idea that his position can be simply characterised as a defense of the role of the party. For example, a very important text such as 'Portrait of an Adventurer' (1950) contains a vivid description of the militant, in addition to the adventurer:

> The Party will be a necessary mediator between [the militant] and his closest friends ... his existence is not a pure abstraction: he knows himself as a member of the class and Party that are making history. He knows that he is defined by precise tasks and by a great hope ... The militant remains halfway between the irreplaceable and the interchangeable: he serves, that is all.[11]

> The militant, sustained and continuously re-created by this project that transcends him, finds himself sheltered from death: the enterprise [*enterprise*] that defines him exceeds the duration of a life by far; hence he works ceaselessly beyond his own death.[12]

Clearly there exists the risk of a subjection of the militant to the party, but Sartre specifies that he finds the militant neither a victim nor a hero, but rather a complex figure, in whom the element of discipline surely plays an important, but not absolute, function. Indeed, the militant identifies fully with the end of the party, to the point of not possessing an autonomous existence from it: in the 'fusion' between such a figure and the purpose (in this regard prefiguring what will later be called the 'fused group'), the party comes to play a decisive role, in which passion and action inextricably intertwine.

While I have until now emphasised an element of discontinuity between the argument of *The Communists and Peace* and both earlier texts and the thesis that would figure in Sartre's subsequent writings, it is necessary to recall an aspect, present in the given work, that instead constitutes a distinctive feature

11   Sartre 2013c, pp. 199–200.
12   Sartre 2013c, p. 202.

of Sartre's entire itinerary: the strong link established between class and action. In other words, class is not conceived on the basis of either an ontological or a sociological hypostatisation, but rather articulated from the dynamic of action: class is not given outside and before praxis. The latter, in some circumstances, becomes revolutionary action, with a co-implication between the individual and collective dimensions:

> In the great moments of the workers' history, the Revolution was neither a future event [*événement*] nor an object of faith, it was the movement [*mouvement*] of the proletariat, the daily *practice* of each [*chacun*] and every [*tous*] worker; not the apocalyptic conclusion of an adventure, but the simple power to make history; not *a* future moment, but for these men exiled in an unlivable present, the sudden discovery of a future [*avenir*]. The Revolution was ... in short, a constant liaison between the individual and the class and between the singular [*singulier*] and the general [*général*].[13]

The revolution is rooted in the 'movement of the proletariat', configuring itself as a daily practice in which the individual and common spheres interpenetrate. In the revolution, the singularity of contingent action and the universality of history converge, such that a fusion is realised between 'each' and 'every'. Only within determinate circumstances does such interpenetration occur: generally, the relation between the two dimensions has an unstable character. Within this scenario, the strict link between class and action emerges with clarity:

> The proletariat forms itself by its day-to-day action. It exists only by acting. It is action. If it ceases to act, it decomposes. I am not saying anything new: you will find this in Marx.[14]

This perspective is compatible with what emerges in the analysis of the *Critique of Dialectical Reason* several years later, in which the link between fused group and common praxis remains stringent. In this way the modality with which the class–action relation is sketched, unlike the question of the valorisation of the party, remains a 'red thread' throughout Sartre's entire trajectory. The writings from this period are distinguished by the attempt to fertilise socialism with the

---

13   Sartre 1968, p. 86. Translation modified.
14   Sartre 1968, p. 97.

dimension of freedom and vice versa. This approach, not without its difficulties and contradictory outcomes, is also testified to by a work such as *Saint Genet: Actor and Martyr* (1952).[15]

In the 1960s, a decisive text for understanding Sartre's political thought and its relation with Marxism is the *Critique of Dialectical Reason*. From the viewpoint of method, the reference to the earlier *Search for a Method* comes to play an extremely important function. Here we see, on the one hand, a critique of dogmatic Marxism, and on the other, an attempt to relaunch Marxism, by 'intercepting' specific Marxian intuitions and making them converse with existentialism.

> [W]hat has made the force and richness of Marxism is the fact that it has been the most radical attempt to clarify the historical process in its totality ... Marxism is still very young, almost in its infancy; it has scarcely begun to develop. It remains, therefore, the philosophy of our time. We cannot go beyond it because we have not gone beyond the circumstances which engendered it. Our thoughts, whatever they may be, can be formed only upon this humus.[16]

Two aspects in particular emerge here. The first, which is the source of some difficulty, is that the reflection is inserted completely within Marxism ('the philosophy of our time'), as if everything could stand on this basis. The second, which poses several other problems, is that Marxism is interpreted as a philosophy. The first aspect consists in the critique of a Marxism that is sclerotised, stiffened, giving birth to that dualism, already examined, between a rigid, dogmatic theory and a practice entirely functional to empirical politics. For Sartre it is instead a matter of activating a link between theory and practice, avoiding however both a consideration of the former in entirely instrumental terms and a 'bending' of the latter into an immediate end. In particular, the importance of philosophy, and its relation with the dimension of truth, albeit complex and never finally concluded, cannot be disavowed. In this way the modality with which the link between theory and praxis is conceived takes on a strong critical valence against any type of positivist approach, which would embrace a sort of 'fetishism' of the object, depriving the discourse of any tension towards a 'beyond' with respect to the 'present state of things'.

---

15   Sartre 2012. See Verstraeten 1972, pp. 348–50.
16   Sartre 1963, p. 30.

In taking this approach, Sartre enacts a strong differentiation between Marx and Marxism, or better, between Marx, Engels, and Marxism. The judgment regarding Engels appears extremely ungenerous, and risks 'philosophical' intellectualism in its repeated insistence on his 'positivism'. In truth, beyond the valorisation of Engels's extraordinary commitment to the organisation of the workers' movement (and his decisive role in the reception of Marxian texts), one cannot silently pass over the substantial inseparability of the personal, political, and theoretical partnership between Marx and Engels. It is not a matter of negating differences between the two thinkers, nor of excluding the presence of problematic elements in Engels's reflection, but the conception of a potent gap between a philosophically fruitful and non-positivist Marx, and a positivist Engels, remains questionable. Beyond the relation between Marx and Engels, Sartre often counterposes various productive intuitions of Marx to Marxism (in many ways 'Engelsian', characterised by the dualism criticised earlier). Which Marxism Sartre alludes to is an open question. Surely the clearest reference would be the Marxism of the Second International, with its deterministic character, however understandable in the political and cultural context of its epoch. Furthermore, there is present a more specific reference to the European and primarily French debate of the postwar period, in which dogmatic, philosophically weak aspects persisted, and at the same time were unable to give a true impulse to revolutionary action. In this regard the polemics of those years must not be forgotten, such as for example those of Lefebvre or even more those of Lukács. On the one hand, the attempt to valorise Marxian elements appears generative, loosening them from the grip of every dogmatic stiffening in order to allow their vitality to shine through (an exercise which moreover was typical of various philosophers within so-called 'Western Marxism', despite their strong differences). On the other hand, the contrast and therefore the idea of a return to an 'original' Marx as opposed to the theoretically and politically mystified versions that would be established in the subsequent development of Marxism remains problematic.

It is necessary to further elaborate on the differentiation between Marx and Marxism. The latter, on this reading, would have undervalued the dimension of the human relation on the basis of a deterministic vision in which the key elements would be represented only by society and the relations of production. But in this way the result would be a notion of human relation that is internally reified, and alienated insofar as any notion of any space of possibility for overcoming the present situation would be negated. Paradoxically we would find a point of contact with liberalism, in the sense that individuals are considered as isolated. With respect to such an approach, it is not a matter of negating the importance of external conditions, and class constraints, but rather of grasping the continuous exchange between the objective and subjective dimensions. Indeed, individuals make history and history makes individuals: individuals simultaneously 'speak' and 'are spoken':

> History is more complex than some kinds of simplistic Marxism suppose; man has to struggle not only against nature, and against the social environment which has produced him, and against other men, but also against his own action as it becomes other. This primitive type of alienation occurs within other forms of alienation, but it is independent of them, and, in fact, is their foundation. In other words, we shall reveal, through it, that a permanent anti-*praxis* is a new and necessary moment of *praxis*.[17]

With respect to Marxism, there emerges a point of discontinuity, or at least problematisation, since Sartre focuses on what has generally been neglected, a 'primitive alienation', founded on the fact that one's own action becomes other. In other ways the reasoning here is also constructed as in continuity with Marx, albeit on the basis of an 'ontologisation' of alienation, and although it is situated within the element of seriality: 'When Marx says that capital speaks through the mouth of the capitalist, he must be taken as meaning that the practical economics of capitalism constitutes itself as a seriality and expresses itself as a particular serial system of polarised relations in a transfinite unity ... Alienation is there at the beginning ... and at the end'.[18]

However, *Search for a Method* also references the question of solitude: for Sartre, the solitude of the individual and the sociality of the collective constitute two sides of the same coin. Here the comparison with Marx is extremely important, as he highlights this co-penetration many times, but in a particularly vivid way in the *1857 Introduction*: 'The human being is in the most literal sense a *zoon politikon*, not only a social animal [*ein geselliges Tier*], but an animal which can isolate itself [*kann sich vereinzeln*] only in the midst of society'.[19] Society does not constitute the opposite of isolation, of 'solitude' – to adopt Sartre's language – but the two dimensions reciprocally require one another. However, for Marx the social link regards individuals as reciprocally indifferent. Sartre certainly takes up such an element. However, if the analysis of seriality is kept in mind, just how strong the co-implication between

---

17   Sartre 2004a, pp. 124–5.
18   Sartre 2004a, pp. 746–7.
19   Marx 1993, p. 84. Translation modified. Cf. Basso 2012, pp. 150–78.

atomisation and 'encaging' in the collective is becomes clear. If Sartre's position radically criticises seriality, the group, with its common action, is precisely aimed at overcoming the dispersion proper to the collective. With respect to Marx, there are further elements provided concerning lived experience, giving rise even to psychological and emotive components. In this sense, the reference to psychoanalysis, while critical in several respects, remains central.

The question here is strongly connected to the theme of alienation, which, moreover, already played an important role in earlier texts (one thinks, for example, of *Notebooks for an Ethics*). In part on the basis of a Hegelian (more than Marxian) matrix, we see a strict, almost coinciding, relation between alienation and objectivation. Maintaining such a position does not mean holding that Sartre did not recognise his own debt to the Marxian approach:

> Marx clearly indicated that he distinguished *human relations* [*relations humaines*] from their reification or, in general, from their alienation within a particular social system. He says, in effect, that in feudal society, based on different institutions and tools, a society which presented different questions, its *own* questions, to its members, the exploitation of man by man did exist, together with the fiercest oppression, but that everything happened *differently* and, in particular, human relations were neither reified or destroyed ... But History itself *does not cause* there to be human relations in general. The relations which have established themselves between those *initially separate objects*, men, were not products of problems of the organisation and division of labour ... [T]he very possibility of a group or society being constituted ... depends on the permanent actuality of the human relation (whatever its content) at every moment of History, even between two separate individuals belonging to societies with different systems and entirely ignorant of one another. This is why the habit of skipping the abstract discussion of the human relation and immediately locating ourselves in the world of productive forces, of the mode and relations of production, so dear to Marxism, is in danger of giving unwitting support to the atomism of liberalism and of analytical rationality. This error has been made by several Marxists: individuals, according to them, are *a priori* neither isolated particles nor directly related activities; it is always up to society to determine which they are through the totality of the movement and the particularity of the conjuncture ... [I]f we do not distinguish the project, as transcendence, from circumstances, as conditions, we are left with nothing but inert objects, and History vanishes. Similarly, if human relations are a mere product, they are in essence reified and it becomes impossible to understand what

their relation really consists in. My formalism, which is inspired by that of Marx, consists simply in recognising that men make history to precisely the extent that it makes them.[20]

Here again Sartre's differentiation between Marx and Marxism emerges. The resumption of the Marxian idea that relations cannot be separated from their reified character in the capitalist mode of production highlights the fact that it remains possible to outline another perspective with respect to the reified 'present state of things', consisting in a situation in which human relations would not remain alienated. A disalienation is possible, albeit through a complex path whose coordinates are not fully predictable. It is necessary to reaffirm this aspect strongly, as too often it is claimed that for Sartre alienation constitutes a permanent, ineliminable element. Earlier I emphasised how, with respect to Marx, in Sartre we witness a strict link between alienation and objectivation. Such a position must however be interpreted by accounting for the complexity of the problem: it is necessary, on the one hand, to avoid surmising an absolute divergence of such concepts in Marx (the immanent character of his argument necessarily prevents a strict differentiation between the negativity of alienation and the positivity of objectivation), and on the other, 'to complicate' the idea of their full coincidence in Sartre. It is true that in Sartre's approach there exists an ambivalence in which sometimes it seems that alienation is ineliminable and remains constitutive of the human subject: however, this presupposes freedom, and thus only a free individual can be alienated.[21] But, as emerges in the passage cited above, alienation *can* be exited, posing a scenario of non-reified human relations. Sartre's perspective is neither subjectivist or antisubjectivist, since he insists both on the fact that individuals make history, and on the fact that history makes individuals.

Some very important texts published after *Search for a Method* and the *Critique of Dialectical Reason* which help to deepen the themes sketched here, particularly the question of subjectivity, are the 1960 lecture at Araraquara University in Brazil, and two lectures given at the Gramsci Institute in Rome in 1961 and 1964 (as well as a series at Cornell University in 1964–1965, which integrate

---

20   Sartre 2004a, pp. 96–7.

21   Gorz's position can be partially accepted. See Gorz 1967 pp. 278 ff., which has the merit of posing the question of disalienation in a polemic with other Sartrean readers who are totally 'closed' on this issue (for example, Chiodi), but also undervalues the presence of difficulty in this regard in Sartre's articulation of the *Critique*. For an overall thematisation of the question of alienation, which also traverses several Sartrean elements, see Gorz 1960, pp. 39–127.

the lectures in Rome and were posthumously published with the title *Morality and History*).[22] The Brazilian intervention focuses on the theme of the relation between Marxism and existentialism, and arrives at a structural and historical anthropology. Sartre's attempt, which is also conducted through a reformulation of Marxism, consists in going beyond the contraposition between subjectivism and objectivism:

> It is unnecessary to speak of subjectivity or objectivity in contrast with subjectivity ... In fact, if we consider the world in the form of understanding, objectivity is total and we are all perfectively objective; it is enough simply to substitute the couple subjective-objective with that of interiorisation-exteriorisation. At this point we can place the one in relation to the other *in situation* ... it is not absolutely necessary to define the subjective, because it does not exist. What is real is simply a totally objective process of interiorisation-exteriorisation.[23]

In the interpretation of the subjective–objective relation in terms of interiorisation–exteriorisation, the inescapable point of departure lies in the Cartesian *cogito*, on which I focused earlier: for Sartre this element constitutes the basis for being able to imagine man as a free being who acts and must not come to be oppressed.[24] The Cartesian *cogito*, while constituting the starting point of the discourse, must be transcended: 'As in other times, it used to be said that the university leads to everything on the condition of leaving it, the *cogito* leads to everything on the condition that we leave it ... and it is here that the *cogito* explodes into the dialectic ... then we find the immediate way out of the *cogito*, because who we find in ourselves is the whoever, that is to say the historical agent, that is to say man, the man of today'.[25] This 'grappling' with Descartes flows into a perspective founded on a dialectical and historical anthropology, in which the Hegelian reference appears as extremely important. The Cartesian setting is eroded (or, in any case, Sartre tries to erode it) from the inside: again, Descartes beyond Descartes.

The reformulation of the subjective-objective relation into the terms of interiorisation-exteriorisation also constitutes one of the decisive aspects in Sartre's two lectures at the Gramsci Institute in Rome. I will focus particularly on the first lecture, given in 1961 (the second, in 1964, brings out the import-

---

22   See Sartre 2005a.
23   Sartre 1991, pp. 87–8. Cf. Badaloni's introduction in Ibid., pp. 7–43.
24   Cfr. Sartre 1991, p. 88.
25   Sartre 1991, pp. 95–6.

ance of morality, although this was never 'systematised' by Sartre in the postwar period).[26] In this lecture, which in French was titled 'Marxisme et subjectivité,' Sartre again attempt to go beyond subjectivism and objectivism on the basis of an interweaving of existentialism and Marxism. According to Sartre, various Marxist threads lead to a perspective in which the element of subjectivity is denied or otherwise underestimated. For example, in his view Lukács's idealist dialectic runs this risk.[27] Sartre unpacks subjectivity in a strong connection with practice, as a response to a situation:

> If subjectivity [*subjectivité*] can be revealed to me, it is due to a difference between what the situation usually demands and the response I make to it ... The response will never be appropriate to the objective demand ... *Subjectivity is outside* [*dehors*], *in keeping with the nature of a response and, to the extent that it is constituted as an object, with the nature of the object.*[28]

The entire lecture is underpinned by the search for the 'singularisation of the universal' [*singularisation de l'universel*]: 'there is subjectivity as a system in interiority, a mediation between being and being, interiorised, in the form of

---

26   Cfr. Sartre 1966, pp. 31–41. Other interventions were presented by Roger Garaudy, Cesare Luporini, Adam Schaff, Karel Kosik, Galvano Della Volpe, Mihailo Markovic, and Howard Parsons. The text of Sartre's speech, recently published in French (Sartre 2015a) (which was available in an earlier, much shorter edited manuscript published in Italian), contains a strong valorisation of morality [*morale*] understood as 'the set of imperatives, values, and value judgments that constitute the common place of a class, a social atmosphere, or an entire society' (Sartre 2015a, p. 16; Sartre 1966, pp. 31–2). In the argument, the norm comes to play a crucial function for the constitution of the subject: 'In this way the norm [*norme*] as unconditioned possibility designates in the agent a subject in interiority [*sujet en intériorité*] as synthetic unity of its diversity ... the norm ... represents *my possibility of producing myself as subject* [*me produire sujet*]' (Sartre 2015a, p. 20; Sartre 1966, p. 34).

27   Cf. Sartre 2016, pp. 3–7. The French edition of the text presents, in addition to the conference Sartre gave in December 1961 at the Gramsci Institute in Rome, a preface by the editors, Michel Kail and Raoul Kirchmayr (Sartre 2013, pp. 5–22), a postface by Fredric Jameson (pp. 177–182) and part of a long and interesting debate (pp. 73–174) between Sartre and important Italian intellectuals who were close to the PCI, including Enzo Paci, Cesare Luporini, Galvano Della Volpe, Lucio Colletti, and Mario Alicata. The recent Italian edition contains, in addition to the conference, a preface by Giacomo Marramao (Sartre 2015b, pp. 7–13), a postface by Fredric Jameson (pp. 59–70), and an extensive appendix by Raoul Kirchmayr (pp. 71–162) which conveys the historical-cultural background and the content of the debate. It is necessary to point out that Sartre's text was already published in Italian, with the title *Soggettività e marxismo* (Sartre 1973) as well as in French, with the title *La Conférence de Rome, 1961. Marxisme et subjectivité* (Sartre 1993).

28   Sartre 2016, pp. 15–16.

having to be a whatever external modification, and the re-exteriorised in the form of an external singularity'.[29] The 'subjective–objective' relation is conceived in terms of interiorisation-exteriorisation: the subjective moment is configured as the mode of being inside of the objective moment.[30] Contrary to a widespread notion, in Sartre we are not faced *sic et simpliciter* with a subjectivistic approach: the link between the subjective and objective dimensions fully unfolds in the moment of praxis, in which subjects, starting from an 'outside', become 'quasi-objects', agents of the destabilising event.

Such a dynamic is characterised as an interweaving of repetition and invention: 'The repetition-invention within a particular, immediate relation, always transcendent to external being, is called projection [*projection*]'.[31] Again the idea of 'inventing the new' returns, understood, however, not on the basis of a simple contraposition with the past, as the emphasis on repetition testifies: the past is there, entirely inside, but must not be conceived in passive terms, instead becoming retotalised. The dimension of subjectivity, between repetition and invention, presupposes a strong valorisation of the 'human' in contraposition to the undervaluation within certain strands of Marxism, with the consequent difficulty of theoretically articulating subjectivity, but, even more, on the basis of a radically different perspective than that of bourgeois humanism.

To return to the *Critique of Dialectical Reason* (and *Search for a Method*), with respect to which, moreover, the Rome lecture is arranged as an explication of its implications and theoretical and political consequences, it is necessary to emphasise that Marxism, or a certain version of it, arrives at a 'fetishised' and reified version of human relations according to Sartre, in which they are completely 'jammed' into objectivity, without allowing the articulation of anything else. Indeed, on the basis of a complete identification between project and conditions, the dimension of inertia cannot but be dominant. Paradoxically this Marxist horizon, according to Sartre, risks appearing compatible with liberal atomism, which reduces every element to the level of competition, despite obviously containing a profoundly different political judgment in this regard. In this way for Sartre, the reference to the 'human' returns, not as an abstract and ahistoric hypostatisation of an 'essentialised' human nature, but on the basis of a critique of real alienation:

[A]ny philosophy which subordinates the human to what is Other than man, whether it be an existentialist or Marxist idealism, has hatred of

---

29   Sartre 2013, p. 55; Sartre 2015b, pp. 41–2.
30   Sartre 2013, p. 72; Sartre 2015b, p. 57.
31   Sartre 2016, p. 26.

man as both its basis and its consequence: History has proved this in both cases. There is a choice: either man is primarily himself, or he is primarily Other than himself. Choosing the second doctrine simply makes one a victim and accomplice of real alienation.[32]

Humanism is presented as an attempt to surpass 'real alienation', which is in several respects in continuity with the Marxian approach:

> But a Marxist aphorism shows how for almost a hundred years, Marxists have tended not to attach much importance to the event. The outstanding event of the eighteenth century, they say, would not be the French Revolution but the appearance of the steam engine. Marx did not move in this direction, as is demonstrated very well by his excellent article The Eighteenth Brumaire of Louis Napoleon Bonaparte ... In a curious way, this Stalinized Marxism assumes an air of immobility; a worker is not a real being who changes the world; he is a Platonic Idea.[33]

These are polemical references to Marxist approaches which, if they do not deny the man-as-worker, conceive him in such a fleshless way that he ends up 'machinised', 'technicised', and thus deprived of any subjective potentiality, on the basis of a sort of Platonic immobilism:

> The Marxist approaches the historical process with universalizing and totalizing schemata ... But in no case, in Marx's own work, does this putting in perspective claim to prevent or to render useless the appreciation of the process as a singular totality [*totalité singulière*]. When, for example, he studies the brief and tragic history of the Republic of 1848 ... he tries to account for this tragedy in its detail and in the aggregate ... he gives to each event, in addition to its particular signification, the role of being revealing ... In the work of Marx we never find *entities*. Totalities (e.g., "the petite bourgeoisie" of the *18 Brumaire*) are living; they furnish their own definitions within the framework of the research ... The open concepts of Marxism have closed in. They are no longer *keys*, interpretive schemata; they are posited for themselves as an already totalized knowledge ... Marxism possesses theoretical bases, it embraces all human activity; but it no longer knows anything. Its concepts are *dictates* [*Diktat*].[34]

---

32   Sartre 2004a, p. 181.
33   Sartre 1963, pp. 124–5.
34   Sartre 1963, pp. 25–8. Translation modified.

If earlier the fact was insisted on that, according to Sartre, Marxism, or at least a certain Marxism, on the basis of a positivistic and deterministic approach, has not known how to grasp subjectivity without conceiving it in a Promethean way, 'collapsing' project and circumstances together, here it becomes clear that Marxism has taken on an increasingly rigid, scholastic character, rather than bearing an expansive function, capable opening new spaces, theories, and practices.

Within this type of setting the element of singularity ends up completely negated, or otherwise has difficulty finding its own place. That is, '[s]ingularity' in the sense of the valorisation both of the subject located in a social context, but never reducible to it, and of the contingency of the political event, which is inscribed in a historical schema but never totally 'absorbed'. According to Sartre, Marx (here the reference is to his analysis of 1848) tries to hold the singular, individual, particular, and specific dimension together with the universal, general dimension: the first sphere should not be subsumed to the second, until it disappears. Sartre's reading of Marx presents some original features, aimed at valorising singularity, in a polemic with any holistic interpretation. However, the entire Marxian itinerary is characterised by the search for individual realisation, obviously not conceived unharmoniously with the social context, and communism is interpreted on this basis, from the earliest to the final writings. The valorisation of such individual *conatus*, in Sartre's *Search for a Method*, takes the form of an interweaving between Marxism and existentialism. In a certain sense, there is a primacy of Marxism over existentialism, insofar as there is a primacy of philosophy over ideology, but the element of ideology, despite its different articulation in Althusser's thought, is important and irreducible to mystification.[35] Indeed, Sartre's reformulation of Marxism achieves the goals of existentialism in a practical, concrete way: on the one hand, existentialism is undervalued with respect to Marxism, but on the other, the modality with which the latter is conceived is strongly affected by existentialist forms.

In pursuing such a theoretical and political path, under the banner of a reference to Marx, in *Search for a Method* Sartre 'uses' Hegel, so to speak, against Kierkegaard, and Kierkegaard against Hegel. The reference to Hegel serves to firmly anchor the discourse to an approach that is both dialectical and historical. However, titling the text the *Critique of Dialectical Reason* does not mean declaring an antidialectical or nondialectical premise. It needs to be added that this work is presented as a critique of historical reason, since in the first part

---

35   On the notion of ideology in Sartre see, among others, Barot 2011, pp. 253–84. With reference to Althusser, see Raimondi 2011.

(which was published), but even more in the second part (unpublished), the reference to history and its meaning is central. Sartre articulates a historical dialectic on the basis of a reprisal of the Marxian method, but tries to give rise to a reflection on history (in part lacking in Marx) that is however presented as a moment of praxis itself. Such an approach can only pose itself in critical terms against positivism: 'It is well known, in fact, that the notion of dialectic emerged in History along quite different paths [with respect to positivism], and that both Hegel and Marx explained and defined it in terms of the relations of man to matter, and of men to each other'.[36] But the reference here also helps show the limits of Kierkegaard's thought, which, within a mystico-religious setting, releases the singular from the social and historical context:

> Of course, as Marx said, the problems are not formulated until the means of resolving them are present; but *everything is already present*: *praxis* as the measure of man and the foundation of truth, and dialectic as the permanent dissolution of analytical Reason ... the universal is the general material interest of any intellectual and ... this universal is realised in potentiality (if not in actuality) by the working class ... But if, like Marx, the theorist *produces* a materialist and dialectical interpretation of History, it is because it is *required* by the materialist dialectic as a rule for working-class *praxis* and as sole foundation of true (that is to say future) universality [*universalité vraie*] ... It must not be supposed that this provides an escape from the need for *situated realism*.[37]

The problematisation of materialism and the adoption of a 'situated realism' do not mean the disappearance of the reference to historical materialism, and thus the recognition of the importance of material, 'objective' factors. It follows that the element of labour appears as central, for which again the Marxian contribution is referenced: 'The essential discovery of Marxism is that labour, as a historical reality and as the utilisation of particular tools in an already determined social and material situation, is the real foundation of the organisation of social relations. This discovery *can no longer* be questioned'.[38]

Within this approach, Sartre highlights the distance between the Marxian and Hegelian perspectives. 'Marx's originality lies in the fact that, in opposition to Hegel, he demonstrated that History *is in development*, that Being is irreducible to Knowledge, and, also, that he preserved the dialectical movement *both*

---

36   Sartre 2004a, p. 29.
37   Sartre 2004a, pp. 801–2.
38   Sartre 2004a, p. 152n35.

in Being *and in* Knowledge'.[39] Paradoxically, there emerges here a point of contact with Althusser in *Reading Capital*.[40] Indeed, Althusser highlights the fact that one of the two fundamental assumptions of Marxian materialism consists in the emphasis on the priority of reality, in Machiavellian parlance the 'effectual truth of the thing', over thought: there is a questioning of the Hegelian homology between real and rational, and thus an awareness of the risk of the complete conceptualisation of reality. Instead, the Marxian approach is founded on the idea of a 'gap' between the two levels. Sartre, albeit on the basis of a much different approach than Althusser, nevertheless reveals, in a Marxian polemic with Hegel, the discrepancy between being and knowing. In *Search for a Method* the reference to Kierkegaard is crucial in this regard. Kierkegaard highlights the failure of the Hegelian articulation, and therefore the relevance of human lived experience, of individual singularity, irreducible to rational transcription. The attempt to carry out a reciprocal interaction between Marxism and existentialism finds its most complete realisation in the formula of the 'singular universal'. In any case, for the purpose of understanding Sartre's interpretation of Marxism, the question of the significance of class and its link with the dimension of action is particularly important.

2   Class and Action

The element of class recurs with great frequency in Sartre's postwar writings, particularly those of the 1950s. In 'Faux savants ou faux lièvres' (1950), Sartre claims the following:

> [T]he oppressed class has 'a universal character through its universal miseries' ... The consciousness of the masses therefore has a practical truth ... The proletariat is thus the negation of the negation; its action [*action*], being destructive, is always all that it can be and achieves its purpose ... This is why Marx insists on the self-emancipation [*auto-émancipation*] of the proletariat.[41]

Some Marxian arguments (primarily those of the young Marx) clearly emerge here, in relation to the proletariat as the non-class class, as a universality of the part, aimed at questioning the present state of things, and, the latter being

---

39   Sartre 2004a, p. 23.
40   Cf. Althusser 2015.
41   Sartre 1950, pp. 29–30.

divided into classes, even (divided) of itself as a class: the subjective charge of class appears clear. In *The Communists and Peace*, the proletariat is on the one hand strongly connected to the dimension of common praxis, while on the other, it is interpreted in light of the party structure, which is necessary in order that its demands be politically effective and concretely realised, rather than dispersed in a centrifugal manner. Sartre clearly distinguishes between *masses* and *class*: he does not criticise the former, but contends that, surely, the latter goes beyond it, or is in any case capable of articulating it politically.[42] The masses, indeed, are described as an ensemble of solitudes – distinctly echoing a subsequent description of seriality and the collective – and therefore as remaining composed of individuals who are not really endowed with their subjectivity but rather incorporated into a mechanism. In this way Sartre uses the category of dispersion, which is typically Kierkegaardian and existentialist, in order to denote their status, substantially neutralising these conceptual origins. This is not to uphold the somewhat questionable thesis of Sartre's 'ultrabolshevism' (to recall Merleau-Ponty's definition), but rather to acknowledge that his distinction between the two is too rigid, as if a contraposition between the 'negative' and the 'positive' exists.

The relation between masses and classes must be interpreted in dynamic terms, emphasising that 'the fear of the masses', a wonderful expression which brings together the objective and subjective senses of the genitive,[43] also indicates an expansive scenario, which cannot be interpreted only by stressing the side of dispersion.

> The worker makes a proletarian of himself to the very extent that he refuses his condition … His human reality is thus not *in what he is* but *in his refusal to be such* … [T]he revolt must contain a principle of union … This movement, directed, intentional and practical, requires an *organization*. It is for this reason that Marx could speak of an "organization into class."[44]

This passage cited for the truth 'complexifies' the theoretico-political framework outlined above, which had the risk of too sharp a distinction between masses and class. Class is configured as a real unity of the masses, but within a historically determinate horizon. From this perspective, in the first place, the nexus between class and praxis is crucial, and thus the reference to daily life,

---

42   See for example Sartre 1968a, pp. 350–1.
43   Cf. Balibar 1997.
44   Sartre 1968a, p. 98. Translation modified.

capable of posing itself in destabilising terms (the similarities with Lefebvre here stand out, despite the polemics between the two). Secondly, we see here a recognition of the necessity of organisation in order to give the movement a political effectiveness.

> The unity of the proletariat lies in its relationship with the other classes of society, in short, it is its *struggle*. But this struggle, inversely, has meaning only through unity ... The unity of the working class is thus its historical and mobile relationship with the collectivity, insofar as this relationship is achieved as a synthetic act of unification which, by necessity, is distinguished from the mass as pure action is distinguished from passion.[45]

The distinction between mass and class is analogous to that between passion and action, in the sense that only with the political articulation of class can action be spoken of in the strict sense, rather than only a revolutionary passion. The reference to passion was particularly relevant in the context of Sartre's earlier work – one thinks, for example, of the conclusion to the final chapter in *Being and Nothingness*, with its definition of man as a 'useless passion'. '[The worker] transforms himself into action when he enters the class, and can assert his freedom only in action. But this freedom is a concrete and positive power: the power to invent [*inventer*], to go further, to take the initiative, to propose solutions'.[46] The idea of 'inventing the new', of opening fresh, even unprecedented horizons returns in *The Communists and Peace*, starting from the present situation but knowing how to go beyond it.

Sartre's confrontation with Lukács's *History and Class Consciousness* is extremely important in the articulation of these problems. There were strong polemics between the two, beginning with Lukács's critique of Sartrean existentialism as a late-bourgeois position. These polemics continued, although I think that Sartre's postwar writings present a number of points of contact with the Lukácsian horizon.[47] The strong valorisation of praxis inspires an extremely vivid image of the proletariat, as an element that is not linked only to interests, rational goals, or an 'instrumental acting', but also to a series of affects, passions,

---

45   Sartre 1968a, p. 129.
46   Sartre 1968a, p. 130.
47   On the Sartre–Lukács relation: Cera 1972, pp. 190–201, although writing from an overall perspective which I do not share, rightly emphasises the strict relation between Sartre's *Critique* and Lukács' *History and Class Consciousness* in regard to the questioning of a scientistic type of gnoseology; see also Koch-Öhmen 1988 and Charbonnier 2011.

and modes of life: the echoes of Lukács are clear. In regard to the question of the class–party nexus, it is also necessary to specify that Lukácsian 'class consciousness' can never be considered abstractly, since it reflects a rearticulation of the passage from class 'in itself', pure objective commonality, to class 'for itself', political class, aware of itself, through the presence of an organisation. Although this 'early' Lukács was criticised by communists for his valorisation of praxis, within this perspective class consciousness is not conceived outside of the organisational moment. Sartre surely takes up such an element. Moreover, from the political point of view in the strict sense, the early 1950s constitute for Sartre the moment of greatest proximity to the French Communist Party, and thus what appears relevant is the reference to the concept of class, strongly linked with Marxian forms, but in particular the role of the party, including some critiques of Rosa Luxemburg.

In this regard Sartre's *Response to Claude Lefort* is also significant, with its valorisation of class that 'makes and remakes itself continuously'.[48] The subjective dimension of class is surely recognisable in the way Sartre characterises class, but articulating such a position does not mean holding that class is always active, mobilised, revolutionary, and thus lacking serial or dispersive elements:

> [T]he proletariat has not only a relationship with its own activity, it has to deal as well with its own inertia and through it – with the activity of the Other class. For it is also through our passion [*passion*] that we have the painful and ambiguous experience of the real … When Marx criticizes Hegel for having stood dialectics on its head, he does not merely contrast materialism to idealism: he wants to show that each moment of the dialectic is a conquest achieved by effort and work, and if necessary by combat, against chance and exteriority … Marxist dialectic is not the spontaneous movement of the Spirit, but the hard work of man to enter a world which rejects him.[49]

Here the characteristics of passivity, dispersion, non-activity, non-engagement in a revolutionary situation are also highlighted: Sartre's discourse is not arranged in immediately affirmative terms, but rather elements of delay, failure, and difficulty are present within a history full of 'holes', and thus a history that is neither linear nor transparent. And the proletariat is conceived as not only

48   Sartre 1968a, p. 97.
49   Sartre 1968a, pp. 270–1.

activity, but also passivity. Class, in its dialectical relation with the party, thus comes to embody that repeatedly invoked singular universal, with its concrete character:

> The working class, such as I conceived it, probably united by the Communist Party, could, in its revolutionary movements, apprehend concrete totalities, that is to say, syntheses of the concrete and the universal: *this* strike, *this* claim. For I see it, in itself, like a concrete universal [*universel concret*]: unique since it was made with these particular men, in these particular circumstances – universal since it embraces an entire collection [*collection*].[50]

In *Search for a Method* and the *Critique of Dialectical Reason* there emerge, on the one hand, an element of continuity with respect to the early 1950s work, which condenses the results achieved there, and on the other an element of discontinuity, which arises not so much from an abstract and intellectual rethinking, but rather from a reflection beginning from 1956, a crucial year both for the Soviet repression in Hungary and for Khrushchev's denunciation of the crimes of Stalinism. From this moment on, Sartre assumes an increasingly critical position (relative to the early 1950s) towards the Soviet Union, and, reflexively, the PCF. *Search for a Method*, written in 1956, is already affected by this new approach. *The Ghost of Stalin* (1956–1957) concerns Stalinism and the phases of destalinisation (real or presumed), which I will return to in the second part of the book, precisely by starting from a critique of the Hungarian repression:

> [T]he socialism in the name of which Soviet soldiers fired on the masses in Hungary, I don't know, I cannot even conceive of it: it is not made for men nor by them; it is a name which is given to a new form of alienation [*aliénation*] ... One can no longer find in the Reason of State which it can invoke today anything but a vague reference to a future socialism; the concrete struggle of the masses [*lutte concrète des masses*] is drowned in blood.[51]

The Hungarian events are decisive for the maturation of a sort of theoretical and political rectification in Sartre regarding the Soviet Union (which does not mean, however, a simplistic liquidation of the socialist experience). In this

---

50   Sartre 1968a, p. 257.
51   Sartre 1968b, pp. 115–16.

sense, Sartre's relationship with Marxism must not be interpreted in abstract, 'doctrinal' terms, but rather on the basis of a continuous interweaving with the events of those years. In order to take up the discussion of the collective subject we must comprehend both the relationship between it and the element of class, since in the *Critique of Dialectical Reason*, the group will play an expansive role.

> Thus we have seen *class-being* as the practico-inert statute of individual or common praxis, petrified in past being, which this praxis itself has to carry out and in which it must finally recognise itself in a new experience of necessity ... In fact *class-being*, far from manifesting itself as an identity of being between independent realities, appears in this investigation as the material unity of individuals or, in other words, as the collective basis of their individuality ... At the same time, *class-being* defines itself for everyone as an inert (untranscendable) relation with his class comrades on the basis of certain struggles.[52]

The link between class-being and the practico-inert is clear: it is necessary to keep the relation open, grasping its constitutively ambivalent character. On the one hand, we see an inert element, a serial horizon, within which class would seem to fully remain. On the other hand, however, a connection between class and the practical dimension is outlined, producing a social articulation of individuality, but beyond the serial horizon, beyond the alienated and fetishised form of relations. In this second sense, the question is posed of the relation between class and group, which is conceived as a possible transcending of the 'present state of things'. Sartre highlights the ambivalence of class several times:

> [C]lass is *praxis* and inertia, dispersal of alterity and common field.[53] The working class is neither pure combativity, nor pure institutionalised apparatus. It is a complex, moving relation between different practical forms each of which completely recapitulates it, and whose true bond with one another is totalisation (as a movement which each induces in the others and which is reflected by each to the others).[54]

It is extremely productive, on a theoretical and political level, to keep this ambivalence open, thereby grasping class in both its passive and active sides.

---

52   Sartre 2004a, pp. 250–1.
53   Sartre 2004a, p. 701.
54   Sartre 2004a, p. 690.

Indeed, class cannot be reduced to one side or the other. On the one hand, the relationship with seriality never ceases, and thus a fully political, revolutionary class, a class which is 'for itself', completely aimed at transcending the 'present state of things', cannot be outlined. On the other hand, class can never be interpreted as entirely internal to that present state. Instead, there unfolds a 'complex, moving relation between different practical forms'. It is necessary to insist on both the dynamism and the differentiated character of this element.

> It is therefore useful to consider the working class as defined by variable statutes (in space or time). The trade union is the working class *objectified, exteriorised, institutionalised,* and possibly *bureaucratised,* but unrecognisable to its own eyes and realising itself as a pure practical schema of unity ... [T]he working class *exists in fact* as a practical totalisation ... This will lead us, as a synchronic determination, to treat the working class – at any given moment of the historical process – not only as an institutionalised organisational group (the 'cadres'), but also as either a fused or a pledged group (the constitution of the soviets, in 1905, appears as an intermediary between a pledged group and an organised group), and as a seriality affected by the negative unity of the pledged groupings. The institutional group, as an abstract skeleton of the united class, is a permanent invitation to unity; indeed it is the sovereignty of the class if it is entirely serial.[55]

We see an oscillation between an 'encaging' in seriality and the attempt to overcome such a logic, but also between institutional articulation and the 'movementist' dimension, for which unions play an important role:

> [W]ith the struggle of a dominated against a dominant class, seriality will always be the product of exploitation [*exploitation*] and the statute which maintains it, *even more than internal dissension. It is seriality* which must be overcome in order to achieve even the smallest common [*commun*] result ... [C]*lass-being,* as past, present, and future seriality, is always the ontological statute of the worker and ... *group praxis,* as a surface dissolution of the relation of alterity inside the class (and therefore on the surface in the worker) and as a conservative transcendence of serial being, is either the present practical reality of the common individual [*individu*

---

55   Sartre 2004a, pp. 682–3.

commun] or his future possibility ... As for the institutional group (union, etc.), it *practically* represents this possibility in its permanence.[56]

In this way the complex intertwinement of seriality and praxis is outlined, as a kind of phenomenology of social groups. Sartre's argument is inserted into a specific analysis of the capitalist system and the alienation that distinguishes it:

> We have shown how class-being (for example, in the working class) is defined by the seriality insofar as it is qualified and determined by pratico-inert exigencies: the primary, negative relation of the worker to the machine (non-ownership), the mystification of the free contract, and labour becoming a hostile force *for the worker*, on the basis of the wage system and the capitalist process. All this takes place in a milieu of serial dispersal and antagonistic reciprocities on the labour market. Alienation is a real and strict process within the system it arises in and through *alterity* as infinite recurrence ... Industrialisation produces its proletariat; it drains it from the countryside, and regulates its birthrate. But, here as elsewhere, a statute of impotence is produced, through the serialisation of the proletarians ... However, the transformation of a class into an actualised group has never actually occurred, even in revolutionary periods. But we have seen that seriality is always being eroded by action groups constituted at various levels and pursuing variable objectives ... Thus, the entire class is clearly present in the organised group which constitutes itself within it; and its seriality as a collective, as a limitation, is the inorganic being of its practical community. It is genuinely a case of *the class* having two forms; the community [*communauté*] is not to be regarded as a Spinozan mode of proletariat-substance, because on the contrary, it constitutes itself as its *practical apparatus*.[57]

---

56   Sartre 2004a, pp. 687–8.
57   Sartre 2004a, pp. 679–80. This passage contains an important reference to Spinoza. On the Sartre–Spinoza relation, cf. Eksen 2017. See also Sartre 2004, pp. 311–13: '[T]he common class-being of the workers in 1830, in the presence of Machine-Destiny and the organs of oppression and constraint, was the seriality of their relations of reciprocity, in that this profound impotence was also a unity ... Exploitation was revealed as the passive unity of all ... in so far as everyone lived the isolation of Others as his own isolation and their impotence through his own. Class as a collective [*collectif*] became a material thing made out of men in so far as it constituted itself as a negation of man and as a serial impossibility of negating this negation ... Every worker feels himself confirmed in his inertia by the inertia of all the Others'.

Here, albeit with a certain genericity of approach and the presence of some transhistoric aspects, the main reference is to the modern, capitalist world, and particularly to the elements of fixed capital materialised in machines, the worker and his labour-power, and the 'mystification of the free contract', with strong Marxist antecedents (especially the first volume of *Capital*).

> [T]he machine could *never* be the particular interest of the worker; on the contrary, it is the *a priori* negation both of his particularity and of any possibility of his having an interest ... *It is not the interest of the worker to work*: the situation is quite different, since, under the constraint of need, his work exhausts him and its ultimate results (the construction of machines) contribute to his elimination.[58]

Sartre articulates an anti-workerist position: factory labour is not the realisation of man, but his de-realisation. It is necessary to point out that any emphasis on a sort of 'ethics of labour' is lacking. Instead, labour is grasped for its exploitative side. In this sense, the Marxian critique of the 'right to work' is criticised, and more generally, those socialist perspectives founded on a hypostatisation of society and labour which saw their condensation in the social-democratic Gotha Program.[59] Behind Sartre's antiworkerist position, behind the critique of exploitation in the factory, the reference to alienation forcefully returns here. The reference to mechanisation is extremely important in this respect: the machine is presented as the negation of human interdependence.

First of all, following this reasoning it becomes clear that the working class constitutes an exemplification of class-being, but not the only possible one: class-being thus cannot be circumscribed exclusively to the capitalist mode of production, even if it finds there one of its most important incarnations. In this sense a very complex discussion can be opened concerning whether classes have always existed or if they rather constitute a distinctive feature of the capitalist mode of production. In Marx the answer appears ambivalent, even if the idea that the class dynamic finds its specific meaning within the capitalist horizon, and thus does not take on a transhistorical valence, In Sartre the articulation of the question is posed in different terms, although the reference to capitalism remains crucial. Indeed, the discourse on class-being finds its focal point in the analysis of capitalism, with the connection of this element to the social dimension.

---

58   Sartre 2004a, p. 208.
59   See Marx 1978, pp. 525–41.

It is on the basis of this being-outside in a field of unifying materiality on the part of everyone that Marx can describe the process of capital as an 'anti-social force' developed within a definite social field and posited itself for itself. But this inertia of impotence ... we can regard it as the *social Being* [*être social*] of man at the fundamental level, that is to say, in so far as there are several people within a practical field totalised by the mode of production ... We shall try to see social Being from the point of view of the pratico-inert in so far as it really determines a structure of inertia from the inside, first in individual *praxis*, then in common *praxis* [*praxis commune*], and finally we shall see it as the inorganic substance of the first *collective beings*: we shall then be in a position to see the primary structure of class as *social and collective Being*.[60]

The idea of the ambivalence of class-being returns, on the one hand as connected to seriality and the collective, and thus the dimension of inertia, while on the other as capable of going beyond such a scenario, on the basis of a destabilising praxis:

We have been considering two classes. In each we have observed three concrete types of multiplicity: the group-institution or sovereign; combat-groups (or pressure-groups, propaganda-groups, etc.); and seriality ... As we have said, unity, at all levels, exists *in mediation* ... [T]he class is connected to its transcendent unity through the mediation of the other class. It is *one* outside itself in the suffered freedom of the Other ... The intransigence of French employers at the end of the nineteenth century was due to the massacres of 1848 and 1871. But this means that they *comprehended in the other class* what it is to have the past of a massacred class.[61]

On the basis of the notion of the division of society into two classes, Sartre evokes two particularly important historical examples, one in 1848 and the other in 1871. These epochal events are characterised by a dramatic clash between 'a massacred class' and a bourgeoisie which has failed in its revolutionary role, during the 1789–1848 phase, and is linked, starting from the June Days of 1848, with the 'party of order' in its brutally anti-worker function.

---

60   Sartre 2004a, pp. 230–1.
61   Sartre 2004a, pp. 794–6. Translation modified.

[T]he *sociality* of common-being [*être commun*] for each employer depends on the historicity of this being as an ineradicable past common-being. But in this past – at the time of the massacres of June 1848 or of the military revenge of the Versaillais – this *common-being* was not a product of the total dissolution of the series or of a pledge: there was a change of class *statute* (an unveiling of oppression) occasioned by government action [*action*]. And this action was itself brought about by pressure-groups. But at the same time it was supported by the series itself, in the classic form of passive activity: panic turning into violence without ceasing to be serial. If we examine, for example, the 1848 Revolution and its consequences in June, it is clear that the bourgeoisie of the notables ... sparked it off ... The fright of the upper bourgeoisie, as described by Tocqueville, was a panic which emerged, in seriality, in all the possessing classes, in the countryside and among the petty bourgeoisie. Lefebvre is right to compare this panic to the 'great fears' of the French Revolution.[62]

Again there emerges the 'politicity' of fear, with the consequences that it activates, and the worsening of the class struggle between the bourgeosie and proletariat that derives from it.[63] 'One important fact of nineteenth-century history is that the workers experienced the absolute intransigence of the employers. They wished (initially) *to reach a mutual understanding as* men; and they gradually realised that this was impossible, *because, to their employers, they were not men*'.[64] In such a scenario the humanistic dimension does not have an abstract meaning, and connects with a radical critique of the 'present state of things': the emphasis on the 'human' is aimed at questioning the structures of domination.

Two particularly important aspects require further elaboration: the nexus between class and action, and the relation between class and group. For the former, Marxian claims can be reactivated. For example, in *The German Ideology* Marx and Engels claim that individuals form a class only in the moment when they lead a struggle against another class.[65] A distinctive aspect of Marx's thought consists in the fact that the element of class, albeit rooted in the question of the relation between capital and labor, cannot be hypostatised onto an ontological or sociological (understood as a social group) level. Radicalising this argument, one could claim that classes only genuinely exist in class

62   Sartre 2004a, p. 759.
63   Cf. Sartre 2004a, p. 765.
64   Sartre 2004a, p. 798.
65   Marx 1978, p. 197.

struggles. In this way a point of contact emerges between Sartre and Marx, precisely in relation to the nexus between class and action: 'In the unity of a praxis ... the workers – who as alienated producers were all really members of the working class – grouped themselves as a class and thereby caused class conflicts to reappear inside their practical community'.[66] In articulating the relation between classes and class struggle, Sartre introduces the concept of the state in a manner explicitly indebted to the Marxian approach:

> Marx was right when he wrote 'Only political superstition imagines today that civil life must be held together by the state, whereas in reality, on the contrary, the state is held together by civil life'. Marx was right, *subject to the* qualification that there is a circular process at work here and that the State, being produced and sustained by the dominant rising class, constitutes itself as the organ of the contraction and integration of the class ... This is particularly important in so far as the State cannot take on its functions without positing itself as a mediator between the exploiting and the exploited classes. The State is a determination of the dominant class, and this determination is conditioned by class struggle.[67]

In the cited passage from *The Holy Family* and still more vividly in *The Communist Manifesto*, Marx emphasises the full subordination of the state to the interests of the capitalist classes. Later, already with the *Eighteenth Brumaire of Louis Bonaparte*, a text that, moreover, Sartre loved, Marx highlights the autonomy (albeit partial) of the state, that is its irreducibility to a mere epiphenomenon, through the analysis of Bonapartism. Sartre's framework approaches this latter consideration, engendering the circularity of the process, and therefore not only the passive but also the active role of the state in securing the production and reproduction of exploitation. Or rather, something more with respect to what has been said unfolds: the state in fact constitutes a field of forces whose outcome is not always predetermined. Again the reference to Marx is productive, and particularly to *Capital*, in the chapter on the struggle to reduce the working day, which culminates with the demand for a 'modest Magna Carta' as a state law.[68] In this sense the state is also configured as a 'battleground', continuously conditioned by the degree and intensity of the class struggle while at the same time capable of conditioning these elements.

---

66   Sartre 2004a, pp. 477–8.
67   Sartre 2004a, p. 639.
68   Marx 1990, p. 416.

The idea of the importance of the link between class and class struggle persists in Sartre, but on the basis of an *Auseinandersetzung* with determinate aspects, in his view problematic, of Marxism:

> Now, the essential point is to establish *whether there is any struggle*. Engels made fun of Dühring for speaking somewhat hastily of *oppression* ... The resulting opposition between capitalists and wage-earners does not merit the name of struggle any more than that between the shutter and the wall it beats against. In *Anti-Dühring*, moreover, Engels takes these schematic ideas to extremes, and goes so far as to disband class struggle in the moment where the rising class, securing the development of the means of production, groups the whole of society around itself ... It would then be possible to speak of *struggle* – in the narrow and purely metaphorical sense of molecular agitations tending in two opposite directions and producing *an average result* ... But this economistic intelligibility is a mere illusion; in the first place, it takes Engels back to analytical Reason ... [T]he conventional transformations and definitions of economic thought are intelligible as long as they are *supported* by the concrete movement of a human, historical dialectic.[69]

Engels's approach in *Anti-Dühring*, with its determinism and economism (true or presumed), or, to adopt the terminology of the *Critique*, its beginning from a merely analytical Reason, depotentiates the practical dimension of struggle, neutralising and 'engaging' it. The expression 'human and historical dialectic' condenses a number of arguments, fostering a strong historicisation and the attempt, with respect to Hegel, to articulate a perspective which adheres to the lived experience of man in his concreteness, in his situated being, and thus in his irreducibility to a generalising schema. On this, Sartre arrives at an antideterministic and antieconomistic reading of the historical dynamic:

> Then the idea of struggle between classes must be given its fullest meaning; in other words, even in the case of economic development within one country, even though the gradual constitution of the proletariat is

---

69   Sartre 2004a, pp. 711–12. In relation to Engels' *Anti-Dühring*, see also: '[O]nly the free praxis of the Other on the basis of material circumstances, through some worked matter, can limit the efficacity [*efficacité*] and freedom [*liberté*] of my praxis. In this sense the explanation of classes in *Anti-Dühring* is correct, although it hardly has any historical value. But, paradoxically, it is correct as a dialectical schema of intelligibility rather than as a reconstruction of a particular social process'. Sartre 2004a, p. 320.

taking place among the poorest sections of the peasant class, and even though the worker 'freely' sells his labour-power, exploitation must be inseparable from oppression, just as the seriality of the bourgeois class is inseparable from the practical apparatuses which it adopts for itself.[70]

In this sense the *politicity* or practical dimension of class is underscored. At the same time, it is necessary to emphasise that the conceptual grasp is never full, and therefore no complete 'welding' between intelligibility and action occurs: Marxism is reproached precisely for the lack, or at least insufficiency, of a theoretical articulation of this problem. Moreover, it is necessary to recall that, in Sartre, class is not conceived on the basis of the idea of a permanent struggle, always 'for itself', to take up old Marxist terminology (which derives from Hegel): instead, a multifaceted vision of class emerges, with its grey areas and its never completely transcended seriality.

Such an approach contains a dialectical and historical character. But it is necessary to make a clarification here: as opposed to Engels (according to Sartre's reading of him), the dialectic, which is a critical dialectic, does not proceed with a linearity in the succession of affirmation, negation, and negation of the negation. On the contrary, history presents an extremely complex course, in which what was negated returns. The dialectic is moreover always situated, rather than abstract and generalising. The fact that we see a historical dialectic (the *Critique of Dialectical Reason* is also configured as a critique of historical reason) thus does not suggest that a generalising and univocal approach is operative, since there emerges an extremely complex structure, endowed with multiple levels. Within this approach the element of struggle is crucial, insofar as, within it, different aspects of praxis merge (and are bifurcated).

> The emergence of dialectical Reason in the working class as a dissolution of analytical Reason and as a determination of the bourgeois class in terms of its function and practice (exploitation-oppression) is induced; it is an aspect of the class struggle ... The conclusion of this investigation is that *the only possible intelligibility* of human relations is dialectical and that this intelligibility, in a concrete history whose true foundation is *scarcity* [*rareté*], can be manifested only as an antagonistic reciprocity. So class struggle as a practice necessarily leads to a dialectical interpretation; and, moreover, in the history of human multiplicities, class struggle is necessarily produced on the basis of historically determined conditions,

---

70   Sartre 2004a, p. 734.

as the developing realisation of dialectical rationality. Our History is intelligible to us because it is dialectical and it is dialectical because the class struggle produces us as transcending the inertia of the collective towards dialectical combat-groups.[71]

This reflection (whose elaboration in the second part of the *Critique of Dialectical Reason*, centered precisely on the question of the meaning of history and its intelligibility, takes on an extremely significant emphasis) gives rise to the historical dimension of Sartre's approach, distinguished by the idea of conflict as the motor of politics and the centrality of the notion of *rareté*.

In relation to the interpretation of class, the specific reference to the Parisian 1848 returns with force in the *Critique of Dialectical Reason*, and therefore the attempt, on the part of class, to go beyond seriality, with the purpose of inaugurating a new scenario: 'The definition of the class by the pressure groups (through their use of directed seriality) becomes the meaning of the repression in Paris. Now, the meaning of repression, lived as Other-Being (class-being), is the concerted transcendence and exploitation of seriality for the purpose of a class *praxis* by an organised grouping'.[72] Another aspect of the problem is represented precisely by the relation between class and group, the latter of which 'defines the struggle it will wage, and its exigencies, and it reveals itself at a certain inner "temperature" in connection with its serial being-outside-itself. It is the suffering class, but above all it is the struggling class'.[73] Here there emerges a 'welding together' of what was maintained earlier at the nexus between class and class struggle, and the conviction of a strict relation between class and group, on the basis of a 'movementist' characterisation. Such an element unfolds in a particularly sharp way in the fused-group, or the oath: 'the group acts for the common interest [*intérêt commun*]: it is the class in action [*classe agissant*]'.[74] An identity even seems to emerge between class and group, as well as their common rooting in the dimension of action: no abstract essence of the group exists, on either the ontological or sociological level. Obviously, however, it is necessary to emphasise that the valorisation of the class-class struggle link does not mean the elimination of a zone of opacity, since seriality never completely disappears. 'Of course, this does not prevent the groups from producing a new seriality'.[75]

---

71   Sartre 2004a, pp. 804–5.
72   Sartre 2004a, pp. 761–2.
73   Sartre 2004a, p. 691.
74   Sartre 2004a, p. 692. Translation modified.
75   Sartre 2004a, p. 685.

Such aspects (the importance of the concept of class, the connection be-tween class and class struggle, and between class and group) push the discourse towards the idea of Sartre having a substantial continuity with Marx. But uni-laterally emphasising such a thesis does not enable us to grasp the specificity of Sartre's thought. First, it is necessary to note that, while class remained crucial in the texts from the early 1950s, in the *Critique of Dialectical Reason* it plays an important role, but the question is understood in partially different terms. Indeed, it is beyond the shadow of a doubt that the key elements for outlining a non-merely-individual dimension are represented not so much by class as by the collective, marked by seriality, and the group, as an attempt to go beyond seriality, starting from an endeavor, an action, a movement, but with difficulty fully arriving at the objective. In this sense, the collective and the group cannot be interpreted *sic et simpliciter* as 'negative' and 'positive': Sartre's representa-tion is much more 'chiaroscural'. Even more generally, it cannot be forgotten that Sartre's critique of capitalism does not agree with the centrality given to the Marxist category of the mode of production, and undervalues elements such as value, surplus-value, and accumulation: the Marxian analytic reper-toire is strongly reduced. The very schema, group versus collective, is rather extraneous to Marx and the Marxist tradition, just as the notion of group con-stitutes a distinctive feature of Sartre's discourse.

First of all, the dimension of class is outlined beginning not with an ana-lysis of valorisation, surplus-value, and so on, but with a theoretical articulation based on the reference to human existence insofar as it is involved in the mater-ial worker and machine. Moreover, class is not presented as durable, revealing itself instead as dynamic: the attempt is to comprehend how the class-being of workers can pass from the serial dimension to an other-being, as a condition of possibility of emancipatory praxis, capable of calling seriality into ques-tion.

Secondly, in Sartre class is 'functionalised' in a number of ways and subor-dinated to the concept of group. At first glance, one could claim that the group constitutes a more general notion than class and thus is less linked as a 'double edge' with a determinate relation of forces on the economic and social level, and therefore with the capital-labour contradiction.[76] He does not exclude this element – and the nexus established with class moves in this direction – but

---

76   Cf. Münster 2005, pp. 174–5: 'Differently than in Marx, *the being in common of the class* in
      Sartre is not ... defined by beginning from the specific economic structure of the workers'
      condition and the will to overcome a state of alienation ... but rather as the fact that the
      situation of being in the class, at the more superficial level of experience ... Outlining the
      proletariat not only as destiny and as negation of destiny, but as *group praxis* ..., Sartre

it does not represent the distinctive feature of Sartre's reflection on the group. We are instead dealing with a wider concept, also because, according to Sartre, the historical process is complex, and the working class itself is split internally: the dynamic of struggle therefore presents extremely diverse characteristics. The group presents several different connotations not only with respect to the Marxian approach, but also to the various structuralist frameworks: it is never configured as totality, but as a totalisation underway, in polemic with any form of Hegelian 'idealism' or determinism. In twentieth-century debates, but also today in debates about the collective subject, Sartre's notion of the group is too rarely referenced. Despite its limits (a certain generality, as well as the difficulty in articulating the passage from movement to organisation and subsequently to institution), Sartre's notion of the group attempts to set up the theme of political intersubjectivity in conflictual terms, with a multiplicity and complexity of planes and levels. The treatment of the group appears crucial for the purpose of interpreting the question of emancipation from a perspective that is never resolved once and for all, but rather through totalisations to be done.

3   'The Realm of Freedom'

For Sartre, emancipation holds an importantly specific weight: it must be understood not in the sense of the stable achievement of an uncontaminated 'place', but rather as an uninterrupted *conatus* of transcending the existing scenario. Various objections can be raised to this approach, particularly those connected to an analysis of the specific manner with which Sartre conceives alienation, and more generally, seriality. Indeed, Sartre sometimes establishes such a strict connection between objectivation and alienation that the two almost seem to coincide at times. In such a case, there would emerge the risk of understanding alienation as a permanent condition of man, from which he cannot escape. However, alienation presupposes freedom, since only a free subject can be alienated. More generally, according to Sartre seriality never fully disappears from the historico-political horizon: beyond the fact that series and group are not conceived on the basis of a temporal succession, the group never completely eliminates the dimension of seriality. It would thus seem to be impossible to escape seriality, of which alienation constitutes an expression.

---

thus maintains the Marxian notion of the *working class* the *practice of a fused group* that is spontaneously constituted as class *"in situation"*'

But the scenario remains more complex with respect to the idea of the permanence of alienation: indeed, it could be maintained that Sartre's entire discourse
is characterised by the tension towards disalienation:

> If, as Marx has often said, everything is *other* in capitalist society, this
> is primarily because atomisation [*atomisation*], which is both the origin
> and result of the process, makes social man an Other than himself, con-
> ditioned by Others in so far as they are Other than themselves ... We have
> also seen that the common interest of the class can only be the negation
> of this negation, that is to say, the practical negation of a destiny which
> is suffered as common inertia ... The worker will be saved from his des-
> tiny only if the human multiplicity as a whole is permanently changed
> into a group praxis ... [W]e can see that the *necessity of some common
> action* [*action quelconque en commun*] can arise only out of an existing
> link [*liaison*] between men and can present itself only as the transcend-
> ence and inversion of this fundamental link.[77]

Once again the idea of alienation as a distinctive feature of the capitalist system
returns. Sociality and isolation constitute two sides of the same coin, since the
other side of society, within the capitalist arrangement, is represented by atomisation, or, to frame it in a more psychological way, solitude. Earlier I highlighted
the substantial continuity of such an approach with the Marxian approach, in
which man is conceived, to take up the phrase from the *1857 Introduction*, as
'*zoon politikon*', as a social animal that only can be isolated in society.[78] Within
such an approach both individuality and society are destructured, on the basis
of the reduction of the former to an atomised dimension, and the latter to a
serialised dimension.

Common action is aimed at overcoming the situation indicated, a 'destiny
which is suffered as common inertia'. The emancipation of the worker, in the
first place, is presented as the emancipation from labour, and not as a realisation in labour: it is not a matter of an individual acting, but a group praxis
which is capable of subverting the conditions on which society is founded. Such
valorisation of acting in common is understood as a change from *Being and
Nothingness*, a substantially *anarchisant* text,[79] founded on a sort of absolut-
ism of individual freedom, with aspects that are both emancipatory and devast-

---

77   Sartre 2004a, pp. 309–10.
78   Cf. footnote 19 of this chapter.
79   Cf. Verstraeten 1972, p. 27.

ating for this element. In the *Critique of Dialectical Reason*, instead, there is a determination, a circumscription of freedom, both starting from the presence of an ineluctable sphere of objectivity, as incarnated by the practico-inert, and by an increasing valorisation of the intersubjective dimension. The 'others' in *Being and Nothingness* are introduced but not really developed: they seem rather to be configured as a sort of *petitio principii*. In the *Critique of Dialectical Reason* emancipation is directly connected to the dimension of the group, the action that involves a multiplicity of individuals: the individualistic footprint is overcome or at least problematised. Maintaining such a thesis does not mean holding that freedom does not have an important function, but it is not conceived on the basis of an idea of the absolute independence of the single individual. '[I]n a common action [*action commune*] (whether reformist or revolutionary), there is both a realisation of class-being and freedom'.[80] Common praxis is not configured as the negation of freedom, but as its affirmation, albeit within the given conditions and on the basis of an intersubjective relation. It is, rather, a matter of understanding in what terms the relation between class-being and freedom should be understood, as well as making eventual 'non-uniform' points arise.

It is necessary to examine the theme of overcoming alienation carefully, since Sartre poses a precise series of limits:

> Thus the other form of class, that is to say, the group which totalises in a *praxis*, originates at the heart of the passive form and *its* negation. A *wholly active* [*active*] class, all of whose members are integrated into a single *praxis* and whose apparatuses organise themselves in unity rather than conflicting with one another, is realised only in very rare [*en certuins moments très rares*] (and revolutionary) moments of working-class history ... However, a number of points should be noted. First, that collective *praxis* [*praxis collective*] can occur only on the basis of a fundamental common-being [*être commun*]; secondly, that it will remain structured by the thing which it transcends and which determines it up to its limits and efficacity ...; thirdly, that it stands in a relation of alterity and, through antagonisms, of seriality to other organisations independent of it ...; fourthly and lastly, that any organisation ... is in constant danger of dissolving into seriality.[81]

---

80   Sartre 2004a, p. 686.
81   Sartre 2004a, pp. 317–18.

In the first place, a fully active class, capable that is of really overcoming alienation, is given only in authentically revolutionary moments. Alain Badiou reformulates this approach in some respects as he maintains the thesis of politics as rare event: 1789, 1848, 1917, the cultural revolution, etc.[82] According to this approach, there were relatively few conjunctures in which the class played a completely active function: indeed, for the greater part of circumstances, it found itself in spurious conditions, with tensions towards change, but also with various aspects that remained linked to seriality. In this sense, the emphasis on the question of 'inventing the new' does not presume a simple rejection of shadow zones or contradictory elements.

However, Sartre's position is decisively more complex than the Badiouian idea of politics as rare event, because in Sartre, particularly in the *Critique of Dialectical Reason*, alongside the attention on the singularity of the political event, there is also present a strong emphasis on the universality of history. We witness therefore a varied and complex relationship (not devoid of internal problems) between the two levels, irreducible to the hypostatisation of the moment of political contingency. Moreover, the group does not fully eliminate the "dross" of seriality but is instead continually affected by what it wants to overcome. The new totalisation, never fully accomplished, cannot but be materially affected by the preceding totalisation. The serial dimension, even when it seems to disappear (for example, during revolutionary events), reappears in the successive development, reconfiguring itself. The event of the French Revolution, central in the first part of the *Critique of Dialectical Reason*, makes this dynamic clear in the passage from movement to organisation to the arrival at institution. In this regard the reference to the Soviet Union is still most emblematic. This reference is central to the second part of the *Critique of Dialectical Reason*, and I will examine it in the next two chapters.

With respect to the idea of a mechanical articulation of revolutionary succession, i.e., the arrival of the Thermidor – and thus the idea of the necessary return to seriality and alienation – it is important to introduce some elements of 'complication'. In Sartre's thought an immediate tactic and a 'long-range' strategy intersect. In more general terms, the question of the 'singular universal' returns here, and thus also the revolution as a 'singular universal', as an attempt to keep together the singularity of political action, in its contingency and rootedness in human existence, and the universality of the project, which is inscribed within a wider and more complex perspective. Here it is noteworthy that Sartre, in a number of texts, points out the failure, in the present

---

82   See for example Badiou 1998.

scenario, of the 'hold' between tactics and strategy, singular and universal. In a passage cited earlier, Sartre adopts an important expression for understanding his treatment of emancipation – 'the everyday *practice* of each and all' – which has strong assonances with Lefebvre. Despite the reciprocal polemics between Sartre and Lefebvre, there exist points of contact on the theme of 'everyday life'.[83] We find a *praxis* (the extraordinary importance of this element in Sartre can never be insisted upon enough) which is however inscribed into everyday life. In this way the revolution is not conceived as 'taking power' (here the assonances with de Certeau clearly emerge),[84] not only because in a Gramscian way there are no longer conditions for a repetition of the Bolshevik Revolution, but also because the revolutionary element must be materially rooted in the existence of individuals, day after day.

The attempt consists in keeping together the 'each', and therefore the freedom of the single individual, and the 'all', and therefore the dimension of equality, understood in a radical sense, not as purely juridical. Balibar's concept of equaliberty could probably be recalled (even if Balibar does not utilise Sartre in outlining the notion) in order to heighten the 'stakes' of freedom and equality, as a constitutive element of a politics of emancipation starting from the French Revolution.[85] However, it is enough to recall the definition of communism as the association in which the free development of each constitutes the condition for the free development of all, provided by Marx and Engels in *The Communist Manifesto*.[86] The fact that, without the free development of each, the free development of all is not possible, testifies to the non-organicist character of Marxian discourse, and its continuous *conatus* towards individual realisation, which is not conceived as unharmonious to common realisation. Sartre himself, in *Response to Claude Lefort*, recalls such a Marxian solution: 'Marx tells us that ... the free development of each will influence the development of all. But first this society must have dissolved its classes, the divisive principle'.[87] From this perspective, the Sartrean 'everyday practice of each and all' can be considered as a possible way of reading communism as the 'realm

---

83   On the Sartre-Lefebvre relation, see Poster 1975, pp. 386–98, who also highlights Sartre's 1968 activism; Gaudeaux 2006, pp. 309–20: 'Lefort's "letter" of Marxism develops a vision of the proletariat to which Sartre violently opposes the "body" of Marxism: an incarnated history' (p. 309). 'Sartre reproaches Lefort for outlining an ideal, indefatigable, and thus necessarily triumphant proletariat' (p. 314); Birchall 2004, pp. 151–55; Kelley 1999; Husson 2011.

84   Cf. de Certeau 1997.

85   Cf. Balibar 2014.

86   Marx 1978, pp. 469–500 (p. 491).

87   Sartre 1968a, p. 235.

of freedom' (without understanding it as a determinate place, deprived of contradictions), on the basis of a coimplication of freedom and equality.

Clearly it is necessary to always keep in mind the dynamic character of the discourse, and thus the crucial emphasis on a movement that never finds a full completion, on the basis of a permanent tension. At the same time, one must not lose sight of the objective of giving life to concrete solutions, of establishing a practical actualisation. It is a matter of reasoning not according to a dualism between movement and organisation, but instead starting from the conviction that, in practice, specific proposals are formed as the fruit of different modalities of operation than those (proposals) which derive from the 'present state of things'. Within this context, Sartre referred in explicit terms, 'positively', to communism, in his writings from the 1950s.

> It is movement [*mouvement*] which holds together the separated elements; the class is a system in motion: if it stopped, the individuals would revert to their inertia and to their isolation. This movement, directed, intentional and practical, requires an *organization*. It is for this reason that Marx could speak of an "organization into class" ... The definition which Marx gives of communism can be applied equally well to the proletariat: "It is not a stable state, an ideal to which reality will have to adapt itself ... (it is) the *real* movement which abolishes the present state of things" ... Marx, when he sketches out a sort of phenomenological description of the fighting worker, finds in him *entirely new* characteristics which arise precisely from the struggle: the proletarians "make of their revolutionary activity the greatest joy of their lives" ... That means that they place their human reality much more in collective *praxis* [*praxis collective*] than in the satisfaction of their personal needs.[88]

In articulating a discourse on communism, between movement and organisation, the theme of the *novum* returns, within a scenario that is not merely individual but collective, a non-hypostatised collective, rooted in the dimension of praxis: we are faced with a 'phenomenological description of the fighting worker'. Sartre also valorises 'true socialism' in the concrete action of individuals and groups in *The Ghost of Stalin*:

> [T]rue socialism [*vrai socialisme*] is not separable from the real praxis of real men [*hommes réels*] who are struggling together against the bosses,

---

88   Sartre 1968a, pp. 98–9.

the cops, sometimes against the State and against its soldiers. And I am still too abstract: for it isn't even a movement; no, it is men on the march who group together [*se groupent*] and carry each other along, who organize themselves and change [*changent*] in organizing, who are made by history and who make it; their action [*action*] is based on their needs [*besoins*] and their needs are as true as themselves.[89]

Such a complex of problems is condensed in the attempt to articulate the communist 'realm of freedom', carried out in *Search for a Method*:

> It is amusing that Lukács ... believed he was distinguishing himself from us by recalling that Marxist definition of materialism: 'the primacy of existence [*existence*] over consciousness' – whereas existentialism, as its name sufficiently indicates, makes of this primacy the object of its fundamental affirmation. To be still more explicit, we support unreservedly that formulation in *Capital* by which Marx means to define his 'materialism': 'The mode of production of material life generally dominates the development of social, political, and intellectual life.' We cannot conceive of this conditioning in any form except that of a dialectical movement (contradictions, surpassing, totalizations) ... But Marx's statement seems to me to point to a factual evidence which we cannot go beyond *so long as* the transformations [*transformations*] of social relations and technical progress have not freed man from the yoke of scarcity [*rareté*]. We are all acquainted with the passage in which Marx alludes to that far-off time: 'This realm of freedom ...' (Capital, III, p. 873). As soon as there will exist *for everyone* [*tous*] a margin of *real* [*réelle*] freedom beyond the production of life, Marxism will have lived out its span; a philosophy of freedom will take its place.[90]

Beyond the polemic with Lukács, it is clear how the element following which the theme of the 'realm of freedom' can be understood within *Search After Method* (and later, in the *Critique of Dialectical Reason*) is the nexus between Marxism and existentialism: the point of departure of the discourse resides in the primacy of existence over consciousness, in partial continuity with the approach of *The German Ideology*. According to Sartre, the Marxian materialist approach must not be understood in the sense of a dialectical materialism, but

---

89   Sartre 1968b, p. 115.
90   Sartre 1963, pp. 31–4. Translation modified.

rather a historical materialism which, is however not articulated in rigid and static terms, namely on the basis of demands which are fundamental to those in existentialism. With respect to the latter, however, the risk of an absolutisation of freedom, and thus an *anarchisant* attitude that remained operative in *Being and Nothingness*, must be questioned, or problematised. In this way the 'realm of freedom' cannot be interpreted starting from the elements just indicated, and therefore by a hypostatisation of the single man at the expense of the social context. In this regard the question of the interweaving of freedom and equality is crucial. It consists not only in the dialectical mediation between such elements, but in a reciprocal implication between 'each' and 'all'. Communism remains connected precisely to the continuous exchange between 'each' and 'all', on the basis of an extreme dynamism. However, it is important to note, in a polemic with the 'sad passions' of real socialism, that we are faced here with an idea of equality not as uniformity, but rather as the differentiation of singularities. Sartre carries out a strong displacement of level with respect to Marx, but it cannot be forgotten that, contrary to an old cliché, Marxian communism does not present an organicist character, but rather is conceived, from the earliest to latest writings, on the basis of the tension towards the realisation of capacities and individual faculties, and not on the subsumption of such elements to a social arrangement. However, it is necessary to scrutinise freedom within a historical horizon and in its specific determination, and thus in its insertion into specific material conditions and specific social and political relations: such reasoning cannot leave aside reference to the practico-inert.

Of the three 'slogans' of the French Revolution – *liberté*, *égalité*, and *fraternité*, the third, often neglected, is strongly valorised by Sartre in the *Critique of Dialectical Reason* and successive writings. In a certain sense, fraternity constitutes the 'glue' between freedom and equality, as an attempt to 'capture' the community among individuals, in its irreducibility to a formal mechanism. Sartre's aim consists in thinking politically the connection between individuals on the basis not only of an abstract rationality (and here the relevance of the existentialist approach returns), but also their passions, their common ways of life, with a call to action. However, the problem remains open of how it is possible to articulate a fraternity different than the terror-fraternity which Sartre examines in the third part of the *Critique of Dialectical Reason*, referring to the Terror but also, more generally, the overall dynamic of the French Revolution. Also on an attempt to 'replay' the three slogans of the Revolution, Sartre outlines communism, at least in *Search For a Method*, by reprising the Marxian realm of freedom (from the third volume of *Capital*), too often interpreted as the sign of a mere prefiguration of a utopian scenario, and not as an attempt at valorising 'each' and 'all' starting from a common practice. The Sartrean definition of Marxism as the 'philosophy of our time' presents a risk of dogmatism. However, 'Marx's statement seems to me to point to a factual evidence which we cannot go beyond *so long as* the transformations of social relations and technical progress have not freed man from the yoke of scarcity ... As soon as there will exist *for everyone* a margin of *real* freedom beyond the production of life, Marxism will have lived out its span; a philosophy of freedom will take its place'.[91]

Hereafter the text will aim to investigate how such valorisation of singularity is connected (and can enter into tension) with the universality of history, and therefore also how the question of the 'realm of freedom', real or mystified, interweaves with the 'thunderstorms' of praxis. In order to go further with such a theoretical and political complex, the second part of the *Critique of Dialectical Reason* is extremely important (and unfinished, in its leaving open a series of problems), centered on the 'short twentieth century', and primarily on the 'unprecedented' event of the Russian Revolution and its successive formation of the Soviet Union, and the search for a meaning, never definable once and for all, of history.

> History is intelligible if the different practices [*pratiques*] which can be found and located at a given moment of the historical temporalisation finally appear as partially totalising and as connected and merged in their very oppositions and diversities by an intelligible totalisation from which there is no appeal ... So far, we have been trying to get back to the elementary formal structures, and, at the same time, we have located the dialectical foundations of a structural anthropology [*anthropologie structurelle*]. These structures must now be left to live freely, to oppose and to co-operate with one another: and the reflexive investigation of this still formal project will be the object of the next volume. If the truth is *one* in its increasing internal diversification, then, by answering the last question posed by the regressive investigation, we shall discover the basis signification of History and of dialectical rationality.[92]

---

91   Sartre 1963, p. 34.
92   Sartre 2004a, pp. 817–18.

PART 2

Sartre and the Twentieth Century

.·.

CHAPTER 4

Common Praxis And History: From the Russian Revolution To The Soviet Union

1   The Dimension of History

The second part of the *Critique of Dialectical Reason*, entitled 'The Intelligibility of History', is decisive for analysing the relation (albeit unstable) between the singularity of political contingency and the universality of history. The second part of the text was to follow the publication of the first, but Sartre never finished it. He worked on it between 1958 and 1962, and it was only published posthumously in 1985. Even indicating 'The Intelligibility of History' as the second part of the *Critique* is questionable, since it is composed of different texts, some of which are contemporaneous to and some of which followed the first part of the text. In spite of this, however, the title has a determinate meaning. Owing also to its incompleteness, the text is a 'work in progress'.[1] At the heart of the argument we find the question of the meaning of history and our possibility of comprehending it or not. These questions arise from the necessity of not being satisfied with watching history from the outside, as if it constituted an objective phenomenon belonging to the world of things that simply exist. It is necessary to go beyond the given by trying to grasp the key elements of history even in their opacity. Such a reflection is irreducible to a sociological approach, while maintaining a relation with sociology. Sartre also proposed an examination of 'disunited societies', namely our Western ones, but we only have fragments of such a thematisation:

> In a bourgeois democratic society, the existence of a group or ensemble of individuals owning a TV is a cultural enrichment which, if I do not have one, causes me an impoverishment ... In relation to the owner, equality [*égalité*] replaces inequality, in the sense that *everyone* will see TV ... That means that the dominant class finds a new means of diffusing its own ideology ... There is a working-class and peasant culture that is prevented from emerging or developing.[2]

---

1   Cf. Aronson 1987, p. 219.
2   Sartre 1991a, pp. 338–40.

Without focusing on the question of the treatment of the means of mass communication, which are only sketched, it is necessary to note that the elaboration of the second part of the *Critique* (which is however very wide) appears strongly focused on Stalinism, 'a shadow and at the same time the guiding-example of the entire analysis'.[3] Moreover, the *Critique* is rightly defined as 'a book of the Cold War', directed in the first place 'against the philosophers of the Western world', but also 'against the philosophy of a part of the communist world'.[4] In this sense, we find here not only a conceptual point, but a position within a particular political and cultural context. Convinced that Marxism constitutes the unsurpassable philosophy of our time, Sartre claims the need to identify another type of thought that takes Marxism into account by overcoming it, by criticising and 'relaunching' it, trying to articulate an overall reflection on history. Such an objective is not abstract but instead must be situated within the context of the Cold War, with respect to which Sartre develops a critical historico-political analysis of both the Soviet Union and the Western countries: the entire argument of the text cannot be grasped without recalling this double object of polemic.

Starting from this specific viewpoint, in the *Critique* Sartre subjects history to investigation, but with the conviction that it cannot be fully conceptualised. Rather, there emerges from the text an awareness of the difficulty of comprehending it in its totality. Sartre claims that history is 'riddled with holes' [*trouée*]: 'its deaths are billions of holes piercing it. And each time, through that

---

3   These are Rovatti's words in Sartre 2006, p. 8. The question of the interpretation of Stalinism is not widely or adequately confronted in the critical literature, despite the relevance of the theme within the economy of the *Critique*. One of the broadest studies in this regard is Birchall 2004. This text has the merit of confronting this theme, but I do not share its approach at a number of points. Indeed, rightly, already in the title, the non-Stalinist character of Sartre's treatment is emphasised, but, as will emerge later in this chapter, the idea that the Sartre of the 1950s presented elements of Stalinism (see pp. 121–70) and the Sartre of the *Critique* became anti-Stalinist remains simplistic. I do not think the former is fully true and the latter must be problematised: Sartre's position is extremely complex and stratified in this regard, and polarising the discourse on categories such as Stalinism and anti-Stalinism risks being misleading for the purpose of comprehending Sartre's thought.

4   Cf. Delacampagne 2005, p. 112: 'the *Critique* is a book of war, a *book of the Cold War*. As such, this book is *in the first place* directed against philosophers in the Western camp. But *also* – because Sartre, despite what his adversaries have said about him, is an independent spirit – against the philosophy of part of the communist camp'. Beyond the point of departure at hand in Delacampagne's article, namely the idea that Sartre's thought constitutes the final philosophy of history (as will emerge in the course of this chapter, my reading is quite different in this regard), the inscription of the *Critique* within the Cold War is accurate, in that the perspective tends to subject both the Western and Eastern scenarios to critique.

fundamental porosity, the fragility of the praxis-process presents itself experientially as the universal presence of its being-in-exteriority'.[5] The *Critique* could be considered as a sort of critique of historical reason, as an attempt to grasp human action in its historical development.[6] In this regard it is necessary to keep in mind the difference between the first part of the work, which develops logical categories, capable of constituting the conditions of possibility of any history, and the second part, in which these categories are lowered into concrete historical effectivity, on the basis of a real diachronic unity.[7] As I emphasised earlier, it can be said that the 'regressive', structural method of the first part of the *Critique* is situated in continuity with the Marxian method of 'from the abstract to the concrete' in the *1857 Introduction*, referring not to the real process but to the order of exposition. Such an approach, while assuming Hegelian elements, differentiates itself from the latter through the emphasis on the 'gap' between the real and thought, which also gives rise to several aspects in concurrence with Althusser. A critique of historical reason, which can therefore completely actualise itself through the second part of the text, with its 'progressive', synthetic method, becomes central for Sartre only after the experience of the war and the Resistance, from which the awareness arose that evil and death are not only rooted in human existence generally understood, but present a historical conditioning. It is precisely death that renders history 'full of holes', since it collides with the experience of nothing and finitude. I remarked that a critique of historical reason comes to be outlined, but it is necessary to add that the reference to the dialectic is decisive, in its capacity of grasping the relation between history and biography, according to an interweaving of the universal and singular dimension.

Sartre does not understand the dialectic on the basis of a linear tendency: '[History] risks fading away before sociology, or juxtaposing institutions and practices, or deriving them from one another at random, so long as it has not understood the dialectical law of circularity [*loi dialectique de la circularité*] and its epistemological corollary, the law of circular interpretation'.[8] Within this complex scenario, we find a 'back and forth [*andirivieni*]' in the form of a spiral, within which what is negated does not disappear but rather is continually reprised:

---

5   Sartre 1991a, p. 313.
6   Cf. Wolin 1990; Simont 2001; Krieger 2005.
7   On the basis of an interpretation that highlights the difficulty of the relation between the first and second part of the critique: Mészàros 1979, p. 267.
8   Sartre 1991a, p. 280.

History appears as a brutal rupture of cyclical repetition: i.e. as transcendence and spirality. These two features represent the inevitable recovery by praxis of its former conditioning. They are generators of immanence and, at the same time, of the practical field: i.e. the sector of the dialectic and the anti-dialectic as determinations of praxis. Making oneself and overflowing oneself ... [9]

However, it is necessary to put dialectical reason to the test. It does not constitute a reason that is applied outside of history, but always remains situated, since at the centre of the discourse we find the meaning of history, in its constant connection with the praxis of subjects, who act and are acted on in the context of complex structures, on the basis of a relation between the 'inside' and the 'outside'.[10] Within this scenario, making and understanding history cannot be strictly separated.

We discussed these views at the beginning of the present work, and showed how the dialectic could not be the object of a critical investigation outside the practical milieu of which it is simultaneously the action (inasmuch as it gives itself its own laws), the knowledge (as dialectical control of action by itself) and the cognitive law (inasmuch as knowledge of the dialectic requires a dialectical temporalization of knowledge). The fundamental identity of *Doing* and *Knowing* thus presented the relationship between a praxis and the historian studying it as the bond of interiority linking *two actions* through a spatio-temporal gap [*décalage*].[11] Comprehension is praxis itself as *accompanied* by the situated observer. Its structure is the very structure of direct action. It grasps the practical temporalization on the basis of its ultimate, future term: in other words, on the basis of its end.[12]

The dialectic outlines a scenario in which knowledge and action, comprehension and praxis, seem to directly constitute an identity. Sartre's position could be interpreted as a sort of reproposition of the Marxist nexus between theory

---

9   Sartre 1991a, p. 334.
10 Cf. Rovatti in Sartre 2009, p. 237: 'From Sartre we learn that the dialectic does not coincide with a synthetic rational law ... Dialectic is thus not a universal law condensed in a center or unfolding in a process: it is instead a determinate relation between inside and outside. This inside is the starting point of subjects, which are plural, determinate, individual, empirical. They do not make history; they are not acted on by history'.
11 Sartre 1991a, p. 303.
12 Sartre 1991a, p. 369.

and practice, but in this regard, it is necessary to make a number of problem-atisations in order to avoid an immediate and simplified articulation of this relation, and instead engender various levels and strata, as expressed with par-ticular efficacy in the use of the term *décalage*. In this way dialectical reason is subjected to criticism, on the basis however of an assumption of the dialect-ical dimension: the confrontation with Hegel in this regard thus presents an ambivalent character, but still marks elements of differentiation.

> Humanist idealism is wrong twice over. The practical integration of indi-viduals could not liquidate the multiplicity of exteriority that charac-terizes those same individuals as substances ... The feature specific to praxis-process [*praxis-processus*] is thus, from the ontological viewpoint, the opposite of that which Hegel ascribes to the movement of conscious-ness in *The Phenomenology of Spirit*. For idealism sees being-in-itself as an abstract moment – that of essence – of the 'becoming-other' of the living substance. It contrasts with the *for-itself* in dissociation, as the raw given of objectification alienated to the negation which repeats and posits itself in the unicity of the subject ... In our dialectical investigation, however, we find the being-in-itself of praxis-process as what might be termed its unassimilable and non-recuperable reality ... So what is revealed to us is not *the anteriority* of being-in-itself in relation to being-for-itself, but its autonomy. Not only does it not need to be known in order to be, but it *on principle* eludes knowledge.[13]

If the relation with the Hegelian dialectic is extremely complex, Sartre's pos-ition towards analytic, positivistic reason is radically critical, since it is incap-able of grasping the coimplication between various aspects, apparently contra-dictory, of reality.[14] The critique of dialectical reason never lands on a resolved

---

13   Sartre 1991a, pp. 308–9. Translation modified. Cf. Sartre 1991a, p. 324: '[T]he movement of our investigation, although it has yielded us formal significations, contrasts with that of Hegelian idealism. The transcendent being of History is being-in-itself assimilating the being-for-itself of interiority without modifying its teleological structure, and becoming the being-in-itself of that being-for-itself ... For the in-itself here comes to the for-itself from its absolute reality. The reflection of praxis upon itself is human, practical and situ-ated *in interiority*'.

14   Cf. Aronson 1987, pp. 221–3: 'The dialectic is not ... analytic reason, positivistic reason, structural or sociological reason ... Analytic reason ... separates ... Sartre resolves the original antagonism between analytic, structural or positivistic reason, and dialectical reason, not – as Lévi-Strauss understood erroneously – by equating them, but rather by strictly subordinating the former to the latter'.

synthesis, unfolding a process of unification that never finds a definitive completion, as emerges from the final considerations of the text:

> The *action* [*action*] struggles against its own alienation through matter (and through men, it goes without saying), inasmuch as it posits itself dialectically as the unifying temporalization transcending and preserving within it all forms of *unity*. So the dialectic appears as that which is truly irreducible in the action: between the inert synthesis and the functional integration, it asserts its ontological status as a temporalizing synthesis which unifies itself by unifying, and in order to unify itself; and never lets itself be defined by the result – whatever it may be – that it has just obtained.[15]

The assumption of a dialectical method, and the tension towards unification, leaves open however a space of practicability. In Sartre we see, on the one hand, a reactivation of the Hegelian dialectic, and on the other, and attempt to get away from it, beginning from an awareness of a 'gap' between reality and its conceptual grasp, as had already emerged in his valorisation of Kierkegaard in *Search for a Method*.

The point of departure of the second part of the *Critique* is that history emerged and develops in the permanent framework of a field of tension generated by *rareté*:

> The man of scarcity [*rareté*], seeking his abundance, seeks it as a determination of scarcity ... Scarcity moves from this moment of satisfaction of needs [*besoins*] to the man who satisfies them ... The scarce man is the one for whom socially scarce objects are abundant ... Scarcity is not just *the milieu* [*milieu*]. Becoming interiorized in the man of scarcity, it first constitutes an initial antagonistic relation between every individual and each and every other. In addition, however, it constitutes the dominant group ambition, violence [*violence*], and a determination to go to the extreme limits of the scarce ... Of course, this in no way means individualism [*individualisme*]. Individualism is a form of interiorized scarcity belonging to bourgeois times.[16]

Here elements already addressed in the first part of the *Critique* return. In particular, the reference to *rareté* is crucial: earlier I emphasised the originality, also

---

15   Sartre 1991a, p. 392. Cf. Védrine 2005, especially pp. 111–12.
16   Sartre 1991a, pp. 421–3.

with respect to the Marxist tradition, of this element, which seemingly contains a transhistorical element, as the specification concerning individualism, which instead presents a specific historical connotation, testifies. Another key notion, strongly connected with *rareté*, is that of need:

> *Need itself* ... is *already* the unity of what is missing – or the unity of what threatens – interiorized and re-exteriorized in the field ... From this viewpoint, life – as a fact of fundamental integration [*intégration*] of the dispersed; as a harmonization of *guided* energy transformation – is the unitary process grounding the dialectical ... The future unity of projected objectives on the basis of need derives its reality from the ontological status of the living being ... The transcendent unity of action comes and grafts itself on to the immanent unity of life, precisely in so far as temporalization ... and overcoming ... represent a fresh solution – not contained in the very principle of life – to fresh problems (posed by scarcity).[17]

Need, being rooted in the dimension of life,[18] is configured as a genuine 'spring' of action. To some extent, the valorisation of this element seems in continuity with the Marxian approach, which, first of all, poses its investigation in the materiality of the needs of single individuals, and secondly, outlines communism in terms of the realisation of human capacities: developing several Marxian intuitions, in the past a sort of Marxism of needs was articulated.[19] In the next chapter I will examine the political implications of this notion in Sartre, with reference to other texts than the *Critique*. It is an open question if a sort of naturalism of needs, understood as 'original' elements, is present or not: the passage in Sartre I just quoted can be interpreted in either direction. In order to examine the overall coordinates of the notion of history further, the most relevant aspect is the connection between needs and conflicts, in adherence to the concrete requirements of individuals: 'For the source of our present struggles [*luttes*] lies not in *theoretical principles or values* ... but ... in the absolute urgency of needs'.[20]

---

17   Sartre 1991a, pp. 332–3. Translation modified. Cf. Verstraeten 2008, p. 54, according to whom 'need is the transcendental as such'; Noudelmann p. 52; Cabestan 2001.

18   Cf. also Sartre 1991a, p. 336: 'life is a precondition which – in one form or another – must always be given. To sow, seed is needed. To fertilize a sea-urchin with sea-water, the urchin is needed'.

19   Although different than the perspective here, see Heller 2018.

20   Sartre 1991a, p. 326.

In this way, within a historical scenario marked by violence, the theme of whether history is intelligible or not finds, as its point of departure, the intelligibility (or not) of struggles, according to a path from the simple to the complex.

> These comments allow us to formulate the two essential problems. The first is this: as common individuals, individuals or sub-groups – if common praxis accentuates their roles – can be the real actualizations within a group of a developing [*en développement*] contradiction ... But, in order to be able to assimilate a fight to a contradiction and its protagonists to be the terms of the developing contradiction, it would have been possible to view them as the transitory determinations of a larger and deeper group, one of whose current contradictions was actualized by their conflict ... It will also be necessary to rediscover in the singularity [*singularité*] of each struggle, on the basis of the group in which it is engendered, the three features of dialectical intelligibility: totalization, particularization and contradiction.[21]

The first question concerns the status of the 'common individual', created by the oath, in its inseparable nexus with a common praxis, on the basis of a framework of dialectical intelligibility that is articulated in these three moments. For Sartre, in a Marxian manner, conflicts constitute the motor of history.

> The other problem is that of the objective process. The struggle [*lutte*] determines events [*événements*], creates objects, and these are its products. Furthermore, in so far as it is itself an event, it must be seen as its own product. But all these products are ambiguous: insufficiently developed, in any direction whatsoever ... they mortgage the future and infect the struggle unleashed by them with their own opacity – their ill-posed questions, ill-resolved problems and ill-performed liquidation.[22]

The analysis of this dynamic highlights the fact that we do not see here a sort of absolutisation of subjectivity, since subjects are 'acted on' by the event, and deeply changed by it. In the earlier chapters of the book I examined such an element with regard to the *exemplum* of the storming of the Bastille, which constitutes 'subject-objects', so to speak, who are overwhelmed by the succession of events. In the annotations to the second part of the *Critique* Sartre emphas-

---

21   Sartre 1991a, p. 11.
22   Ibid.

ises the disruptive force of the event, with its transformative character, without conceiving of it on the basis of a sort of fraternity-terror, but rather through an action that suddenly induces obedience.

> So the historical event appears as the exterior transforming interiority from the interior, but without any necessary action of the exterior upon exteriority (praxis-violence) and without an immediate act of interiorization. The event comes *like a thief*. An ultimatum: either I must *be other* (and there is a good chance I will not be able to manage it), which means *make myself an other*, or I must kill myself, otherwise I shall remain in bad faith throughout my life.[23]

'The event comes *like a thief*', without the subject noticing, but, from that moment on, no longer being able to move in continuity with the past, since it is at stake. The biblical image, connected to the element of the event, could make one infer that there are affinities between this perspective and Benjamin's. Sartre's formulation actually seems to be different with regard to the reactivation of the past, and the struggles of the defeated, which remain operative in Benjamin, particularly in the *Theses on the Philosophy of History*. Rather, in Sartre the reference to the Kierkegaardian approach returns, with the centrality of the dimension of choice, which cannot be evaded: one is faced with an either-or, in which either one is transformed, acted on by the event, or remains in the earlier condition, but now with bad faith. However problematic this latter concept appears for a variety of reasons (particularly, the risk of an existentialistic 'moralism' returns here, which weakens the political articulation of the theme), there is no doubt that the power of the event stands out, with its disruptive consequences on the status of the subject. From this treatment there emerges a crucial element of Sartre's argument, namely the objective character of subjectivity. Too often, reprising in an uncritical way the various *querelles* of the 1960s and 1970s, absolute distinctions are made between Sartrean subjectivism and structuralist anti-subjectivism: without denying the strong differences between them (beyond the fact that, among the thinkers who are labeled structuralist, there are many significant differences as well), hypostatising such incommunicability does not allow the full complexity of the questions posed to be grasped. Sartre's framing of subjects as 'quasi-objects', insofar as they are acted on by events, raises doubts about the presence of an approach that is *sic et simpliciter* subjectivistic.

---

23   Sartre 1991a, p. 398.

[Struggles] precisely represent the manner in which men live scarcity in their perpetual movement to transcend it ... As long as abundance – as man's new relation to the Universe – has not replaced scarcity [*rareté*], the displacements of scarcity ... are interiorized and transcended as displacements of human struggles. Although it is classes which through their opposition create struggle, it is the permanent existence of these struggles which creates classes at a certain level of the technical development of production.[24]

In this framework the centrality of struggles emerges, as well as their rootedness in the dynamic of *rareté*, and the fact that classes can only fully be grasped starting from the dimension of conflict. Insofar as Sartre ambivalently interprets the element of *rareté*, and often seems to conceive it as a natural given (it is necessary to keep in mind that in the first part of the *Critique*, on the basis of the structural, regressive method 'from the abstract to the concrete' method we examined, the fundamental categories of human action are outlined), the set of arguments of the second part of the text pushes the discourse in the direction of a historicisation of this question, which is inserted into a detailed social and political horizon. More specifically, in the passage just examined, the notion of *rareté* is thought within the capitalist context, marked by the reference to classes. In this regard it is productive to recall the Marxian idea, presented in a particularly incisive way in *The German Ideology*, that individuals form a class at the moment in which they lead a common struggle against another class: in that sense, the element of class is not hypostatised on either the ontological or sociological level, instead receiving a political articulation. Such an idea appears relevant insofar as the Marxian approach is frequently attributed a sort of 'sociologism' of class which obscures the political dimension of class. Moreover, what is also of crucial importance is the fact that in the third volume of *Capital*, the chapter on classes was never completed, and in that context the reference to income as the defining element of class is rejected. To return to Sartre, within such a political interpretation of class, the labour–conflict relation is crucial, starting from the awareness that

> ... our history is a singular case among all possible histories, and that history is a particular relation and a particular case of the systems of possible relations within practical multiplicities ... [T]he problem of the intelligibility of the transformations under way within riven societies is

---

24   Sartre 1991a, pp. 13–14.

fundamental. For a theory of practical ensembles claiming to be universal, however, the developments envisaged present themselves with all the contingent richness of a singularity ... In the framework of scarcity, constitutive relations are fundamentally antagonistic.[25]

Here that unstable dialectic between singularity and universality, which we have recalled on a number of occasions, appears to be at work, placed into the dimension of struggle by Sartre. Sartre genuinely wrestles with Marxism, trying to foster its relaunching, but on the basis of a critique of certain problematic tendencies:

> For if we consider the Marxist interpretation carefully, it must be acknowledged that it relates simultaneously to two terms that seem opposed, without troubling to establish their compatibility: while presenting class struggle to us as the motor of History, it simultaneously reveals to us the dialectical development of the historical process. ... In other words, Marxists have concerned themselves with the material success of their hypotheses ... But the formal problem of intelligibility has struck them as not useful, or at any rate premature ... Marxism is strictly true if History is totalization. It is no longer true if human history is decomposed into a plurality of particular histories ... Our aim is solely to establish if, in a practical ensemble riven by antagonisms (whether there are multiple conflicts or these are reduced to a single one), the very rifts [*déchirures*] are totalizing and entailed by the totalizing movement of the whole. But if we actually establish this abstract principle, the materialist dialectic – as movement of History and historical knowledge – needs only to be proved by the fact it illuminates.[26]

In the discussion with Marxism two tendencies emerge which are potentially contradictory: Marx remains aware of the problem but does not manage to carry out its consequences. Within the framework indicated, attention comes to be focused on anti-labour as antagonistic activity, aimed at the destruction of the 'present state of things': 'the group – by maintaining it in its internal field – manifests a real adaptation of the product of anti-labour to the common situation, inasmuch as it is actualized by all organs and all common individuals. There is a practical meaning of anti-labor that dialectical Reason can

---

25   Sartre 1991a, pp. 14–15.
26   Sartre 1991a, pp. 15–16. Translation modified.

discover and positivism will not discover'.[27] In order to grasp this dynamic of labour and anti-labour, according to Sartre, it is necessary to adopt a dialectical approach, since any positivistic approach is dualistic, therefore revealing itself as incapable of interpreting reality in its complexity. It is necessary to note that the contrast between dialectical reason and analytical reason contains, insofar as it starts from the shared critique of a dualistic conceptual framework, the risk of a *reductio* of the second element to a simplified schema. Sometimes this argumentative approach arrives at a critique of the human sciences or in any case their subordination to philosophy, whereas Sartre had strong interest in psychology, psychoanalysis, anthropology, and sociology. In order to focus on the questions which remain open in the text, the reference to the Russian Revolution and the Soviet Union is decisive, in the same way that, for the first part of the *Critique*, the French Revolution was the decisive reference.

2   **Between Stalin and Trotsky: 'Socialism in One Country' and 'Permanent Revolution'**

The second part of the *Critique of Dialectical Reason* contains perhaps the most extensive philosophical analysis of the Soviet Union. Indeed, while there are numerous historical studies of the USSR, from a purely philosophical viewpoint the question is posed in different terms: references, whether in agreement or radically critical, have been continuous, but few are based on thorough investigations. We can add to this the fact that Sartre's analysis presents an articulated character, configuring itself in an indisputably critical way, but at the same time starting from a complex framework, completely irreducible to any anticommunist perspective. But the text in question has had a rather unfortunate reception, from two perspectives. First of all, it was criticised from opposite directions, often accused of ending up in a sort of Stalinism, and other times, on the contrary, of fostering a perspective that is incompatible not only with Stalinism but also with Marxism: in both cases, the framework of the analysis ends up strongly simplified. Secondly, the text has not received the broad debate that it merits. In Italy it is noteworthy that the translation of the second part of the *Critique* was released much later, without generating an especially thorough discussion. The present investigation even finds its *ratio existendi* in the inadequate consideration of the text. In my analysis I will particularly focus

---

27   Sartre 1991a, p. 98.

on 'socialism in one country', in which several particularly important knots are contained for Sartre's interpretation of the Soviet Union.

Sartre broadly focuses on two opposing projects in the wake of the Bolshevik Revolution: the construction of socialism in one country (Stalin), and the permanent revolution (Trotsky).[28] Although both depart from the awareness of the fragility of the constitution, the former wants only to protect all that was already acquired, and the latter maintains that instead, in order to safeguard this, it is necessary to spread it. For Sartre the situation tore apart what had to be seen in a unitary way: the two projects are actually intrinsically interdependent.

> Critical investigation will show us: (1) that this slogan ['socialism in one country'] was a product of the conflicts rending the leading bodies; (2) that beyond and through these conflicts, it represented certain contradictions and transformations of Soviet society as a whole; (3) that inasmuch as it survived, it created other verbal formulae that supplemented and corrected it.[29]

Stalin and Trotsky should not be interpreted as materialisations of radically opposed positions, on the basis of a recourse to analytical reason, but on the contrary must be viewed within a dialectical horizon. Indeed, they constitute two polarities of the same practical field, reciprocally interpenetrating one another much more than what might appear:

> So the two leaders and the fractions they represented could seemingly agree on a minimum programme, as required by the actual situation: to embark at once on building the new society, without for the time being relying on any outside help ... There was another point, too, on which it was possible for Stalin and Trotsky to agree: poverty cannot be socialized.[30] Trotsky, a remarkable man of action when circumstances required it, was nevertheless first and foremost an intellectual ... Stalin, by contrast, always represented an intermediary between the émigré leaders and the Russian masses. His task was to adapt directives to the concrete situation and the real men who would do the work ... [T]he universality [*universalité*] of Marxism – although, of course, he spoke about it – constantly eluded him ... What he wanted to preserve at any price was not principles, or the movement of radicalizations: it was the incarnations – or, if you

---

28   Cf. Barot 2011, pp. 134–7.
29   Sartre 1991a, p. 98.
30   Sartre 1991a, p. 99.

like, the Revolution itself inasmuch as it was incarnated in that particular country, regime, or internal and external situation.[31]

In this way Stalin's position can only turn out to be hegemonic, more 'practical', realistic, even cynical, with a capacity of continuous adaptation to the present conditions.

> Stalin had relied on the Right to exclude Trotsky from the government because he was hostile by *nature* (i.e. by the interiorization of his praxis as a militant) to principles, to radicalism, to the Permanent Revolution ... In fact [Stalin] *did not understand* his Left opponents and, without being strictly speaking opportunistic, the only decisions that inspired him with confidence were those *demanded* by circumstances ... Nothing to do, according to him, with any intellectual *apriorism*: the idea was the thing itself.[32]

Stalin remained adequate to the circumstances in which he moved, providing a series of practical solutions calibrated to them, which were not configured as a sort of 'flight in advance', disconnected from the materiality of the status quo. In any case, at the basis of his victory is the idea of the conservation of the nation, if anything its consolidation and not the construction of something radically new. One of the reasons of the success of the Soviet Union can be found precisely in Stalin's insistence on national pride, a widespread demand among the population. A fundamental difference between Lenin and Stalin consists in the fact that, in the former, there was a tension present that was radically critical towards the state, on the basis of an attempt to articulate communism beyond the state. In Stalin, however, there remained a 'conservative' element towards the state, which was in fact not only maintained, but dramatically strengthened. In this sense, there are various points of contact between Stalin and the history of tsarism. As Mario Tronti has emphasised, the problem of the Soviet Union was not represented by the excessive rapidity of the revolutionary phenomenon, but the specific modality with which socialism was subsequently formed:

> The Bolshevik October, the conquest of power, did not necessarily foresee the immediate construction of an alternative society. It was the start of a

---

31   Sartre 1991a, pp. 100–1.
32   Sartre 1991a, pp. 195–6.

long process, of construction of the material conditions and subjective presuppositions, of anthropological differences, of another way of being together in the social relation of human persons. An enormous project ... The error was not the revolution right away. The error was socialism right away. Lenin, in fact, had understood this right away. The NEP will be the other brilliant intuition, indeed, after October. A sort of socialist way of capitalism, even of the realisation of the development of capitalism in Russia directed, led, and oriented by the Bolshevik seizure of power. A model, today, not at all extinct. The reruns of history are not precipitated on it, but on the continuation of the affair, which that model has suddenly contradicted.[33]

In order to turn to Sartre's treatment of the two polarities of the Revolution, in the moment in which Stalin and Trotsky enter onto a collision course, monstrosities are born.

This formula ['socialism in one country'] was a monstrosity inasmuch as it said more than was necessary. In other words, it falsified the precise exigencies of the situation by giving them a synthetic unity whose motivations were contemporary, but which claimed to be based on distant objectives and the total praxis in its future temporalization ... [T]he socialist Revolution was universal and international only when it remained ideal – i.e. before its incarnation ... And no positivist Reason can comprehend that presence of Trotsky at the heart of a determination that disowned him, since presence and interior negation – in their indissoluble synthesis – represented the singular incarnation of a multidimensional conflict, i.e., its totalization in the object by the two adversaries.[34]

In the first place we find a contradiction – an incomprehensible element within positivistic logic – and the Russian reality develops dramatically through such

---

33   Tronti 2015, p. 24. See the continuation of the argument, concerning the post-Stalin phase (p. 27): 'The Leninian NEP was one thing – the workers' use of capitalist development, from the height of power – the Khrushchevian staging will be another: we talk, we trade, but we will not bury you. The USSR withstood political confrontation in the Cold War, but has not withstood peaceful coexistence on the economic model. And not because that was war and this was peace ... The permanent revolution was not possible in the state of permanent war communism which capitalism forced upon socialism'.

34   Sartre 1991a, pp. 103–4.

contradiction, which presents a dialectical character rather than being configured as an absolute opposition between the two perspectives. In this scenario the formula 'socialism in one country' says more than it should say, and
thus already establishes a synthetic unity, which predetermines the future temporalisation, placing those who were in the minority with their backs to the
wall. In this way an absolute predominance of Russia and a subalternity of
the Western proletariat is confirmed. Any workers' internationalism is put into
question: or better, this ultimately comes to be conceived, on the one hand,
as an abstract and far away ideal, and on the other, as a functional element to
the interest of the Soviet Union (and real socialism, of which the Soviet Union
constituted the pivot). Thus we arrive at a monster-institution, on the basis of
the putting into question of every concrete hypothesis of internationalism and
revolutionary struggle.

The second question to examine again concerns the formula 'socialism in
one country', but by focusing attention on the fact that it represents, through
the conflict between Stalin and Trotsky, precise contradictions and transformations of Russian society.

> What the Soviet revolutionaries were perhaps less prone to mention –
> though they certainly accepted its results – was that the Russian Revolu-
> tion itself, as praxis, was partly responsible for the defeats and divisions
> of the Western proletariat: because of the abortive attempts it stimulated
> more or less everywhere (Hungary, Germany, above all China); because of
> the debilitating conflict that sprang up everywhere between social demo-
> cracy ... and the new Party identifying with the USSR ... In this sense, it can
> be said that its incarnation was in direct contradiction with its universal-
> ization ... [T]he proletarian Revolution in the USSR, instead of being a
> factor in the liberation [*libération*] and emancipation [*émancipation*] of
> Europe's working-class masses – as it should have been – was achieved at
> the cost of plunging them into relative impotence.[35]

We thus arrive at an only apparently paradoxical outcome: not only did the
Russian Revolution not need the West as a source from which it could draw
practical inspiration, it also produced practical changes in the West, render-
ing the West even more impotent. Such a dynamic made a 'qualitative leap'
with the Soviet Union, and therefore with the process of the institutionalisation of the proletarian revolution. The Soviet Union generated, in fact, more or

---

35   Sartre 1991a, p. 105.

less successful attempts at communism, as well as a dialectic, within the West, between social democratic and communist parties, which however remained linked to the CPSU (Communist Party of the Soviet Union) as the leading-party of real socialism. In this sense, the West, differently than what Marx predicted, certainly did not have a vanguard function, but on the contrary moved, in one way or another, on the basis of a hostility or, on the contrary, a subalternity in relation to the Soviet Union, with a substantial impotence, or an attempt at emulation. In this way the formula 'socialism in one country' gives rise to a practical necessity, which, Sartre judges, even Trotsky would have had to face. Trotsky, if he had prevailed over Stalin, would not have started from that slogan but from a position of radical universalisation, only later finding himself forced to circumscribe the formula of the 'permanent Revolution' within a determinate situation.

> When Stalin's policy is attacked, Stalinists often reply: "Perhaps, but if Trotsky had been in power, we should be honouring the memory of the late Russian Revolution like that of the Paris Commune." I do not know if that is true or false. Above all, moreover, we shall be seeing how much importance should be attached to "ifs".[36]

Regardless of the Stalinist claim, what remains cogent is the presence of a 'practical necessity', with respect to which Stalin's tactics and strategy were dramatically adequate.

In this way Russia, which had come to take on a historical significance, finds itself not in a real interaction with the West, but rather in a condition of isolation, an element that can even possess, in some ways, a vanguard character.

> Soviet isolation was first and foremost that of a monstrosity: an underdeveloped country passing without transition from the feudal order to socialist forms of production and ownership ... [A] universalist ideology and practice, born in the most industrialized countries of Europe and imported by circles of revolutionary intellectuals towards the end of the nineteenth century, in a country that its economic and geopolitical structure seems to designate, in the name of Marxism itself, as a particularity – i.e. as a nation so 'backward' that Marxist practice (mobilization of the working-class masses, etc.) does not seem to be able to develop there, at least not without profound modifications.[37]

36   Sartre 1991a, p. 209.
37   Sartre 1991a, pp. 107–8.

The Soviet Union takes the form of a 'monster' with respect to the traditional Marxist schema, according to which a capitalist development would necessarily be observed, before the possibility of the realisation of socialism could be imagined (for reasons I emphasised earlier, beyond the terminology Sartre adopts, in this regard it would be more correct to speak of 'socialism' than 'communism'). Instead, the Soviet Union passed directly from feudalism to socialism, and, in order to actualise socialism, wanted to proceed in stages and thus forced a consistent industrialisation, with the highest human costs. The discourse needs to be 'complexified', highlighting, with respect to what Sartre claims, that one cannot speak of a *sic et simpliciter* feudal country, since, in the final decades of the nineteenth century, in Russia a process of industrialisation began, albeit slowly. But, despite such an element, and despite the interest of the 'late' Marx on Russia,[38] we surely find a situation that could be interpreted as a particularity, insofar as it was still not capitalistically developed, within a traditional Marxist schema.

> [Acclimatizing Marxism in Russia] was thus bound to mean particularizing it, since it would be asked to guide revolutionary praxis in a feudal country where the proletariat represented practically nothing, while the rural masses constituted virtually the totality of the population. Before 1917, however, Russian Marxism was still universalist and abstract, since it was a doctrine and a strategy for working-class militants, intellectuals and émigrés. After the Revolution, it became the basis of the culture of the masses ... [Marxism] was incarnated by becoming a popular and national culture ... as reality lived and perpetually produced by the Soviet masses.[39]

Marxism, before 1917, was not widespread among the masses in Russia, and would be developed only after both the Revolution and the formation of the Soviet Union. But obviously it must come to be adapted, becoming a national-popular culture, in one country, which was in many ways still predominantly agrarian. From this point of view, what takes shape is a 'denaturalised' Marxism, a particularistic Marxism.

> [T]he theoretico-practical ensemble that was Marxism dissociated its unity as a universalist dialectic into two particular universalities. The uni-

---

38   Cf. Basso 2012, pp. 94–109.
39   Sartre 1991a, pp. 108–9.

versality of the several revolutionary movements of the West became abstract ... The particular universality of Russian Marxism, on the other hand, was to alienate itself in the history of the USSR, precisely inasmuch as it objectified itself in it ... No doubt things would have been different if a sequence of revolutions, diversifying the incarnations of Marxism, had allowed it to rediscover via new contradictions a living and concrete universality.[40]

It is very important to insist on the doubling that has come about. Marxism in the West maintained that universalist dimension belonging to Marxian discourse, but at the price of acquiring an abstract character. Later I will turn to the status of the universal, which presents an ambivalent connotation: Sartre provides a complex and layered reading. The spread of Trotskyism in the West is inscribed in such a vision, apparently more 'Marxist', but at the same time lacking a material basis. The reality to keep in mind is that there were no associated revolutions in the West, and, even from a symbolic perspective the defeat of Rosa Luxemburg's council experience was very heavy. Moreover, references to the Luxembergist approach remain very important in Sartre's work after *The Communists and Peace*, on the basis on an articulation of the movement-organisation relation no longer 'squashed' into the party element. In Marx (and Engels), the idea of a coimplication of revolutions in the West and East was present, but a decisive function was attributed to the West: in the period in which Sartre writes, conversely, the West languishes, or so it seems.

3   The Incarnation of the Russian Revolution and Totalisation

The situation in the Soviet Union, the country of the proletarian Revolution, was completely different, witnessing the formation of the first socialist state and thus a concrete incarnation of Marxism, but at the price of its particularisation.

> [Stalin] incarnated the dialectical intelligibility of all the inner poverties of the practical field, from the shortage of machines to the peasants' lack of education. But an incarnation [*incarnation*] is not a symbol. He did not limit himself to tranquilly reflecting those shortages. If he incarnated them, he also synthetically added the shortage of men, through

---

40   Sartre 1991a, pp. 109–10.

his own inadequacies – inasmuch as these would produce deviations ...
Incarnated and singularised [*singularisée*], the working-class Revolution
deviated to the point of demanding the sovereignty of a single person
[*souveraineté d'un seul*].[41]

Moreover, the extreme importance of incarnation in the *Critique* (already
decisive in *Being and Nothingness*, but on the basis of a partially different
approach) makes it clear that Sartre attempts to valorise the 'flesh' of Marxism,
through an existentialist priority of existence over essence. In several ways, the
polemic with Lefort examined earlier can be interpreted by starting from precisely this demand. It is not a matter, however, of counterposing flesh and body,
elements that are not separated, just as the dynamic of the social cannot be
unlinked from the process of totalisation that provides organisation.[42] Instead,
we observe a situated materialisation of forces, on the basis of a praxis, which
exist thanks to their becoming-body. In any case, incarnation, while rooted in
rareté, is not reducible to it and even contains a partial autonomy, giving rise to
a deviation. Such deviation, which is configured as a differential with respect
to the mere codification of scarcity, comes to indicate a radicalisation of the
argument, carried out by Stalin's domination.

> Stalin defeated Trotsky *precisely in so far* as the proletarian Revolution,
> *by being born Russian*, was nationalized and, observing the ebb of the
> revolutionary movements outside, undertook a movement of withdrawal
> into itself – partly the product and partly the source of Soviet mistrust
> of the European proletariats. In other words, when the Revolution *was*
> *incarnated* in the USSR, it automatically effected a weakening of the inter-
> nationalist emigration in favour of the national militants. Thus, from the
> moment of Lenin's death, there was an obvious adaptation of Stalin, the
> Georgian militant, and of the revolutionary incarnation.[43]

The importance of incarnation in the *Critique* for understanding the political
dynamics cannot be overstated: even the question of subjectivity becomes the
question of incarnation. While this concept is important throughout Sartre's
work, in the second part of the *Critique* it is presented as a genuine fulcrum
of the argument, constituting the outcome of the analysis of the situation
which followed the Russian Revolution, with the contradiction between Stalin's

---

41   Sartre 1991a, p. 226.
42   Cf. Bourgault 2005, especially p. 498.
43   Sartre 1991a, p. 212.

'socialism in one country' and Trotsky's 'permanent revolution'. Such a dynamic remains crucial for the interpretation not only of the distinctive features of the Soviet Union, but also of the changes that have taken place, and the difficulties that are present in Western countries. In this text, incarnation finds a particularly important expression in the long example of boxing: the effectivity of social struggles is at work in the ring and the participation of the spectators.[44]

The Marxism incarnated in the Soviet Union, with its particularism, inevitably possessed a nationalistic character. It is not necessary to reiterate the fact that Marxism is configured in internationalist terms, thus Sartre is critical of any nationalistic approach. Obviously, however, from a historical point of view, struggles for emancipation, working-class (but also anticolonial) struggles, often take on a national hue. Marx himself, as time passed, was forced to reevaluate, at least partially, the national question, but interpreted it as an initial moment rather than an end. Instead, the formula 'socialism in one country' does not contain only a politically motivated character, and was not reducible to a "realistic" or even cynical tactic, but rather was the expression of elements strongly rooted in the Russian people. Moreover, the Soviet Union constituted a state-power, with a hegemonic rule, from a certain moment onwards, over half the world. Such particularistic, nationalistic Marxism thus rests on precise needs, but comes to be 'monstrous'.

> This monstrosity, unintelligible as a verbal idea or theoretico-practical principle, was comprehensible as a totalizing act which, at that precise moment of action, kept together and united the theoretical and the practical, the universal and the singular [*l'universel et le singulier*], the traditionalist depths of a still alienated history and the movement of cultural emancipation, the negative movement of retreat and the positive movement of hope. Its singularity [*singularité*] as an ideological deviation was a totalized totalization [*totalisation totalisée*], since it expressed and simultaneously reinforced revolutionary praxis in the historical singularity of its incarnation – i.e. in the particularity of its objective tasks, inside the community [*communauté*] under construction and outside in the practical field.[45]

---

44   Cf. Coorebyter 2001, p. 189: 'any boxing match is presented as a totalising incarnation of all of the tears that run through the society in which it is organised'; Aronson 1987, pp. 51–75.

45   Sartre 1991a, pp. 111–12. On the overall relation between incarnation and deviation, see Noudelmann 1996, especially pp. 133–9.

Here we find an alteration of the principles of historical materialism and, at the same time, its conservation in terms that are, however, purely ideal. In this way a 'totalised totalisation', the fruit of that aforementioned particularist incarnation, is produced. An important aspect concerns the attempt, on the part of this totalising 'monstrosity', to keep universality and singularity together. It is interesting to observe that Sartre, in order to note the victory of Stalin's hypothesis of 'socialism in one country' and the successive totalisation it came to form, returns to the notion of historialisation. In *Truth and Existence*, a text distinguished by an intense confrontation with Heidegger, historialisation is interpreted starting from the dimension of the project of the 'for itself' in history, on the basis of a differentiation with *historicité*, 'the pure expression of the epoch'.[46] In the second part of the critique this concept presents a more complex character:

> [T]he movement of historialization [*historialisation*] has three phases. In the first phase, a common praxis [*praxis commune*] transforms society by a totalizing action whose counter-finalities transform the results obtained into practico-inert ones. In a second phase, the antisocial forces of the practico-inert impose a negative unity of self-destruction upon society, by usurping the unifying power of the praxis that has produced them. In a third phase, the detotalized unity is retotalized in the common effort to rediscover the goal by stripping it of counter-finalities.[47]

Within such a tripartite articulation, which gives an account of a movement irreducible to a mechanical and linear dialectic, the third moment of historialisation allows the distinctive features of Stalin's Soviet Union to become comprehensible, insofar as it is an incarnation of Marxism and a totalisation that tries to keep universality and singularity together.

> This totalizing reality was thus characterized by the *immanence* [*immanence*] of the bonds uniting the elements that made it up (synthetic structure of the field) and, at the same time, by the presence of practico-inert concretions producing collectives within it and tending to reify human relations ... Without the internal existence of the practico-inert, the totalization [*totalisation*] would be a totality [*totalité*] or it would not be at all.[48]

---

46   Cf. footnote 62 of chapter 1.

47   Sartre 1991a, pp. 120–1.

48   Sartre 1991a, p. 278. Cf. Rizk 2011, especially pp. 189–212 (here p. 203): 'The *totalising* charac-

Unlike totality, totalisation, which is anything but impermeable by the prac-tico-inert, is never complete and has an internal dynamism:

> [W]hat is involved is a temporalization: i.e. an interior passage from minus to plus, from plus to minus, from a quantity to a quality, and vice versa. In short, this presupposes a detotalization [*détotalisation*] in act – or threatening – against which the totalization is perpetually effected. Otherwise, there would be merely a *totality* ... So totalization resembles unification [*unification*]. But it is not comparable to the rigorous unifica-tion of a body (an army, for example) attempted by groups in the govern-ment.[49]

The emphasis here on the temporal dimension of the question and individu-ation of a link (but not a coincidence) between totalisation and unification comes to assume a political importance: interpreting the Soviet Union in the name of totalisation rather than totality, and even less so totalitarianism, is heavy with ramifications. The rejection of the category of totality clearly shows a will to get away from Lukács's position, and the notion of totalisation anticip-ates in several ways the idea of territorialisation in Deleuze and Guattari, who praised Sartre's analysis: 'Civilized modern societies are defined by processes of decoding and deterritorialization. But *what they deterritorialize with one hand, they reterritorialize with the other*'.[50] Sartre in any case does not establish a

---

ter of struggle is mixed with the character of incarnation proper to singularity ... Incarn-ation presents two important properties of the idea of totalisation: on the one hand, it seems that totalisation is a principle of individuation if singular being, finding the differ-ential relation series-group at its own basis, while on the other, individuation necessarily implies negation'; also cf. McBride 1991, pp. 103 ff.; Poster 1975, p. 276; Aronson 1987, espe-cially pp. 33–50.

49   Sartre 1991a, p. 448.
50   The entire passage is worth quoting: 'Sartre's analysis in *Critique de la raison dialectique* appears to us profoundly correct where he concludes that there does not exist any class spontaneity, but only a "group" spontaneity" whence the necessity for distinguishing "fused groups" from the class, which remains "serial," represented by the party or the state. And the two do not exist on the same scale. This is because class interest remains a function of the large molar aggregates ... The problem is situated there, between uncon-scious group desires and preconscious class interests ... Civilized modern societies are defined by processes of decoding and deterritorialization. But *what they deterritorialize with one hand, they reterritorialize with the other*'. Deleuze and Guattari 1983, pp. 256–57. Translation modified. Cf. Jameson 2014, p. 115: 'The vocabulary of "totalization" developed in the *Critique of Dialectical Reason* will arouse now perhaps ancient or dormant repu-diations of notions of totality as such, despite the fact that Sartre's term was meant to substitute a process and an activity for this inert and substantified noun; and without any

'pacified' framework deprived of internal tensions. In order to note his representation of the Soviet Union, the category of totalitarianism is inadequate: 'Totalization here does not mean the suppression of conflicts, a mediation; it means that every conflict is the incarnation of the most general conflicts, and of unity'.[51] Investigating the incarnation of the proletarian revolution in the Soviet Union thus does not mean being confronted with a scenario characterised by a total unification, fixed once and for all.

In a passage cited earlier, Sartre adds in this regard the unfolding of a 'totalised totalisation', since 'totalisation ... is transcendence [*transcendance*], always induced to retotalize itself and control its deviations ... In this sense, [totalization] is always *creative*'.[52] The dimension of transcendence is not conceived as counterposed to the dimension of immanence:

> [the goals of the praxis-process] are at the same time immanent and transcendent ... *Transcendent in their immanence*, since the character of non-shared goals necessarily refers to the agent who *does not share* ... Immanent in their transcendences, since ... their inner relation to the agent remains etched in the ontological affirmation of transcendence ... [T]his relation represents the irreducible structure of the act, the objective moment of praxis *as necessity of freedom* [*nécessité de la liberté*].[53]

The question of the nexus established between immanence and transcendence must be interpreted by starting from a view of the former as concerning the relation of each individual with one another internal to the dynamic of praxis, and the latter as indicative of a process of unification of the operative relations and a tension towards overcoming the given – the 'present state of things'. The notion of incarnation inscribes itself within this problematic complex, presenting an open character on the theoretical and political level, since it fosters the modality with which a concrete lived experience can develop the set of totalisations underway, on the basis of a scenario that is not predetermined.

---

particularly scandalized awareness of its continuing use, in only slightly modified form, in the Deleuzian trinity of territorialization, deterritorialization and reterritorialization'; Jameson 2004.

51   Sartre 1991a, p. 431.
52   Sartre 1991a, p. 345. Cf. Rademacher 2002, p. 125: 'Totalisation is a theory of the process of political change. Such a theory holds that antagonistic relations are necessary for social transformations'.
53   Sartre 1991a, pp. 322–3.

In 'going beyond' the process is supported by a *conatus* of invention:[54]

> This operation is ... an *invention* [*invention*], in so far as the complex cat-
> egory of *unity* ... is a category *of Doing* ... i.e. in so far as it determines the
> orientation of an *absolute production* (or *creation*).[55] So action [*action*] is
> a succession of inert processes, in so far as the overcoming [*dépassement*]
> of the original situation towards the restoration of interiority *invents* the
> unity of these processes as the immanent meaning of temporalization
> ... Invention as synthetic unity – at whatever level it may be produced –
> is necessarily the projection of the living synthesis as an exigency *in the*
> *future* [*avenir*].[56]

A tension towards the *novum*, never fully reached, unfolds here on the basis of a
projection into the future – the crucial temporality of Sartre's discourse: 'invention is precisely only another name for the dialectical overcoming of a given ...
But transcendence is nothing but transformation into concrete practice [*transformation en pratique concrète*]: each *operation* is totalization and compression
of all the given into a transcendent relationship of regulated transformation
of the practical field'.[57] The reference to 'dialectical overcoming' takes on a
significance different from the Hegelian approach, remaining connected to
the practical, transformative function of the Marxian dialectic, on the basis
of an awareness that the homology between "the real" and "thought" does not
hold. In any case, within an overall historical dynamic such as was executed
in the formation of the Soviet Union, the dimension of invention, insofar as it
steps beyond the given, contains varied and complex characteristics: one is the
'invention' carried out by the Bolshevik Revolution, another is the 'invention'
of the Soviet Union as an institution. '[T]he inventor as a singular individual
[*individu singulier*] is further conditioned by his own needs and by his desire
(for money, glory, honours, etc.): i.e. by the incarnation in his practical person
of the objective exigencies of the ruling class. Invention is a mediation between
this incarnation and the exigencies that it incarnates'.[58]

Within the Soviet situation, even if the dynamic of events moved in the
direction of an overcoming of the status quo, this scope was only partially actualised, and objective difficulties remained.

---

54   Cf. Sartre 1991a, p. 364: '*invenire* (to find) is the source of a French word meaning "to cre-
      ate"'.
55   Sartre 1991a, p. 361.
56   Sartre 1991a, p. 355. Translation modified.
57   Sartre 1991a, p. 82. Translation modified.
58   Sartre 1991a, p. 377.

From this point of view, through its common activity [*activité commune*] the group supports the monstrosities generated by anti-labour ... Each common individual and each sub-group supports and nourishes the monstrosity, inasmuch as it presents itself as an intelligible and practical transcendence of their contradictions. This certainly does not mean that such transcendence is the true synthesis of, and solution to, the objective difficulties.[59] There is still ... the case where the conflict is adopted as its own by the entire group, and where every common individual belongs to one camp or the other. In such circumstances, the intelligibility of products tends to disappear. But this is because a split is immanent.[60]

The formula 'socialism in one country' represents, through the conflict between Stalin and Trotsky examined earlier, specific contradictions and transformations of Russian society. The permanence of contradiction shows that totalisation is never complete, perfect, or lacking internal tensions. In this regard, and also on the basis of some observations Hobsbawm makes in *The Age of Extremes*,[61] it is necessary to question the limits of the category of totalitarianism, in many ways an abstract theoretical model that has never been completely realised, but which has also enjoyed a boundless fortune in the historical, philosophical, and political debate. Without reconstructing the entire genealogy, it is necessary to note that the concept of totalitarianism increasingly functions as an ideological apparatus, in which the decisive feature, beyond appearances, is anticommunism, due to Cold War events. Arendt's study on totalitarianism itself is not immune to a series of problems in this regard, and is even adopted precisely in this direction.[62] There is a 'politicist' risk which consequently removes the social: the summoning of a demonic face of power

---

59   Sartre 1991a, p. 113.
60   Sartre 1991a, p. 114.
61   Cf. Hobsbawm 1995, pp. 393–94: 'Brutal and dictatorial though it was, the Soviet system was not "totalitarian", a term that became popular among critics of communism after the Second World War, having been invented in the 1920s by Italian fascism to describe its objects. Hitherto it had been used almost exclusively to criticise both it and German National Socialism. It stood for an all-embracing centralized system which not only imposed total physical control over its population but, by means of its monopoly of propaganda and education, actually succeeded in getting its people to internalize its values ... the [Soviet] system was not "totalitarian", a fact which throws considerable doubt on the usefulness of the term. It did not exercise effective "thought control", let alone ensure "thought conversion", but in fact depoliticized the citizenry to an astonishing degree. The official doctrines of Marxism-Leninism left the bulk of the population virtually untouched'.
62   Arendt 1951.

which does not allow the distinctive social features within the situation to be grasped. Moreover, there is also an undervaluation of the operative centrifugal forces, and thus of the never-fully-accomplished 'normalisation' of society: in this sense Sartre's category of totalisation is advantageous since, differently than totalitarianism, it retains a dynamic character.

In the second part of the *Critique of Dialectical Reason*, the notion of 'totalisation-of-envelopment' [*totalisation d'enveloppement*], which takes on particular importance in relation to the Soviet Union,[63] is crucial. Totalisation-of-envelopment refers to the integration of individuals, through praxis, into an organised group. Theoretically we could consider such an element also in relation to 'disunified', 'non-managed' societies such as in the West, but, since Sartre's references are relatively few, the question must be investigated in relation to the Soviet Union.

> [T]he totalization-of-envelopment [*totalisation d'enveloppement*], if it exists, must not be a mere rule – or even a synthetic schema – ensuring the temporalization of particular events from outside. It can be realized as a singular incarnation [*incarnation singulière*] – at a given moment, and in a given fact (or a given action) – only if it is itself, in itself, singularity and incarnation. This, moreover, is what constitutes its historicity; and it is in the name of this historicity that we discover the Russian Revolution as a unique adventure and the Stalin regime as a quite singular phase of its development.[64]

Totalisation-of-envelopment springs from the entire reflection on incarnation: it exists when it remains possible to interpret every praxis of an individual or group as the incarnation of the totalisation underway, on the basis of the extension of this dynamic to the entire society. 'The term *praxis-process* has no function other than to designate the totalization-of-envelopment, inasmuch as it forges its passive syntheses and these reintroduce multiplicity ... into it,

---

63   Cf. Münster 2005, pp. 245–6: 'Sartre does not define the *totalisation-of-envelopment* ... as a being or a rule ... It is thus *objectivation* of *praxis* – and *incarnation*'; Guigot 2001, p. 21: 'The totalisation-of-envelopment constitutes a genuine renovation of the notion of causality ... Volume 2 [of the *Critique*] is the most decisive in this regard, insofar as the schemas *incarnation* and *idiosyncrasy* and *diachronicity/synchronicity* take part ... The deviations and counter-finalities participate in a sort of *incomplete* human causality, which we can call 'a-causal' by insisting on the circularity that plays a role in the historical movement *and* in the movement of representation'; Kirchmayr 2005; Catalano 2010, pp. 134–6.

64   Sartre 1991a, p. 188.

as an internal risk'.[65] In relation to the Soviet Union, in the preparatory writings to the *Critique* Sartre establishes an identification between totalisation-of-envelopment and system:

> this system (totalization-of-envelopment) is at once the inner framework of the undertaking and its *drift*. It supports this undertaking, expresses it and deviates it. But this undertaking [*entreprise*] closes over the system, because – to the end – men are held responsible for the drift. Praxis-process.[66]

Totalisation-of-envelopment is configured as the objectivation of praxis and as incarnation, but on the basis of a multilayered approach, which thus contains many levels, irreducible to one plane: from this perspective, there is a critique of substantialistic approaches, which tend not to grasp such a varied and complex dynamic. This element can be interpreted as signifying a circular trend, whose figures constitute specific historical moments: it is characterised as praxis-process and as the set of respective deviations.

> Thus circularity alone can reveal the totalization-of-envelopment to us. And as the latter is a movement never completed [*mouvement jamais achevé*], that circularity – in the perspective of temporalization – becomes a spiral. Of course, this can under no circumstances mean that only circular relations exist in the society under consideration: the relationships may be simply vertical, oblique or horizontal. Only it must not be forgotten that they are established through a movement of spatializing temporalization, which gives a certain curvature [*courbure*] to every new fact.[67]

Insisting on circularity however does not mean interpreting it *sic et simpliciter* as a sort of repetition, on the basis of the idea that the past, reactivated, returns. Moreover, Sartre explicitly rejects conceiving relations in only circular terms, and not 'vertical, oblique or horizontal' terms as well, and remarks instead on the presence of a curvature, which impedes reading the events on the basis of a simple linearity. Circularity is not configured in terms of the 'eternal return of the same': rather, such an element fosters the precarity of the path. Circularity moreover concerns, more than the historical process, the critical experience

---

65   Sartre 1991a, p. 335.
66   Sartre 1991a, p. 433.
67   Sartre 1991a, p. 236.

from which the developments in Sartre's text begin: as a result, history does not remain closed, and "becoming" appears cleaved by an internal tension. From this perspective, there is no longer an outline of a sort of historical 'grand narration', since no completely constituted history exists, since it is to be done, according to complex coordinates. At the foundations of such an approach is the possibility of developing, in the *creases* of the real, new spaces of political practicability.

The question of the *mouvement jamais achevé* is crucial: the emphasis on the character of *inachevé* allows us to grasp not only the manner in which Sartre interprets the Soviet Union but also the structure of the *Critique of Dialectical Reason* itself, above all the second part. Investigating a totalisation (which is not a totality, but rather if anything, a mirage of totality)[68] means grasping in it the double face of unification and dispersion. Every praxis is totalisation in the measure in which it is configured as an overcoming in view of a goal, but such totalisation presents precisely a double, ambiguous, but never perfectly transparent character. As Sartre explained in his 1961 lecture at the Gramsci Institute, we find an interiorisation of exteriority, on the basis of a perspective irreducible either to a unilateral valorisation of exteriority, as happened within several strands of Marxism, or a unilateral, antimaterialist valorisation of interiority: singularity in this way is conceived as a sort of exteriority of interiority. The use of an approach of this type also comes to play a specific function in the case of an analysis of a 'managed' society such as Stalinism. The critique of this society does not mean the adoption of a simplified schema, such as an easy taking of position in favour of Trotsky against Stalin, as if they did not constitute the two polarities of the same practical field. It is a matter of contextualising the errors and even the crimes of Stalin within the 'solidification' of his sovereign praxis, on the basis of a qualitative and not merely quantitative investigation of the existing transformations.

We arrive now at the third question posed by Sartre in relation to the formula 'socialism in one country': as it is used, this slogan has been given additions which are attempt to correct it. Indeed, if the 'monstrosity' survives, various adaptations and corrections are necessary, on the basis of a continuously chan-

---

68   Cf. Caeymaex 2005a, pp. 45–63, particularly pp. 62–3: 'All praxis, insofar as it is individual or collective action, is totalisation, or overcoming in view of an goal, a *project* ... Thus practical totalisations ... are themselves constituted by irreducibly double relations, always practical, always inert and reciprocal: "exteriorisation of interiority" and "interiorisation of exteriority". Only the mirage of totality, the motor of dogmatism, can nourish the illusion of a history that is completely in the inertia of exteriority (dogmatic materialism), or illuminated by its own interiorisation'.

ging situation. In order to examine this theme, it is necessary to focus on the concept (and practice) of socialism, and its relation with communism.

> The slogan "socialism in one country" actually involved a certain inde-termination from the outset, since the word "socialism" was fairly ambigu-ous. In Marxist writing, the words "socialism" [*socialisme*] and "commun-ism" [*communisme*] are, in fact, often used interchangeably to denote a single order: the society that the proletariat has the task of realizing in the future. In this case, the word refers as much to the withering away and disappearance of the State as to the elimination of classes, and the own-ership by all workers of their instruments of labour. On the other hand, however, inasmuch as social democracy too identifies with this key word but claims it will reach the socialist society at the end of a long reform-ist evolution, the term "socialism" undergoes a slight alteration in that it can serve to denote the reformist illusion of social democracy. In this case, the term "communism" will have the advantage over it of exactness: it will denote the order in question precisely in so far as this can be realized only through Revolution.[69]

On the one hand, the word 'socialism' seems superimposable over 'commun-ism', thus referring to the overcoming of capitalism with a collectivist-type sys-tem, founded on workers' common control. On the other, it also presents some reformist tendencies, as testified by the fact that it was adopted by social demo-cratic parties in Europe, sometimes with anticommunist hue during the Cold War. In this sense, insofar as the relation with the state remains entirely other than what is univocally outlined within the socialist perspective, for Sartre it is more adequate to speak of 'communism' than of 'socialism', since the former presupposes in clearer terms that a revolution will have taken place.

After this Sartre considers another sense of socialism: socialism as a phase of transition that precedes genuine communism, the communist society beyond the state. In this regard, the *Critique of the Gotha Program* could be revisited, thereby evoking some problems that remain open. In particular, it could be claimed that socialism presents as its own basis a sort of non-state state: on the one hand, the state is maintained, while on the other, a sort of counter-use of the state takes place, whereby the characteristics are transformed and given an expansive meaning. According to Sartre in such a transition phase:

---

69   Sartre 1991a, p. 114.

The State continued to exist. It was the body by whose agency the proletariat exercised its dictatorship ... Later Stalin was not to shrink even from adding that class conflicts intensify as socialist achievements grow in number and importance ... Indeed, official Marxists gradually began to raise the question of the "contradictions of socialism". Taking on these new meanings under the pressure of circumstances, the term "socialism" changed its signification. It came to denote more narrowly (but still inadequately) the singular regime [*régime singulier*] that was progressively established in the USSR, and that presented itself as transitional.[70]

With 'socialist' coming to designate the system of the Soviet Union, it is no longer characterised by the lessening of the dimension of the state and, at the same time, class conflict: Stalin makes precisely this element emerge with force. In a certain sense, it is possible to maintain that it was a transitory situation. But maintaining such a position creates more than a few problems. First of all, we find a transition that is tough and protracted, and which, when it ends (if it ends), does not become communism but rather something else. In the second place, it is controversial to assert that the Soviet Union truly constituted a proletarian system, if one thinks of the perverse effects of bureaucratisation, and the formation of a nomenklatura increasingly delinked from the social fabric.

In order to be able to comprehend the key elements of such a scenario, which will be explored in more detail in the next chapter, it is necessary to articulate the reasoning not on the basis of an 'organicist thought', but by unearthing the conflictuality, the presence of unresolved tensions: in a word, the character of totalisation underway, and not the accomplished totality. In addition to reprising aspects detailed in the earlier chapters, concerning the first part of the *Critique*, it is important to remark upon the substantial extraneity of Sartre – albeit with a series of ambivalences – towards organicist temptations: here the critical reference to the conception of the group as a 'hyperorganism' is crucial. The group presents a 'fusional' character, but in relation to the destabilising event (the storming of the Bastille, the storming of the Winter Palace ...): such a dynamic is not fully solidified in a community, and, when this occurs, it remains the object of Sartre's critique. The object of such a critique consists in keeping open the discourse from a theoretical and political perspective, since every totalisation is an 'inventing the new', and at the same time involves deviations, as well as a series of elements that impede it, thus not coming to outline a linear path.

---

70   Sartre 1991a, p. 115. Translation modified. Cf. Carpi 2015, especially pp. 138–42.

Organicist thought [*pensée organiciste*] is everywhere, slipping in behind practical thought every time it is a question of hypostatizing action [action] by cutting it off from the agent [agent] ... The whole, if it is to have an ontological status, must produce itself – through a continued but purely *affirmative* creation – as the new being of diversity [*diversité*] (with the diverse no longer being an obstacle, [any more than] an incitement, to unification, but – in an immobile transcendence of itself – becoming the means of which *totality* as a real being is *the end*, and finding in this totality as a realized end its meaning and its raison d'être: as though totality had retrospectively engendered diversity only to produce itself through the liquidation into it of the diverse as such, and through its preservation as a qualitative variety in unity). Totalization, for its part, is transcendence, always induced to retotalize itself and control its deviations ... In this sense, [totalisation] is always *creative*.[71]

---

71   Sartre 1991a, pp. 344–5.

CHAPTER 5

Seriality And Bureaucratisation: A Reified Equality

1 The Construction of the Soviet Man

The events of "actually existing socialism" (and particularly the Soviet situation) that Sartre examines paradigmatically exemplify the dynamic of group institutionalisation, with its disciplining effects on single individuals. It is enough to think of bureaucratisation and the decisive role played by the party, with its extremely hierarchised structure and the tendential way it 'extinguishes' the tension towards change that belongs to the fused group.[1] According to Sartre, that dialectic between the soviets and the Communist Party which Lenin kept open was closed with the development of the Soviet Union, while the nuclei of 'democracy from below' constituted by the soviets, with their rootedness in the world of labour, became substantially powerless. In such a context the Communist Party thus became absolutely hegemonic, a genuine 'Leviathan' in its inseparability from the state. This reflection could be interpreted according to a contraposition between the 'positivity' of the first, 'heroic', revolutionary, 'hot' phase, which is marked by the praxis of the 'fused group', and the 'negativity' of stabilisation, and thus of a socialism that made itself into an institution. However, Sartre's argument is irreducible to this kind of dichotomy.

Despite the problems indicated, the Soviet Union was founded on the collective appropriation of the means of production:

> [T]he formula ['socialism in one country'], which was false, became true provided socialism was made into a *praxis-process*, building an order on the basis of machines and a fundamental socialization of the land, in emergency conditions and through the perpetual sacrifice of everything to the most rapid intensification of production rates ... [T]he emergency conditions – with the practical consequences these entailed (commandism, authoritarian planning, idealist voluntarism, strengthening of the State apparatus, bureaucracy, terror, etc.,) – necessarily entered into the definition of that order-undertaking [*régime-entreprise*].[2]

---

1 Cf. Barnes 1974, p. 129.
2 Sartre 1991a, p. 116.

In this way we observe a praxis-process which realises socialisation, but at the price of a sacrifice of the needs and capacities of individuals, and therefore with the highest human costs, within a scenario of continuous emergency, necessitated by the encirclement in which the Soviet Union found itself. Such a development can only lead to a regime of terror:

> [T]he ruling praxis was real, material and coercive, based on a party and a police that gave it its true weight ... And unity was not that of the "kingdom of ends", or the unity which idealism terms a mutual agreement of minds: it consisted in an integration obtained *by a labour* – by the pretty disgusting labour that cops execute upon suspects (i.e. everybody) in a dictatorship (even a socialist one). But it really was a labour. Tracking down, arresting.[3]

Sartre had already dwelt on the problem of 'fraternity-terror' owing to the Reign of Terror during the French Revolution (as well as the Revolution's overall dialectic). Such a dynamic goes through the strongest escalation with the Soviet regime. In this respect, the entire analysis of the second part of the *Critique* can be considered as a continuous dialogue with Merleau-Ponty's *Adventures of the Dialectic*. In outlining his own political thought after *The Communists and Peace*, Sartre certainly reexamined the political conjuncture, particularly with reference to the events of 1956, but he also thought at length about Merleau-Ponty's critical moves. In the *Critique* (and the texts immediately prior to it) there is a clear Merleau-Pontean influx with regard to the critique of fraternity-terror, and the specific modality with which the relation between fused group, organisation, and institution was articulated in the Soviet Union: the subordination, albeit with some ambivalences, of class to party, which is present in *The Communists and Peace*, ends up being radically called into question. Maintaining such a position does not mean claiming that there is a convergence between the *Critique* and *Adventures of the Dialectic*, since Sartre's critique of the Soviet Union remains complex and does not imply the loss of an intense relation with Marxism, however much it is reformulated. Sartre's philosophical and political orientation is not harmonious with Merleau-Ponty's, but this does not exclude the persistence of some important consonances between them, as will also emerge in this book's conclusion. In any case, the valorisation of the subjective dimension of the group (and class), in its irreducibility to a serialising structure, cannot but lead, for Sartre, to a critical analysis of bureaucracy, an element that is anything but extraneous to the Marxian approach.

---

3   Sartre 1991a, p. 246.

Indeed, it is necessary to remark that in Marx there remains operative, contrary to what has become an old commonplace, a strong questioning of bureaucracy as an apparatus of the state. Although there are controversial aspects (for example, with regard to the transitory phase, the continuity of the state order), the Marxian approach cannot contain any 'statolatry' in which, inevitably, bureaucracy plays a decisive role. Notwithstanding the extremely long polemic carried out against him by Bakunin, Marx's outline of communism remains entirely extraneous to the legitimisation of the bureaucratic 'iron cage'.[4] Turning back to Sartre, already in *The Ghost of Stalin* there is an emphasis that bureaucracy does not constitute a class, and therefore the removal of the bureaucracy does not mean the presence of a politics of class.[5] Sartre further explores the question of the status of bureaucracy in the second part of the *Critique*, in terms that are strongly critical but substantially confirm the earlier judgment that questions the class character of bureaucracy.

Communists saw in the privileges of the Bureaucracy only the derived recompense of the bureaucrats' absolute dedication to socialization. Anti-Communists argued as though the material interests existed *first* and the leading circles – in the name of these interests or, as was usually claimed, out of *self-interest* – had allocated to themselves the lion's share (had systematically diverted the major share of the national income into their pockets) ... [P]raxis becomes the instrument of individual selfishness or the particularism of certain groups. In other words, the ambiguous position of this Bureaucracy – which has *given itself interests on the basis of its absolute dedication to the Cause*, and found itself "interested" even before understanding what was happening to it – all vanishes, in favour of a rapacious and logical activity that inflexibly combines its means with a view to attaining selfish ends, and unfailingly achieves its goal ... [F]rom the outset ... it was the leaders who ... deviated praxis in favour of themselves, and deliberately sacrificed the revolutionary ideal to their own interests. And all of this without changing themselves: they were *already* self-interested.[6]

---

4 Cf. Basso 2015.
5 Cf. Sartre 1968b, pp. 71–2: 'At first the Plan engenders its own instruments: it develops a bureaucracy of experts ... It is absurd to pretend that this bureaucracy *exploits* the proletariat and that it is a *class*, or then words no longer have meaning ... Born of the Plan, it is the Plan which legitimizes their privileges ... This total alienation allows them to consider themselves as organs of the universal to the extent that the Plan must be established by their efforts ... Between these "organizers" and the masses, the Party claims to play the role of mediator'.
6 Sartre 1991a, p. 241. Translation modified.

Such an analysis of bureaucracy and bureaucrats strongly 'complexifies' the idea of their functionality to the socialist cause, with respect to which they would merely have the role of executing: we note their autonomisation, starting from their anchoring in selfish interests and goals. Despite this, bureaucracy comes to be posed in disciplining terms: 'everyone was modified, even in his self-awareness, by a bureaucratic ossification that – inasmuch as he *was not* a bureaucrat – was not produced directly within him, but – inasmuch as he was linked to the Bureaucracy, at least by the immanent relation of obedience [*obéissance*] – *determined him from afar*'.[7] Such 'bureaucratic ossification' produces a 'grammar' of obedience.

In this way, with Stalinism we observe a hypertrophy of the state, a continuous expansion of its functions and thus an accentuation of its repressive character.

> [W]hat was left as a distant objective – as the non-incarnated other side of the daily struggles and of the whole undertaking – was the communist order itself. This is what still defined itself, abstractly, as internationalization of the Revolution, disappearance of the State, abundance, liberty. *Socialism*, in this theoretical synthesis, was essentially *homogenous* with communism, in so far as the radical transformation of economic and social structures was carried out in the very first years of the Revolution. It was simply the mediation between the abstract moment of *socialization* [*socialisation*] and the concrete moment of *common enjoyment* [*jouissance commune*]. This meant that in certain historical circumstances it could be a synonym of *Hell*.[8]

Hell, which in the 'early' Sartre remained connected with the overall human condition, here comes to be set next to socialism, but only in 'determinate historical circumstances' and not absolutely. It is necessary to add that even if an identification between socialism and communism seems operative, communism is actually configured as a distant, purely ideal goal: 'the effective truth of the thing' was socialism. The slogan 'socialism in one country', with the passage of time, begins to enter into crisis:

> Thus the Stalinist formula – at first false, then more and more true – eventually decayed and lapsed into an honorific role when the situation no longer justified it: i.e. when the Chinese Revolution and the appearance

---

7   Sartre 1991a, p. 254.
8   Sartre 1991a, p. 116.

of the people's democracies in Central Europe abolished the 'socialist isolation' and required another praxis on the part of the Soviet government. Meanwhile, of course, the counter-finalities of that transcended praxis has transformed the USSR: stratifications, practico-inert structures. That singular incarnation [*incarnation singulière*] was progressively singularized in the process of institutionalization. The adaptation of such a highly specific reality to the new exigencies was to be long, arduous and obstructed.[9]

In this way Sartre articulates a response to another crucial theme concerning the formula 'socialism in one country': in the measure in which it continues to be used, that slogan has created other verbal determinations that add to it and correct it. Other socialist systems are formed in Eastern Europe and other places: in particular, the case of China is especially significant, i.e., a communist system in a gigantic country, but with a different orientation than the Soviet one. In this sense we no longer find ourselves faced with a single state, nor only to entities dependent upon the Soviet Union. The slogan, initially false, became true and finally was put into question.

'The transformations might be violent, but they would no longer have the character of a revolution [*révolution*]'.[10] We thus arrive at a result which initially seems paradoxical, namely at a neutralisation of the revolutionary dynamic. Violence was not eliminated; rather, the very possibility of a thoroughgoing transformation became foreclosed: instead, internal changes and small adaptations take place. Moreover, such a element, upon closer inspection, is less paradoxical than it may seem: revolution, with its 'constructivist' character, always entertains an ambiguous relation with the state-form, and thus with its authoritative structures. Indeed, differently than a revolt, it comes to form a new politico-juridical order, with the risk that it establishes a new modality of 'discipline and punish'. In this regard it is necessary to take up Sartre's considerations on the passage from movement to organisation and institution, with its particularly dramatic consequences in the Soviet Union. The analysis of the slogan 'socialism in one country', in some ways a monstrous formula, has highlighted several distinctive features of the construction of the Soviet Union and its successive development. But Sartre's position presents a complex and overall character, thus remaining irreducible to the simple idea of the conversion of the Revolution into its opposite, and the counterrevolutionary character of

---

9   Sartre 1991a, pp. 116–17.
10   Sartre 1991a, p. 117.

its development. Sartre's treatment of the Soviet Union evinces a sort of historical prudence, such that the critical approach never flows into the complete demolition of that experience, on the one hand, or the defense of Western liberal democracies, on the other.

> Through this internationalism – a future unity of peoples – the Soviet citizen discovered that *his* country was *designated* (by History itself) to draw all nations into the convergence of a single destiny. At the time of nationalism, this people was discovered as *the* nation that would save all the others from their national solitudes ... Future history of the USSR and past history of Russia were illuminated by a reciprocity of lights ... In this, properly speaking, there was neither mystification nor 'fetishization'. It was more a matter of the necessary interaction between two popular cultures (one folkloric, but partially alienated by the religious and social ideology of the old regime; the other materialist, but imbuing the people on the basis of sovereign decisions and with the inflexibility of praxis).[11]

The question of Russian nationalism is central in Sartre's account, but starting from an overall reflection on the history, and an analysis of the different temporal dimensions – past, present, and future. There seems to emerge the meaning of History with a capital H, since one feels like the bearer of a bright future, of which the Soviet man and the Russian-Soviet people must take charge. Such an element does not present a merely rhetorical function: not by chance, the image of an elected people is evoked. We find here an interweaving of the temporal dimensions: from a glorious past, through a disruptive present, one arrives at a bright future.

> As forced labour (or rather, forced consent to the mode and to the norms of labour) proceeded and the first results of action made themselves known, *Soviet man* was created. His *pride* sprang from his first achievements (*although* – and above all *because* – most of them ... were not just destined directly to raise his standard of living). His *toughness* was just interiorized oppression (he was tough and disciplined, quick to denounce as slackness the relaxation of his neighbour) ... [T]his 'Soviet man' – the first *really* to define the present in terms of the future (and on the basis of the past) and his individual future in terms of the socialist future ... this type of man would never have been produced in bourgeois democracy ...

---

11   Sartre 1991a, p. 123.

Or, if you prefer, education and propaganda had eventually determined in each individual a zone of almost pledged inertia.[12]

We thus find the construction of the Soviet man, with his discipline, a discipline that is interiorised and appropriated as one's own, even in the absence of concrete results. Such a scenario is supported by a powerful ideological dispositive, without attributing a reductive meaning to the element of ideology. As Althusser has remarked, in history there occurs a continuous production of ideology, and the question of ideology cannot be circumscribed within the events of the short twentieth century. Sartre, while articulating the notion of ideology in different terms than Althusser, does not reduce it to false consciousness or mere mystification, as the elements indicated are also important for comprehending its distinctive features.[13] It is necessary to further examine the relation between past and future: the tsarist past, glorious in its own way, also made of ancient traditions, however important, and the communist future, under the banner of emancipation. The two temporalities interweave in a peculiar way. In this way the idea returns that the prevailing hypothesis – Stalin's – presented points of continuity with tsarism, remaining much more 'conservative' than Lenin's.

In order to reach the goal of keeping together the traditionalist tsarist past and the materialist future, it was necessary to move according to a rigorously unitary logic, attempting to realise the common property in all sectors in order to implement a substantial equality among individuals, while at the same time producing an elite, formed by the summits of the bureaucracy and the Party. In the face of a situation, such as that present on the eve of the revolution in Russia, a country which lacked a genuine working class and in which the social base was more or less constituted by peasants with a low education rate, the choice taken went in the direction of a strict 'disconnect' between the Party leaders and the rest of the population. For Stalin there reemerges the question of the necessity of the five-year industrialisation plans, in order enable the production of a working class which at that point existed only to a lesser extent. Such planning, with its exacerbated human costs, could only lead to a process of centralisation, and thus to the presence of a managerial element, on the basis of increased verticalisation. Being a 'common individual' meant remaining adequate to that order, and thus accepting one's subjection to a strong discipline.[14]

---

12   Sartre 1991a, pp. 161–2.
13   Cf. Barot 2011, pp. 253–84; Bourgault 2001.
14   For a valorisation of some aspects of Sartre's analysis of the Soviet Union, see Negri 1999, p. 298: 'Sartre concludes without coming to a conclusion, the urgency of the synthesis has

In this way a discourse of uniformity is articulated to a sovereignty, a constituted power, albeit one resulting from the proletarian revolution. There emerges a logic of sovereignty, in this sense adequate to the state-form, with the internal differentiations that follow. We find a paradoxically elite element – 'paradoxically' in the sense that the Soviet Union should have been founded on the dictatorship of the proletariat and equality among Soviet citizens. The shape of the group is significantly different than the 'heroic' phase of the fused group. A reification of relations ends up being implemented:[15] the capitalist system is criticised for its atomisation, yet there is a risk of finding oneself, under false pretenses, in another, albeit different, form of atomisation. The fundamental term for comprehending this process is 'serialisation', which is an index of uniformity, the mirage of equality rather than equality. In the first part of the book I emphasised repeatedly that the group arises from the negation of seriality, in the direction of a community among individuals, but with the institutionalisation of the group (and, in a particularly emphatic way, in the specific case of the Soviet Union), there is a risk of returning to seriality, albeit according to different coordinates than the seriality which preceded the formation of the group (without however understanding the series-group relationship as a mechanical temporal succession). 'The Institution [*Institution*] – as a reversal of worked materiality – gives human praxis its inert-being, for the simple reason that it imposes its indispensable practical synthesis on the multiplicity of agents'.[16] By itself the institution is linked to the presence of an element of inertia and seriality: the possible nexus between institution and seriality traverses Sartre's entire account. With regard to the development of the Soviet Union, there remains operative an organised, disciplined seriality which thus tends to neutralise any *conatus* towards the overcoming of the 'present state of things'. This new seriality leads to a strict separation between leaders and followers: in this way, the nexus between seriality and bureaucratisation appears very tight.[17]

---

become stronger and stronger and because the dialectic has wanted to be restored at all costs ... The singularity of constituent strength is broken and recomposed in the dialectic of absolute differences. Stalinism is the representation of all of this ... Any singularity of the Marxist and Leninist constituent potential is subjected to an administrative decomposition and to an executive recomposition, whose definitive sign is the absoluteness of constituted power'.

15   Cf. Sartre 1991a, pp. 367–8.
16   Sartre 1991a, p. 342.
17   See Desan's analysis (1965, pp. 171–81) regarding the role of institution, with particular reference to the Soviet Union and its 'extreme centralization and bureaucratization' (p. 194).

According to Sartre, Trotsky's project could not but be defeated by Stalin's, because, in addition to the limits already noted, it did not take into consideration a decisive factor such as the shortage of time. In this regard it is worth recalling the great historian of the French Revolution, Georges Lefebvre. Although he interprets this event substantially as a bourgeois revolution, he does not adopt a rigid monocausal explanation, and indeed shows the presence of various 'French Revolutions', so to speak: the revolution of the Third Estate, the revolution of the *sans culottes* in the city, and the revolution of the peasants in the countryside. What is particularly important in Lefebvre's treatment is the dimension of the countryside, with its revolts, which are also important for understanding the development after the events of the Revolution (one thinks of the Thermidor). Sartre reworks the question of the peasants in his analysis of the Soviet Union. Trotsky thought that, not being able to produce consumer items, industry would provide the countryside with machines, and that such a dynamic would accelerate the mechanisation of agriculture. This process, together with the education of the rural masses, could only have happened in and through collectivisation. Trotsky had in mind a broad overall project of the mechanisation of agriculture: an ambitious and strenuous attempt to involve the peasants. For the reasons indicated, Stalin's hypothesis prevailed, which led to a 'particularist, but concrete' position, founded on the cynical awareness of the fact that Trotsky's proposition would take too much time, and that it was thus necessary to 'skip steps'.

In this way there arrives, through Stalin's will, a forced urbanisation. A constitutive part of his revolutionary optimism, and therefore of his voluntarism, his 'constructivism', resides in his elimination of 'traitors', those who hinder the revolutionary process. The operation that was implemented is that of a radical collectivisation, which also had the effect of increasing control and thus integration. There is a destruction, or at least a strong erosion, of rural communitarian elements, owing to a continuous escalation of urbanisation. The society increasingly found its center of gravity in the city rather than the countryside. It is necessary to add that the workers were not really in solidarity with the peasant resistance, and thus the peasants had to yield in some way, not only due to Stalin's 'military' management of the situation, but also due to the fact that the concrete development of events, and the material forces in play were entirely to their disadvantage. In this regard an overall analysis of the role of the city and countryside in the Russian Revolution is necessary, as well as a comparison with the Chinese Revolution. While having its own basis also with the peasants, the Russian Revolution found in the workers, in a working class still in formation, its center of gravity.

In the Soviet situation the peasants tried to resist, but at the same time they absolutely did not want to return to the tsarist epoch. The repression of the peasants' struggles acquired a brutal character and was arranged as a 'fraternity-terror', on the basis of a genuine dictatorship. There was a strict displacement from the Marxian dictatorship of the proletariat, as emerges in the crucial function fulfilled by the bureaucracy. Within such a autonomous practice institutionalisation leads to an ossification of the existing order, and thus to an elimination, or at least a neutralisation, of the dimension of political subjectivity. For these reasons the process outlined comes to be configured as a conflict distinguished by a 'progress towards unity', endowed with coercive elements. However, the latter cannot be understood as the elimination of the peasantry *tout court*: rather, there agriculture is mechanised and what emerges is the hegemony of workers over peasants, and city over countryside. The Russian peasants are transformed into Soviet men, permeated by a 'Marxist' ideology. Within such a process the logic of Soviet sovereignty has strictly prevailed. Starting from the given conditions, the peasant resistance appeared as 'backwards', and Stalin's sovereign practice as 'progressive': it is not a matter of attributing these elements a positive or negative valence, but rather of grasping their specific function in the historical dynamic. Clearly, such 'progressivism' also presents a 'compositional' character, but the discourse should not be reduced to the enunciation of such a critique. Rather, Sartre 'encompasses' the notion of progress within totalisation:

> whether progress [*progrès*] exists in History or not, the fact of giving a name to the total meaning of History is an *extrapolation* of its *primary meaning* ... Progress is necessarily a totalization ... So in progress we go towards what we want (goal) and what we could neither want nor predict (totalizing end).[18]

Amidst such a complex of questions, there emerges the theme of the meaning of history, which is central to the second part of the *Critique*:

> It is at this level – i.e. at the level of *meaning* [*senso*] and no other – that the question is posed of the person with her objectives rationally defined, never wholly achieved or wholly unachieved; always overwhelmed by the transcendent meaning of what she realizes, and never being anything other than what she does ... The *meaning* is the synthetic indication of

18   Sartre 1991a, pp. 403–8. For a different interpretation, cf. Aronson 1992.

the tasks to be accomplished – both regressive and progressive. Taking the term in this sense, we can say – adopting this time the viewpoint of historical reconstruction – that praxis-process is disclosed as a temporalization that has taken the form of *realization of a meaning*.[19]

2   The 'Sovereignty of a Single Individual' and Stalin's Ghost

In order to further unpack this line of reasoning, it is necessary to focus on two related questions, which do not enable a complete synthesis (which Sartre neither desires nor is able to arrive at), but rather identify certain conclusions, however unstable, of the *Critique*. The first concerns the 'sovereignty of a single individual', and the second the definition of such a dynamic in terms of Stalinism. The totalisation-of-envelopment, within a managed society such as the Soviet Union, is arranged in terms of the sovereignty of a single individual, Stalin.

> So what was the totalization-of-envelopment during the Stalin phase of socialist construction? It was Stalin ... Soviet society assimilating Stalin, being individualized by him ... i.e. the deep assimilation of a fatherland as a semi-abstract entity with a person as a non-transcendable limit of the concrete ... In this singularizing incarnation [*incarnation singularisante*] that was Russia on the march towards socialism, every worker's obligations were singularized by the face and voice of the one who imposed them ... The cult of personality was the first known attempt to change into a pledged group [*groupe assermenté*] a society in which, at the outset, the dissemination of peasants outweighed (in terms of the number of scattered individuals) the working-class concentrations.[20]

The 'agent's indissoluble unity' is crucial for overcoming dispersion, and the cult of personality which derives from it finds its *ratio existendi* in a social composition still more agrarian than industrial, in which the conditions of possibility for the passage from capitalism to socialism thus seem to be lacking without the 'singularising incarnation' of Stalin. The reasoning turns on incarnation, with its character of both unification and dispersion, which flow together in the comprehension of the Stalin phenomenon.

---

19   Sartre 1991a, p. 294.
20   Sartre 1991a, pp. 233–4. Translation modified.

Stalin made himself the man of the situation [*situation*] by the reply
he gave to the exigencies of the moment. In other words, the day when
the first Plan was decided, a specific and individualized praxis replaced
a hesitation and greater or lesser oscillations ... But this praxis func-
tioned *by* a recasting of the leading group (and – in a circular manner – occurred *as* a recasting of that group), which replaced collective
leadership by the sovereignty of a single individual [*souveraineté d'un
seul*].[21]

The incarnation comes to be configured in the 'sovereignty of a single individual', Stalin, 'the man of the situation'. We thus see not a questioning, but
rather a reinforcement of the state-form. Such a dynamic can cut through the
reference to the notion of sovereignty, which gives rise to all of the difficulties
present in the order of the Soviet Union. Indeed, the action of the fused group
during the Russian Revolution (just as, within a different scenario, during the
French Revolution) was aimed at destabilising the element of sovereignty, with
its disciplining impact on individuals. If anything, the attempt consisted in
rearticulating authority on the basis of mobile coordinates, rejecting rigidly
stable hierarchies. Sartre's perspective characterises the element of sovereignty
with a radical critique, despite the risk recalled earlier of a sort of abstract
'anti-juridicism'.[22] Instead, the Soviet Union represents, *mutatis mutandis*, the
'stigmata' of sovereignty. It is necessary to focus on the second part of the
expression 'sovereignty of a single individual', and thus on the 'single individual', Stalin.

[The Russian Revolution] demanded a sovereign who would be a dogmatic opportunist ... [T]he very fact that the experience was singular
demanded that he should adapt action to *singular circumstances* [*circon-
stances singulières*], without any reference (other than formal) to principles ... Was *that Georgian former seminarist* really necessary? There will
be a temptation to answer yes, if one of the themes developed in *Search
for a Method* is recalled. I showed there, in fact, that the child, through

---

21   Sartre 1991a, pp. 196–7.
22   Cf. Desan 1965, pp. 179–81: 'Sartre seems to maintain that every sovereignty is a *pisaller*
      ... This sovereignty becomes a more complex concept when it is viewed not solely as a
      phenomenon of the group, of all groups, but when it is seen as operating in society at
      large ... This ensemble also has a sovereign, and this sovereign is called the "State." ... The
      State does not express the wishes of the multitude, according to Sartre; this would be mere
      mystification'.

his family situation, realizes the singularization [*singularisation*] of generalities ... Nevertheless, a relative autonomy of mediated sectors must be considered here, within the living totality ... In other words, Stalin's harshness and inflexibility, inasmuch as they had their source in his earliest childhood, were indeed the results (the preservative transcendences) of the social contradictions which, taken in their full dimensions, were certainly among the fundamental factors of the Russian Revolution.[23]

The entire treatment tries to highlight the reasons Stalin's 'practical particularism' prevailed over Trotsky's 'abstract universalism': what emerged was the 'man of the situation' with his capacity to adapt to 'singular circumstances' and his in many respects instrumentalist use of Marxist principles. The notion of situation plays a decisive function in Sartre's project, starting from his earliest writings, with its capacity of keeping together the dimension of freedom with the reference to the objective conditions in which it is inscribed.

In order to comprehend the praxis of someone within a circumscribed situation, it is necessary to examine their entire trajectory. To recall *Search for a Method*, for the purpose of grasping the characteristics of a specific individual, an analysis of their life existence is necessary, without neglecting the period of childhood: determinate Marxist threads are thus criticised for having considered the human being only from the moment he becomes a worker, without examining his earlier itinerary. This 'move' gives rise to the extreme importance of psychoanalysis in Sartre's thought, in spite of his self-representation and his numerous critiques of Freud. Moreover, the monumental work on Flaubert, *The Family Idiot*, is precisely supported by the attempt to conceive an epoch by focusing attention on a singularity, examined starting from trauma suffered in the years of childhood and adolescence. Applying this reasoning to Stalin, a double-articulation is reached. On the one hand, for reasons already explained, the examination of his biography plays an important function, and is irreducible to a secondary and purely adjunct element. On the other, however, it is necessary to make a series of mediations, in order to grasp the 'systematic' contradictions present within the Russian Revolution. In any case, the use of the term 'singularity' in relation to Stalin gives rise to the hidden side of such a notion: moreover, singularity, in the second part of the *Critique*, is adopted contextually, and in some ways is 'functionalised' to the element of totalisation-of-envelopment.

---

23   Sartre 1991a, pp. 215–16. Translation modified.

So it is not a matter of knowing whether historically and practically an other could have played Stalin's role, or whether Stalin could have played his own differently ... But what is given in each person is merely their *contingency* [*contingence*] ... the total praxis of Soviet society in the course of industrialization is imbued, down to its deepest layers, with this contingency. Far from presenting itself – as the engineers of the Plan would like – as the necessary response to questions posed by the necessary development of objectivity ... There can be no doubt but that this reinforcement can and must have positive results (at least in the 'ascending' period of action). It was the Russian Revolution's fortune that its voluntarism should be incarnated in the will of the 'Man of Steel'. But *by the same token*, certain negative features found themselves exaggerated by the singularization of the sovereign [*singularisation du souverain*]. Stalin being less cultured than Trotsky, the sovereign as a whole would reproduce his shortcomings. The bureaucrat ... hastily acquiring knowledge that was always new and always inadequate – would be characterized, *inasmuch as he was Stalin himself*, by a universal incompetence. Marxism ossified into a hardened dogmatism.[24]

The argument is aimed at giving rise to the crucial nature of the element of singularity, on the basis of a valorisation of contingency. Any 'objectivist' approach which attempts to resolve the theme into necessary terms is subjected to critique. But such a formulation does not arrive at a subjectivist outcome: moreover, the situation keeps together, albeit in an unstable way, the freedom of singularity and its rootedness in material conditions. The overall structure of Sartre's approach appears chiaroscural, obviously irreducible to an apology for the role of Stalin as well as to a simplistic demolition. At least in the initial phase, the incarnation of the Russian Revolution (and its incarnation of the proletarian revolution) in Stalin had a propulsive function, or in any case, as a deviation, allowed Bolshevism to survive,[25] and at the same time gave rise to those structural problems examined earlier, in relation to the 'sovereignty of a single individual', with devastating implications at the level of practice as well as theory.

---

24   Sartre 1991a, pp. 204–5. Translation modified. Cf. Kirchmayr 2005, p. 122: 'Stalin is a historical example of the possibility of recognising, in a singular individual, the product of a society in a given historical moment as well as the mode in which this society and this moment is incarnated in him. Singularity is thus a sort of crystal in which forces historically materialise through practices that, in turn, become an inertial force thanks to their becoming-body ... At the same time, the solidifcation of praxes leads to a modification of *praxis* itself'.

25   Cf. Aronson 1987, especially pp. 226–7.

This theoretico-practical complex is often denoted with the term 'Stalinism': it is a matter of investigating the latter, in order to understand within it a critical, but also complex, interpretation of the Soviet Union. This notion, first, is assumed as a generic formula. '[T]his praxis, unaware of itself in many sectors, was to begin the grandiose, terrible and irreversible temporalization that in History was to take the name of *Stalinism*'.[26] It is necessary to problematise this term.

> Meaning, as an orientation of the temporal spiral, is itself a practical signification and can be comprehended only in and through temporalization [*temporalisation*]. All those, for example, who present what they call 'Stalinism' as a strict mechanism that starts as soon as it is wound up, like a musical table-mat, are losing sight ... of the fact that if Stalinism – can be described in the form of a permanence ... this mechanical interconditioning of the elements that make it up is just a purely theoretical view ... For – however, and via whatever mediation, I may combine the notions of planned growth in an underdeveloped country, bureaucracy, idealist voluntarism, cult of personality, etc. ... the constituted ensemble will present itself as a *prototype* ... [T]he prototype as an object of concepts ... loses its temporal determinations and is universalized ... [the *meaning*] is Stalinism-as-a-venture, containing within it its own temporalization, and not Stalinism-as-a-prototype.[27]

Such observations of Sartre's appear particularly contemporary to today's situation, or at least to the scenario following 1989, in which the conformist banalisation of the reflection on the Soviet Union, the result of a will to cancel the spaces opened by the 'profane experiment' inaugurated with the October Revolution,[28] has led to a simplified and ascientific usage of '"Stalinism"', which brings out the extreme consequences referred to by the schematism. According to the mechanical meaning, 'Stalinism' functions as a sort of *passe-partout* which can be applied to various situations, stretching it like an accordion: what is completely concealed in this way is the temporalisation, which is the element that constitutes Sartre's analysis of 'Stalinism-as-venture'.

But Stalinism enters into crisis with the passage of time.

> Between 1948 and 1953, Stalin's praxis became a monstrous caricature of itself. He could not resolve the problems posed by the existence of new

---

26   Sartre 1991a, p. 195.
27   Sartre 1991a, pp. 295–6.
28   Cf. di Leo 2012.

socialist States. The man of retreat and solitude felt only mistrust when Russia emerged from isolation: quarrel with Tito, absurd and criminal trials in the people's democracies, resurgence of political anti-Semitism – nothing was lacking. The same mistrust led him to condemn Mao for wanting to resume hostilities. At home, the rise of new generations and the growing number of technicians alarmed him: he returned to Terror and purges. The fact was that he had grown old and become the pure product of his former praxis ... However, the society he had produced required a policy radically different from his own.[29]

The analysis of Stalinism as incarnation of the Russian Revolution (and in turn, as incarnation of the proletarian revolution) established an extremely complex framework, with a critical position in this regard that does not indulge in immediate simplifications. Moreover, the conflict itself between Stalin and Trotsky is interpreted by highlighting the way the two share the same practical field: although Sartre was close to militant Trotskyists, it cannot be claimed that the *Critique* presents a 'Trotskyist' platform. Further, the Soviet Union constituted the 'Other' with respect to the Western societies subjected to critique. In this sense, from both a theoretical and political perspective, Sartre's position appears extremely complex. But, facing a changed situation, on both an internal and, above all, external level, Stalin's practice (beyond any ethical and political judgment of it) is entirely unproductive, insofar as it reproposes old schedules and thus is no longer capable of really being adequate to existing conditions. In this regard what appears important is the references both to countries in Eastern Europe (above all Yugoslavia) and to the increasingly disruptive role of China: in both cases, Stalin's posture reveals a sort of 'anxiety of encirclement'. Stalinism, which had in any case given clear signs of difficulty and aging in the postwar period, ends with the death of Stalin.

> The sclerosis of society would be incarnating in the ageing of society; and the latter would maintain it *beyond* the time when new contradictions, without him, could have exploded it. Furthermore, the end of one phase of the Revolution would coincide with the sovereign's death. Our investigation has shown, in fact, that Stalinism outlived itself, making the new structures of the society produced; and that the end of Stalinism can well and truly be identified with Stalin's death.[30]

---

29   Sartre 1991a, pp. 235–6.
30   Sartre 1991a, p. 203.

This observation is perfectly consistent with the idea that Stalinism must be read according to its temporalisation. In this way such an element, in its processual and not abstractly atemporal character, cannot but disappear with the end of the sovereign.

Sartre draws a sort of balance sheet on the reflection as follows:

> We have just shown that in a society whose sovereign [*souverain*] is a dictator, practico-inert rifts, conflicts and disharmonies – far from breaking the unity of praxis-process – are at once the consequences of that unification and the means it chooses in order to tighten up still further. Thus the historian must be able to comprehend dialectically ... the vast historical upheaval which, between 1917 and 1958, has produced Soviet society as we see it. These conclusions are not in themselves either optimistic or pessimistic. We do not claim that the struggle was not atrocious, or that (innumerable) individual disasters do not irredeemably damn certain practices ... At the level of dialectical investigation we have reached, we do not even have the right to say that it was impossible to proceed otherwise (nor, moreover, the opposite right: we simply do not yet know anything about the possibles).[31]

There is no organic conclusion to the reasoning, and in any case even the conclusion of the text itself must be interpreted by keeping in mind that the work was never published by Sartre himself. What has emerged from the path we have taken is the efficacy of the praxis-process of the Soviet Union, with the effort towards a 'progressive' unification. We observe a totalisation, which does not mean totality, and, even less so, totalitarianism: totalisation is always imperfect, unfinished, presenting shadow zones as well as centrifugal thrusts. Otherwise, it would never end. As emphasised earlier, Sartre's investigation of Stalinism is a critical analysis, on the basis of a complex argumentation, not simplistically indulging in an absolute opposition either between Trotsky and Stalin, or between West and East in favour of the West. The concluding observations taken from Sartre, with their provisory and unfinished character, are neither optimistic nor pessimistic.

I will conclude this chapter with two considerations which I will reprise at the start of the next chapter. The first is that Sartre's traversal through the genesis and development of the Soviet Union has the merit of taking on a sort of historical prudence as the method of analysis: in a Spinozan way, 'it is a matter

---

31   Sartre 1991a, p. 183.

of neither laughing nor crying, but understanding' the functional logic, with its temporalisation, clearly starting from a determinate point of view, through an attempt at relaunching Marxism in continuity and discontinuity with respect to specific 'Marxist' theoretical and political experiences. Sartre's *conatus* of the valorisation of singularity, with its shared character of unicity and differentiation (but also on the basis of an awareness of the presence of a hidden side), is clearly critical of reified equality, as in the Soviet Union, in which the 'slogan' of *égalité*, the great legacy of the French Revolution, risks being identified with seriality, connected to bureaucratisation, which neutralises the vitality of individual and collective needs and capacities. Such a critical investigation, although not conducted in dichotomising terms, and acutely grasping various important articulations, arrives however at an impasse that is both theoretical and political.[32] This is testified to by the fact that Sartre wrote the parts that we have between 1958 and 1962 but never concluded the text, which was published posthumously. The crucial adjective Sartre attributes to history could be applied to the work itself: *inachevée*. The incompleteness is an indication of a difficulty in outlining a theoretico-political perspective. If anything, the major interest and reason for contemporaneity of 'The Intelligibility of History' resides on a theoretico-analytical level as well as due to its 'negative' force.

In this way, what turns out to be profitable is an approach founded not on totality but rather a totalisation underway, a totalisation that is precisely *inachevée*, insofar as it is an attempt at reasoning starting from historical conditioning, but at the same time with the awareness that history is never accomplished, nor already given, and thus does not immediately appear available to the eye. From this perspective, it is problematic to designate Sartre's perspective as historicist,[33] precisely owing to the presence of a *décalage*, which

---

32   Cf. Birchall 2004, p. 223.

33   I have adopted the term 'historicism' because the question of the relation with it acquires a determinate meaning in the *Critique of Dialectical Reason*, which is also presented as a critique of historical reason: the reference to Dilthey is clear. I have not examined the theme of the philosophy of history more deeply (only referring to Hegel's *Philosophy of History*). An investigation into the characteristics of the modern philosophy of history would be extremely complex: too often, in 'postmodern' approaches (or, conversely, in the frameworks distinguished by a 'total' critique of modernity), it is established with a simplistic representation as the exaltation of progress by means of a full linearity. Reinhart Kosselleck's work provides several useful coordinates for the sake of a historico-conceptual articulation of the problem. These works highlight (albeit with a certain rigidity in their lines of demarcation) that what is found at the basis of the philosophy of history, starting from the 'epochal threshold' of the second half of the eighteenth century, is the acceleration of the passage from the plural *historiae* of the premodern scenario to the modern

makes history never fully conceptualisable. At the same time, it tries to establish an overall articulation, however inevitably unfinished and unresolved,
starting from the conviction of the unavoidability of a historicisation of the
categories: the relation with the Hegelian philosophy of history appears complex in this regard, presenting both traits of continuity and discontinuity, as
already clear by the title *Critique of Dialectical Reason*. Specifically, the Soviet
Union is not interpreted in 'mechanical' terms, but on the basis of a qualitative analysis, given by a situated character, of the transformations running
through it. Such a posture presents a critical potentiality in relation to both
nineteenth century 'grand narratives' and late-twentieth century postmodern
visions. Indeed, on the one hand, any linear conception of history comes to
be questioned, since its meaning instead reveals that opacity on which I have
repeatedly focused. On the other hand, the position does not arrive at a representation of an 'interchangeable' multiplicity of interpretations and perspectives.

The second consideration is that in the *Critique* there remain operative (or
at least, there can be extracted) further elements than what have been outlined
so far, also in the direction of the activation of other individual and collective
subjectivities with respect to those 'functionalised' in the construction of the
praxis-enterprise of the Soviet Union. In this sense, three of them seem to me
to be important theoretico-political articulations (which will be explored further in the next chapter), connected to the struggle, to the attempt, more or
less successful, with lights and shadows, of 'inventing the new' in the course
of the 'short twentieth century'. The first is given by the reference to other
socialist experiences than the Soviet Union: it is enough to think of China
and Cuba (but also, for example, Yugoslavia). The second consists in the stra-
tegic importance that the question of the critique of colonialism has taken on,
which undoubtedly 'complexifies' a Marxist approach as traditionally understood. The third key element, which would find a concrete articulation in 1968,
is connected to the valorisation of a 'movementist' dimension, not necessarily
on the basis of a total negation of the element of institution, but at least with a

declination of history as 'collective singular'. Cf. Koselleck 2004, pp. 26–42. Cf. Chignola
and Duso 2008. For an interpretation of historical time on the basis of a sort of 'contemporary prehistory', against any idea of the 'end of History', which 'derives from the apparent
liquidation or surpassing of prehistory', see Virno 1999 (here p. 139). Beyond the fact that
what is intended by 'philosophy of history' often remains opaque, for reasons I explain
throughout this chapter I do not think that we find in Sartre the outline of a philosophy of
history (here I disagree with Delacampagne 2005), but, whatever it is, maintaining such a
position does not mean negating the presence of a strong historicisation of the categories.

critical 'charge' in its confrontation with the latter, as emerges by making inter-act the fused group, in the *Critique*, with the *prise de parole* contained in more contingent writings, linked to specific struggles.

CHAPTER 6

The 'Spectre' Of 1968: Critique Of Colonialism And New Spaces Of Emancipation

1   Another Socialism Is Possible?

Our analysis of part two of the *Critique* has brought out a critical approach to the Soviet Union and Stalinism. On the one hand, Sartre embraces certain aspects of Merleau-Ponty's position in *Adventures of the Dialectic*, while on the other, he articulates the question in terms that are profoundly different. Indeed, Sartre's vision is not presented as a demolition of this experience, but rather has a varied and complex character: as emphasised earlier, we do not find a total juxtaposition of Stalin and Trotsky, since they constitute two poles of the same practical field. And even less so can Sartre's discourse about the Soviet Union be characterised as offering an apology for Western societies. With regard to Stalinism, it is necessary to reiterate that Sartre's critique does not focus on an indiscriminate use of such a category, as if it constituted a sort of *passe-partout* applicable to all possible situations. Rather, this category is temporalised and historicised. In any case, the *Critique* ends up in an impasse, rather than a sort of delineation of an alternative socialism with respect to the one already examined. However, in Sartre's work there are elements of complication, of problematisation of the framework, observable in the attempt to highlight other forms of socialism than that constituted by the Soviet Union.

For example, before the *Critique of Dialectical Reason*, there is a very interesting text entitled 'Faux savants ou faux lièvres' (1950), which Sartre wrote as a preface to Louis Dalmas's *Communisme jugoslave*. Here one cannot speak of a genuine exaltation of the Yugoslavian experience, in its detachment from the Soviet Union, and moreover it is necessary to emphasise that in those years, Sartre had a political position rather proximate to the Soviet Union. Still, there are some important things worth noting about this text. Right from the start, Sartre defines Yugoslavia as an 'ambiguous and moving [*mouvante*] reality'.[1] Already these two adjectives vividly highlight the ambivalence of Sartre's approach.

---

1   Sartre 1950, p. 24. Cf. McBride 1991, p. 89: 'The principle theme of the essay ... is a critique of the "objectivism" ... into which Soviet Marxism has degenerated: Titoism, Sartre asserts, has restored a healthy element of subjectivity'. For a more critical evaluation of the Yugoslavian

Insofar as [Dalmas] does not hide his sympathies – which I share – for the Titoian regime, he conceals neither the risks of error nor the external threats ... He is one of the few, in France, to produce first-hand documents on Tito's dissidence ... He has not applied any *a priori* principle to this historical fact: he has allowed it to develop before us in the perspectives of the Marxist dialectic, but instead of strongly explaining it in the name of a particular Marxism, he has considered it as an experience realised by history, which verifies the method that allows it to be interpreted, complete on certain points and modified on others.[2]

This consideration is situated in continuity with Sartre's constant valorisation of the experiential dimension, on the basis of an interweaving of phenomenology and existentialism, and therefore according to a priority of existence over essence. As such, it is not a matter of establishing the abstract essence of Titoism, in the same way that Sartre does not attempt to examine the abstract essence of Stalinism. The Yugoslavian affair, while referring to an overall vision as the fruit of a rearticulation of Marxism, must be investigated in its singularity, and with the subjective *conatus* contained in it. 'Tito's half-victory reintegrates subjectivity [*subjectivité*] into Yugoslavian leaders'.[3] Here the question of the relation between the objective and subjective dimension emerges, also in relation to Sartre's reading of Marxism, in his attempt to go beyond a dogmatic objectivist vision.

[E]ither Tito's success is explained through the objective conditions of Yugoslavia in the perspective of an objectivism that destroys itself, or it is explained through political errors – committed by USSR or Yugoslavian leaders – and thus a certain efficacity, a certain consistency to the subjective [*subjectif*] needs to be recognised. This dissident Yugoslavia was impossible.[4] Socialist realism ... must resolve this new antinomy; thesis: the subjective is a secondary structure of objectivity – antithesis: objectivity depends on a subjectivity that assesses and anticipates phenomena and that modifies them in the service of its assessments. This extreme

experience, cf. Birchall 2004, p. 116: 'Sartre ... also showed some sympathy for Tito's Yugoslavia, which seemed as though it might be in some ways a preferable alternative to Stalinist Russia ... Sartre stressed the "ambiguity" of the Yugoslav experience. Unlike some on the left he rejected the idea that Belgrade was the new "workers' Mecca"'.

2 Sartre 1950, pp. 24–5.
3 Sartre 1950, p. 28.
4 Sartre 1950, p. 50.

embarrassment of Soviet leaders reveals itself in the contradictions of the communist press, which fails to define Tito.[5]

The attempt here is to go beyond the juxtaposition between objectivism and subjectivism. What stands out most forcefully is the critique of objectivism (which also belongs to specific Marxist currents), but Sartre's approach is not reducible to a subjectivist position. In my view, such a position is not identified with the Hegelian idea of the mediation between objectivity and subjectivity. Rather, at the base of Sartre's argument is experience in its specificity, in its irreducibility to a generalising schema, and, at the same time, in its inscription within a determinate scenario: in a word, the 'singular universal'. In the case in question, it is a matter of inserting the Yugoslavian affair within an overall historical path while grasping its distinctive characteristics, which make singularity emerge.

> [T]he leaders of a small country without industry are obligated to consider at all times the external forces that can ruin their efforts. Their destiny is only partially in their own hands ... even the most skilled politician can be impotent in averting a catastrophe that arises in other regions of the globe and extends soon to the rest of the earth. In this way a new form of subjectivity appears; the leader takes risks, evaluates them, assumes them.[6]

In examining the Yugoslavian dynamic, Sartre valorises Rosa Luxemburg's approach, which emphasised that the errors eventually committed by a really revolutionary workers' movement are more productive than the infallibility of the best central committee: the emphasis on the emergence of subjectivity returns. 'In a word, the pressure of objective circumstances and the contradictions of objectivism have often led ... to a revalorisation of subjectivity; but this valorisation, in turn, requires a theoretical rearticulation; Marxism needs to be rethought, man needs to be rethought'.[7] It is a matter of relaunching Marxism, trying to make subjectivity emerge, and situating it within the specific context of the Yugoslavian situation.

'In a word, the state apparatus plays the role of the Hegelian intellect; it analyses, specifies, clarifies, but also determines and limits. Against this limitation, the movement of concrete collectivity must be permanently carried out; it

---

5 Sartre 1950, p. 52.
6 Sartre 1950, p. 60.
7 Sartre 1950, p. 66.

must make the frameworks explode'.[8] The emphasis here on the movementist, insurgent dimension is strong. Moreover, Sartre conceives class in its structural relationship with the dimension of action, in its character of radical critique of the 'present state of things'. It is a matter of understanding how this approach is situated within the analysis of Titoism.

> [T]he *chance* of Titoism, born from an error, from a conflict between two contradictory infallibilities, is that it cannot pretend to be infallible. The sole way in which it can defend itself against the USSR, in the eyes of the Yugoslavian masses, is not by opposing one dogmatism to the other ... but by asserting, against every dogmatism, the leader's right to error and presenting the socialist construction as a risk.[9]

In Sartre we do not find a sort of juxtaposition between the Soviet Union and Yugoslavia, and the identification of the latter as a model, but rather the attempt the identify it as a singular 'risk' which 'complexifies' the socialist framework.

> We can conclude: Tito's half-victory has taught us by itself the importance that it had in covering our Western eyes. It is not a question of creating a new International or making Belgrade a new "Workers' Mecca". Simply the existence of a socialist Yugoslavia, independent from the Kremlin, must act from within on the consciousness of our communist militants by making them discover their own subjectivity ... I do not say that militants must never be led to have sympathy and comprehension for the Titoist movement, but only that a socialist society, if it is established and lasts against the Soviet leaders and the Cominform, must necessarily illuminate for Western communists the nature of their activity ... But if there is something else, it was a vague flash, very far away, an ambiguous movement, whose origin is a quite cloudy schism, but here it remains that, if it holds, it does not cede to the Soviet threats and does not corrupt from American gold, then the worker proves for himself that his adhesion to the Party does not result from the effect of a simple automatism.[10]

We return to the initial definition of Yugoslavia as an 'ambiguous and moving reality', which allows for an interpretation of this reference, and the reference to

---

8   Sartre 1950, p. 63.
9   Sartre 1950, pp. 64–5.
10   Sartre 1950, p. 67.

other socialist realities than the Soviet Union, on the basis of a strong interest, though rejecting the idea of an 'absolutely other' to the Soviet Union. It is precisely this complex, nuanced judgment that is significant.

As already emphasised earlier, another very important moment for Sartre's historico-political reading of socialism is 1956. In particular following the Soviet repression in Hungary and Khrushchev's denunciation of Stalin's crimes, Sartre assumes a critical position towards the Soviet Union. *Search for a Method* and *Critique of Dialectical Reason* are affected by this painful reflection.[11] As emerges from *The Ghost of Stalin*, the analysis of the Hungarian situation is also decisive for the comprehension of the characteristics of the Soviet Union in its presentation as an incarnation of Marxism: moreover, '"socialism in one country", or Stalinism, does not constitute a deviation from socialism; it is the detour [*détour*] that is imposed by circumstances'.[12] And the Hungarian repression cannot be considered as a mere deviation of the Soviet Union:

> [T]he politics of the Party were wrong ... the bureaucratic apparatus underestimated the revolutionary force of the masses and did not take their aspirations into account at all ... With everything weighed, French communists should be advised not to shout too loudly that the Soviet intervention could not be avoided.[13]

> Foreign intervention appears ... as the logical conclusion of an abstract and false politics that led to economic catastrophe and must engender, by itself, counterrevolution ... The over-industrialisation and accelerated collectivisation *were already criminal*: these carried in them *from the first day* the Budapest massacres as their outcome.[14]

In this sense, for Sartre the reference to Hungary as well as Poland comes to be connoted in terms of de-Stalinisation, and the latter is presented as a form of democratisation, understanding this term in relation to an expansive practice:

---

11   Cf. Gray 2011; Mészàros 1979, p. 250; Birchall 2004, pp. 159 ff.
12   Sartre 1950, p. 233.
13   Sartre 1950, p. 159. Cf. Sartre 1950, p. 245: 'In the popular democracies, the brutal dissolution of the fronts and the Stalinisation of the communist Parties produced this fracture [*coupure*] *in advance* and discredited the new politics when it had not yet had time to prepare'.
14   Sartre 1950, p. 158. Cf. Poster 1975, pp. 184 ff.

No one can doubt that the events of Poland and Hungary are the direct consequences of what is here called *de-Stalinisation*. De-Stalinisation, democratisation.[15] [C]ommunism in Hungary cannot be saved without entirely reconsidering the relations between Hungarians and Russians. It is on this social basis that all of those who reclaim democratisation instinctively rest.[16]

Sartre's position on real socialism presents a double character, as the entire investigation of the second part of the *Critique of Dialectical Reason* will subsequently highlight. On the one hand, we find a critique of the Soviet Union, with its 'serial' institutionalisation that has moved away from 'true socialism'. On the other, there is a realistic awareness of the importance of the Soviet Union on the global chessboard, in its opposition to capitalist countries.

> [T]rue socialism is inseparable from the real *praxis* of real men who struggle against the owners ... But that socialism in whose name Soviet soldiers have fired on the masses in Hungary, I do not know, I cannot even conceive: it is neither made for men nor of them, it is a name given to a new form of alienation [*aliénation*] ... But when the USSR returns to retractable politics, socialism and nationalism, inseparably, become the reason of State. It is no longer a matter of saving men, of workers' achievements, the concrete future of a socialism underway, but of conserving with force the positions that, in the perspective of a global war, are able to favor the Soviet nation, its armies and its military industries. Certainly, it is necessary that the USSR lives, it is necessary *for the cause of communism*: all men of the left recognize this. But it also needs to continue being socialist.[17]

Support for Hungary is not presented here as the identification of a sort of model. Despite the extreme differences between the situations, an articulated position emerges analogously in regard to Yugoslavia:

---

15   Sartre 1950, p. 250. Cf. Ibid., p. 270: 'De-Stalinisation is at the origin of events in Poland, Romania, and Hungary; in turn, the USSR must suffer the backlash of disturbances [*troubles*] in central Europe'.

16   Sartre 1950, p. 177.

17   Sartre 1950, pp. 275–6.

it is a matter, if one wants, of deep knowledge but neglect of a negative identity. It is what explains the original character of the insurrection: it is sporadic, confused ... But the insurrection will remain a many-headed hydra until the end.[18]

Despite the awareness of numerous limits, the image of a 'many-headed hydra' vividly expresses Sartre's valorisation of these attempts at 'true socialism', despite their defeats.

After the references to Yugoslavia and Hungary (as well as Poland), in the years that followed the reference to Czechoslovakia is particularly important. In an interview entitled 'Communists are Afraid of Revolution' Sartre strongly valorises the 1968 insurgency: 'In Czechoslovakia ... a revolt [*révolte*] is underway against the dehumanising system of production-for-production that is focused in this moment on a claim to freedom'.[19] In an interview with Rossana Rossanda and militants from *il manifesto*, 'Masses, Spontaneity, Party', there is a further observation on the serial character of Communist Parties:

> If the cultural apparatus of the Communist parties is practically null, the reason is not that they lack good intellectuals, but that the mode of existence of the parties paralyses their collective effort of thought. Action and thought are not separable from the organization. One thinks as one is structured. One acts as one is organized. This is why the thought of Communist parties has come to be progressively ossified.[20]

One of Sartre's toughest texts with regard to the Soviet Union, which precisely begins from a critical analysis of the Soviet repression in Czechoslovakia in 1968, is crucial for confronting such themes: 'Czechoslovakia: The Socialism that Came in from the Cold'. Before investigating this event, Sartre examines the situation that preceded it in Czechoslovakia, showing however the specific differences with respect to the Soviet Union:

> Czechoslovakia, by contrast, had long since passed the phase of primitive accumulation and was merely encumbered by the type of socialism so kindly bestowed [*octroyait*] on it. The country had no urgent need to

18   Sartre 1950, p. 182.
19   Sartre 1972a, pp. 219–20. Cf. McBride 1991, p. 186: 'Nowhere is Sartre's ultimate judgment about "the system," the rigid and deviated socialism practiced in the USSR and the countries within its orbit, expressed more mordantly than in this essay'.
20   Sartre 2008c, pp. 131–2.

develop heavy industry since its resources were already mainly derived
before the war from prosperous manufactures ... In fact, the inordinate
expansion of its output and especially the absurd reversal of its priorities
rapidly forced it to *produce for the sake of production*, when it should on
the contrary have reorganized its existing industries to satisfy the needs
of its own people.[21]

This economic and social structure cannot be immediately compared with that
of the Soviet Union, and, from this perspective, Soviet politics was decisively
myopic, incapable of adhering to the specific characteristics of Czechoslovakia.
'Czechoslovakia could have been the first power to accomplish a successful
transition from an advanced capitalist economy to a socialist economy, offering the proletariat of the West, if not a model, at least an embodiment of its
own revolutionary future. It lacked nothing, neither the means nor the men'.[22]
The Czechoslovakian situation, more advanced than other Eastern territories,
was 'encaged' by the Soviet protectorate, and configured as an '*octroyé* socialism':[23]

> Everything had changed, and nothing had changed. Khrushchev gave
> public notice of this when the Hungarian made an inopportune attempt
> to draw conclusions from the Twentieth Congress. Obviously, the
> Czechoslovaks no longer believed the institutionalized lie, but they were
> much afraid that they had now nothing left to believe in. They had hither-
> to lived in what one of them calls a 'socialist fog'; now that the fog was
> lifting somewhat, they could survey the damage that it had hidden. A dev-
> astated economy was on the point of collapse ... The country had literally
> no idea of its real situation, for official lies and falsification of statistics
> had ... destroyed previous elements of knowledge.[24]

As such, in several respects there emerges a line of continuity between the 1956
Hungarian and 1968 Czechoslovakian revolts. Moreover, Sartre's position on
Marxism, understood not in doctrinally abstract terms but in its connection
with political practice, cannot be understood without constantly keeping in
mind these two events. 1956 established, as emphasised earlier, the full awareness of the distinctive characteristics of the Soviet Union, which led Sartre to

---

21   Sartre 2008c, p. 89.
22   Sartre 2008c, p. 89.
23   Sartre 2008c, p. 90.
24   Sartre 2008c, p. 102.

recalibrate his own position with respect to the past: *Search for a Method* and the *Critique of Dialectical Reason* refer to such a path. From a number of viewpoints, but surely also with a strong reference to the Czechoslovakian revolt, 1968 (as will be demonstrated later) constitutes a possible political outcome of the *Critique*: it is enough to think of the strong valorisation of the fused group, and therefore a movementist tension, in contention with the sclerotisation carried out by party and state structures. In the context of '*octroyé* socialism', Prague 1968 played the productive function of unmasking the 'institutionalised lie' of the USSR.

> [A]t present the struggle of Czechoslovakia for its cultural autonomy is part of a much wider struggle, waged by many nations – large and small – against the policy of blocs and for the achievement of peace.[25] [I]n 1968, after twenty years of Stalinism, the situation was very different for Czech and Slovakian workers. To start with, they too had been sated with lies, though just how sick of them they were only now becoming fully aware. The dictatorship of the proletariat was the dictatorship of a party that had lost all contact with the masses ... to the very extent that they became conscious of their maximalist demand for councils, the full truth – as theoretical and practical knowledge – became indispensable to them ... Thus within a vast revolutionary movement, workers and intellectuals constantly radicalized each other.[26]

The question of the critique of the Soviet Union and the neutralisation of the dictatorship of the proletariat returns here, in a situation wherein the indistinguishable nexus between state and party eliminates, or at least neutralises, the emancipative tension, the 'real movement abolishing the present state of things'. In the Czechoslovakian context there is a cooperation between workers and intellectuals, and the former understand perfectly that the critique of the 'institutionalised lie' does not constitute a purely accessory element with respect to immediate material needs.

> The intellectuals realized that this great popular movement represented a radicalization of their own thought, and now radicalized themselves, intensified their struggle against the system, without turning against the new team of leaders ... What was most striking to a Westerner was that

---

25   Sartre 2008c, p. 110.
26   Sartre 2008c, pp. 114–15.

the battle of the intellectuals for complete freedom of expression and information was supported by the workers, who very quickly decided that the right to unrestricted information was one of their basic demands.[27] There is no doubt that all the agents of this process were far from knowing where they were going and what they were doing. But neither can there be any doubt that they were trying to *achieve socialism* by liquidating the system and establishing new relations of production ... Everyone knows the sequel. Before it was even full-born, this socialism was smothered by counter-revolution. This is what *Pravda* claims, and I am in complete agreement with the Russian newspaper except on the minor question of cardinal points: the counter-revolutionary forces did not come from the West ... The leaders of the USSR, terrified to see socialism on the march again, sent their tanks to Prague to stop it ... Nothing had changed, except that a prefabricated [*octroyé*] socialism, now become an oppressor socialism, had become unmasked.[28]

With respect to the scenario outlined in the second part of the *Critique of Dialectical Reason*, it is a matter of understanding if identifying other perspectives is possible. The entire structure of the *Critique*, with its extremely complex character, is not presented as a total, unproblematic demolition of the Soviet Union and Stalinism, nor as focused on the immediate articulation of 'another socialism', or another 'workers' movement'.[29] Moreover, we are far from the idea of a history of the defeated, by way of the reactivation of Benjaminian and Blochian messianic elements,[30] as testified to by the overall structure of the *Critique*. We thus do not find another, already outlined perspective, perhaps rooted in mythologised traces of the past, but rather an attempt, risky and lacking, in this case in Czechoslovakia, to '*achieve socialism* by liquidating the

---

27   Sartre 2008c, pp. 113–14.
28   Sartre 2008c, pp. 115–16.
29   I borrow the expression here from Roth 1974.
30   From this point of view, I do not share Münster's (2007, pp. 156 ff.) interpretation. See Fergnani's (1978, p. 253) considerations: 'In the revolutionary perspective in an eschatological perspective hinted at by Walter Benjamin and developed on several sides by Ernst Bloch, there is or must be a struggle for the emancipation of the "oppressed past" ... Sartre's position appears more drastic and disenchanted, faithful to an assumption of the finitude of existence and its destiny, and distanced from the religious-messianic suggestions of redemption and final *renovatio* (renewal)'. Although affinities can sometimes be found with Bloch, and despite the same use of the term '*novum*', in the title of chapter three, which lends itself to Blochian suggestions, I share Fergnani's reading.

system and establishing new relations of production'. Of this experiment it is necessary to emphasise, on the one hand, that it was not carried out by liberal, anticommunist subjects, but by communist subjects who tried to articulate socialism in terms other than those of 'real socialism', and on the other, that its enemies were not Western imperialists, but Soviets. The latter were mobilised militarily in order to save *'octroyé* socialism', which had lost the tension towards change by sclerotising it.

From the analysis we have carried out, through several texts on Yugoslavia, Hungary, and Czechoslovakia, a red thread emerges: Sartre valorises socialist experiences (thus situating himself within real socialism, albeit in critical terms and without being pro-Western) inasmuch as they are different than the Soviet Union, a deviation which is articulated in various ways (as a matter of differentiated geographical, historical, and politico-social situations). Such an approach reveals, on the one hand, a presupposition of the *Critique* (one thinks, in particular, of the Hungarian revolt in 1956), while on the other, one of its possible outcomes (particularly the Czechoslovakian revolt of 1968). More generally, at the basis of Sartre's discourse stands a movementist tension, and thus the questioning of the serialising effects of the process of institutionalisation. Moreover, even in a text such as *The Communists and Peace*, which is distinguished by a strong valorisation of the role of the party and by a certain favourability of judgment towards the Soviet Union, the complex between class and action remains crucial. The *conatus* indicated, as will emerge following the treatment, can only find its 'condensation' in 1968, which is moreover the theoretical and political context of the Czechoslovakian revolt.

If we wanted to continue on this path, aimed at highlighting elements that are eccentric to the Soviet Union while at the same time related to it, it would be necessary to widen our gaze beyond Europe. Various examples could be provided, but, on the level of international weight, the reference to China is particularly significant. Moreover, it is not necessary to linger on the enthusiasm for China within communist intellectual environments in Western Europe (above all in France), on the basis of a sort of neo-Maoism. I will not delve into Sartre's position on China here but instead limit myself to remarking on his strong interest in this regard, which is not separate from a distance taken in several ways. Sartre makes various references to China but does not carry out a systematic analysis. Surely, however, there emerges a valorisation for a political reality that was detached from the reference to the Soviet Union, thus giving life to an autonomous path of socialism. But in several writings, such as for example 'Les maos en France', the reference to Maoism is oriented not so much to an investigation of China as to a theoretico-political analysis of the specific role played by French Maoists, on the basis of an overall judgment.[31] From the start of the essay Sartre specifies that he is not a Maoist,[32] thus showing that he does not fully share their position, and that he has the clear desire not to alter the coordinates of his own thought by starting from such a political platform. In any case, Sartre also valorised several aspects of Mao's thought in the 1970s as antideterministic:

> Mao's method is not "scientific", but applied to a different sector ... It is not a thought founded on determinism, because it studies the relations between men (classes, groups, assemblies, armies) which precisely excludes deterministic explanations and can only be understood dialectically. Soviet Marxism instead went straight to determinism.[33]

Here the constitutive reference to dialectical reason as a critique of analytical reason returns, distinguished from a dualistic logic, but also any dialectical approach (more or less Hegelian) which outlines the movement of affirmation, negation, and negation of the negation in linear terms. We find a critical, open dialectic, indebted in several ways to the Marxian framework, and endowed with a situated character. Sartre distinguishes between the constituted dialectic, relative to a practice already unfolded, and a constituent dialectic, connected to the making of practice, on the basis of an intelligibility which, however, presents zones of opacity, never being fully transparent. Such a framework, starting with *Search for a Method*, identifies the determinism underlying analytic reason as a constant polemic reference. In this passage Sartre 'deploys' the reference to Mao with an antideterministic function, precisely on the basis of trying to rethink socialism beyond the Soviet Union.

We thus do not find a purely historico-theoretical question, but a *prise de parole* in a specific situation: in Paris, Sartre had a close relation with the Maoists, who asked him to take leadership of *La cause du peuple*. In particular, during the 1970s his partnership with Benny Lévy, who would move away from neo-Maoism (and Marxism) towards politically ambiguous and problematic positions, was quite intense. According to Sartre, the French Maoists had

---

31   Cf. Gaudeaux 2006, pp. 375–84: 'Sartre was at once internal and external to the French Maoists' (p. 375). 'Before and after May '68, the Maoists gave Sartre a practical exemplification of what he anticipated in the *Critique of Dialectical Reason* ... But Sartre, to the Maoists, does not concede anything of his philosophy, of his work' (pp. 381–2); Bourgault 2011.

32   Cf. Sartre 1976b, p. 38.

33   Sartre 1974, p. 100.

the merit of cultivating a violent opposition, both theoretical and practical, against the capitalist horizon and the seriality that arises from it.

> [T]his aspiration to freedom [on the part of the French Maoists] has noth-ing idealist about it and always finds its source in the concrete and mater-ial conditions of production ... Violence, spontaneity, morality: such are, for the *maos*, the three immediate characteristics of revolutionary actions ... From this agility to invent and realise local actions whose origin is always found in the masses ... The classic parties of the left remained in the nineteenth century, in the age of competitive capitalism. But the *maos*, with their antiauthoritarian praxis, seem to be the only revolution-ary force – still in their beginning – capable of adapting themselves to the new forms of class struggle, in the period of organised capitalism.[34]

In this sketch, various aspects of Sartre's approach return, such as the central-ity of the tension towards freedom, the concrete rooting of this in the sphere of production, the moral dimension of the discourse, and the acceptance of viol-ence in a revolutionary sense. The most interesting aspect is that Sartre tries to interpret the question of Maoism (or neo-Maoism) not in abstract terms, but on the basis of the conviction of the adequacy of the French Maoists' political practice in relation to the specific contemporary situation, which presented a scenario different from nineteenth-century competitive capitalism. By itself, Sartre's valorisation of the French Maoists leaves more than a few doubts, but the fact that Sartre remarks on their Marxism (albeit understood in nondog-matic terms) appears important, as he also discusses in relation to an earlier conversation in Cuba: 'It goes without saying that the *maos* are Marxist in the sense in which Guevara told me in 1960: "It is not our mistake if the truth is Marxist"'.[35] The line of reasoning on China, or better on the Maoists in the West, leads back to what was said earlier about the valorisation of the potentially revolutionary force in the West. This movementist tension remains strongly connected to the theoretico-political path examined, which found two key moments in 1956 and 1968. In order to complete the reflection on the extra-European socialist reality, an absolutely crucial reference for Sartre, already broached in the reference just made, is the Cuban Revolution.

The development of the Cuban situation was directly considered by several scholars as the main reason for Sartre's choice not to complete the second part

---

34   Sartre 1976b, pp. 46–7.
35   Sartre 1976b, p. 45.

of the *Critique of Dialectical Reason.*[36] Two events which allow for a partial reopening of the *inachevé* character of this text are the Cuban Revolution and the Algerian liberation. With regard to the former, it is necessary to emphasise that it provoked much enthusiasm in Sartre, after which a number of doubts took over. Sartre had already visited Cuba in 1949, before the Revolution, and then, together with Simone de Beauvoir, returned in February 1960 for almost a month, meeting Castro, Che Guevara, and students in an assembly at the University of Havana.[37] The situation in Cuba had radically changed since 1949. Sartre identified the expansive character of the Cuban Revolution starting from an immanent critique of the countries of real socialism throughout various articles, particularly a sort of *reportage* for *France-Soir*, 'Ouragan sur le sucre'.[38]

Beyond the praise of Castro[39] and Guevara,[40] one aspect which immediately strikes Sartre is the 'youth' of the revolution, consisting in a complete change of the leading class, which testifies to the radical social and political shift:

> [I]f a common thread [of the revolution] is needed – and it does provide one – the youth clearly stands out immediately ... labour relations, class conflicts, all come together around a fundamental relation; that of the youth who experienced their life with suffering, against the older people

---

36 For a broad interpretation of Sartre's writings on Cuba, which moves in a direction aimed specifically at commenting on the decisive nature of this situation for understanding the impasse of the second part of the *Critique*, see Ireland 2009. Such a thesis, albeit a bit excessive, clearly grasps the importance of the Cuban events for Sartre's political thought. See also Murphy 1996.

37 For a different perspective than what I outline here, see Birchall 2004, pp. 204–5: 'Sartre has been much criticised for the sympathy he showed to Castro's Cuba in the late 1950s and 1960s. Again this must be set in the context of the period, when Sartre's pessimistic assessment of the French left meant that he was looking for new sources of inspiration ... The full story of his relation with Cuba was complex and contained a number of contradictions. But if his support for the USSR between 1952 and 1956 was genuinely tragic, Cuba was no more than a one-act farce ... [Sartre and Beauvoir] felt undoubted enthusiasm for the new regime ... Yet in private Sartre remained deeply suspicious ... [H]e was seeking some alternative to post-Stalinist communism'.

38 The texts on Cuba were not collected into a book in French, but Sartre's *reportage* 'Ouragan sur le sucre' appeared regularly in *France-Soir* between 28 June and 15 July 1960. A Spanish edition was produced, and part of these texts were translated into Italian. See Sartre 2005b, as well as Paolucci's introduction in Ibid., pp. 7–21. Translator's note: I have used the Italian edition to translate from Sartre's 'Ouragan sur le sucre'.

39 Sartre 2005b, pp. 126 ff.; 159; 181 ff.

40 Sartre 2005b, p. 143: 'radical in his decisions, violent as a soldier during execution, Guevara was the most learned man and, after Castro, one of the most lucid intellects of the revolution'. Cf. Sartre 2005b, pp. 185 ff.

who have instead made their lives. Today, in the songs, in the fields, or inside a ministry, *labour is young* ... This means that the regime produces and manifests a radical upheaval of human relations. If we wish to understand these transformed relations, it is necessary to search in all fields for the consequences of this historical event, the invasion of Cuba by barbarians.[41]

The revolution carries out a *tabula rasa* over all that constituted the material and symbolic bases of society. Such a dynamic is implanted in specific characteristics in Cuba, with the presence of an 'old' and brutally hierarchical society. Against this situation, the revolutionary energy is disruptive, even barbaric, capable of producing a 'radical upheaval of human relations'.

> The revolution is medicine for horses: a society breaks bones with a hammer, destroys its own structures, unsettles institutions, transforms the regime of property and redistributes its goods, orients production towards other principles, tries to improve the growth rate as quickly as possible, and in the moment itself of most radical destruction, tries to reconstitute, with all of its force, as with bone transplants, a new skeleton; the remedy is extreme, often needing to be imposed with violence. The extermination of the adversary and some of those allied is not inevitable, but prudent to prepare for. After this, nothing guarantees that the new order will not be crushed by an internal or external enemy, nor that the movement, if it wins, will not deviate from its struggles and the victory itself.[42]

Even if the outcome is not obvious, as Castro wished, resignation turns into anger, and inertia into revolution.

> The Cubans understood, in the period of their immovable degradation, that it is History that makes men. It was up to them, now, to demonstrate that they were instead the men to make History. They need to grab Destiny, this scarecrow planted by the rich in the sugar cane fields.[43]

It is necessary to emphasise that Sartre, in the years that followed, revised or weakened his positive judgment on Cuba in some ways, highlighting the

---

41   Sartre 2005b, pp. 183–4.
42   Sartre 2005b, pp. 89–90.
43   Sartre 2005b, p. 125.

decline of the regime, which was also due to foreign threat, while still express-
ing solidarity for the isolation in which the Western countries had put it.

However, it is necessary to further elaborate on the reasons for Sartre's
enthusiasm in 1960. It should not be forgotten that while Sartre was in Cuba,
the Algerian war for liberation, with which Sartre had forcefully sided, was alive
and would come to an end in 1962. Moreover, the question of revolution in Latin
America, and more generally, the Third World – on the basis of the idea of the
coimplication of different social and political situations – becomes crucial for
Sartre. Indeed, the *prise de parole* against colonialism plays an essential function in Sartre's rearticulation of revolution. In an interview in Brazil in 1960,
released immediately after his time in Cuba, Sartre establishes a parallelism
between Algeria and Cuba on the basis of an internationalist platform.[44] In
this context he would also write about his positions in solidarity with Indochina and Vietnam. The first element, which is more general and also connected
to a specific reading of the events in the Soviet Union and satellite states, consists in the conviction of the difficulty of revolutionary activity in the West, and
conversely, in the possibility of expanding developments in the so-called Third
World, leveraging the situation in the countryside, more than the working class,
which Marxism had traditionally centred.

> [T]he Cuban revolution would have been a peasants' revolution or it
> would not have happened. This necessity came from things more than
> men and nothing could be done about it. In the distance, the cities were
> crushed by impotence. The countryside imposed its aspect on the rebel-
> lion, even before participating.[45] The revolution must be put in the hands
> of three million men. But the distrust of these men would be difficult
> to annul unless it proved itself done for them ... If the peasants were to
> become rebels, the rebels had to become peasants: they took part in the
> labor of the fields. It was not enough to know the needs and miseries of
> the countryside, they needed to suffer them and fight against them at the
> same time ... [Castro] decided to beat the regular army in order to have
> free hands and realise the agrarian reform ... The agrarian reform was the
> guerilla. But the guerilla was the true reform.[46]

One particularly relevant but problematic aspect of Sartre's argument is the
idea that this is a revolution without ideology. This is the thesis of the essay

---

44   Sartre 1960c.
45   Sartre 2005b, p. 133.
46   Sartre 2005b, pp. 134–5.

'Ideology and Revolution', which Sartre did not publish in French, perhaps testifying to the fact that he was not fully convinced by the content.[47] Starting from a critique of real socialism, Sartre recognises in Cuba the presence of a revolutionary energy deprived of ideological dogmatism: what would be lacking is an ideology extrinsic to the concrete flow of the destabilising event. It is necessary to emphasise that such an approach remains unsatisfactory for interpreting the element of ideology. Indeed, ideology is here understood in purely negative terms, and also reduced in comparison to the articulation provided in other texts. Generally, Sartre does not only highlight the mystifying side of ideology but also outlines it by distinguishing it from philosophy. For example, I noted how, in *Search for a Method*, Marxism is considered as a philosophy, as 'the philosophy of our times', and existentialism as an ideology, as its practical exemplification, which testifies for Sartre to the superiority of Marxism, but also to the non-irrelevance of ideology. In this sense, in this essay on Cuba there is an excessive devaluation of ideology, but also of theory, as if it was possible to obtain such elements from practice *ex post*, which risks falling back into that 'empiricism without principles' criticised so much in *Search for a Method*.[48] Theory seems to be subordinated to practice *sic et simpliciter*, and experience is considered, in an immediate way, as the point of departure for the discourse: every conceptualisation seems to remain false and residual. Moreover, from another perspective, maintaining that the Cuban Revolution was deprived of ideology appears problematic on a historical and political level.

If such a conviction of the non-ideological character of the Cuban Revolution creates a series of quandaries, it is possible to rearticulate the question in other terms, focusing on the reasoning about the more generative element in this regard, namely the connection between the Cuban Revolution and the centrality of the critique of colonialism. Moreover, Sartre himself identified points of contact between the Cuban Revolution and Algerian liberation, oriented toward a dislocation of the struggle for socialism in the countries of the so-called Third World. The emancipative practice of Cuba, with its anti-imperialistic character, can be presented as a sort of *exemplum* for its capacity of 'inventing the new', of giving life to a 'revolution of the youth', within a scenario that is geographically and politically far away from the traditional

---

47   Sartre 1960b.

48   Cf. Paolucci in Sartre 2005b, pp. 20–1: '[Sartre maintains that] ... *no general theory* can be used to guide the course of the revolution. This is a thesis that does not fail to amaze when recalling that it comes from a thinker who dedicated the major part of his own life to maintaining the importance of thought and the word in the transformation of society'.

geometries of class struggle.[49] It is a matter of understanding in what sense the constitutive reference to the 'wretched of the earth' can 'replay' the question of revolution, after the critique of the Soviet Union contained in the *Critique of Dialectical Reason*.

2   Between Race and Class: the Struggle of the 'Wretched of the Earth'

The question of the critique of colonialism is a 'red thread' throughout Sartre's entire postwar period, particularly in the 1950s and 1960s. This element thus plays an essential function for understanding Sartre's arguments both before and after the *Critique*. In many ways, it can be argued that this theme constitutes both a presupposition of the *Critique* and its outcome, or at least an element that lends itself to further development from this text. Here I will not carry out an analytic reconstruction of the entire theme, from the writings of the immediate postwar period through the 1960s, but instead start by referring to Sartre's postwar investigation of antisemitism and its relationship, as well as difference, to racism.

In order to understand his investigation of antisemitism, the text 'Anti-Semite and Jew' is central. Published in 1946, it contains only very brief references to National Socialism, instead attempting to grasp the distinctive features of antisemitism. The latter, for Sartre, constitutes a passion rather than a thought. It is the anti-Semite who 'creates' the Jew:

> Far from experience producing [the anti-Semite's] idea of the Jew, it was the latter which explained his experience. If the Jew did not exist, the anti-

---

49   Several years later, Sartre valorises the Cuban Revolution but also highlights the problems that arose after, with reference to the dynamic of institutionalisation he examined in the *Critique*: 'there was something particular, and it is that, just as the terror was in front of them, there was a state of happiness and consensus that I had never seen. This kind of revolution which was a party was remarkable ... I think that, despite everything, it is necessary to give fidelity [to Cuba] until it fails ... Then after, it depends, if it finds itself then having a bureaucracy, it is necessary to deal with it as with all bureaucracies: against. There is no doubt. But the beginning was there in any case' (1977, pp. 119–20). Sartre also interprets the Cuban Revolution by beginning from a *conatus* of freedom, the bearer of a new spirit, in *On a raison de se révolter*: 'First of all it must be noted that life is not acceptable. Cuban life under Batista was not acceptable. Thus the choice of freedom or death means that if there is no freedom, it is death anyways ... You are forced by example to choose to overthrow Batista' (1974, p. 196).

Semite would invent him.[50] If then … the anti-Semite is impervious to reason and to experience, it is not because his conviction is strong. Rather it is because he has chosen first of all to be impervious.[51]

Antisemitism is a form of Manicheanism, connected to the destructive character of the 'sad passions' and the absolute incapacity to imagine a different horizon than the status quo:

> His task is therefore purely negative: there is no question of building a new society, but only of purifying the one which exists … [A]nti-Semitism channels evolutionary drives towards the destruction of certain men, not of institutions … If all he has to do is remove Evil, that means that the Good is already *given*.[52]

The antisemite does not at all want to articulate a 'positive' scenario, but limits themself to accepting given values, wishing to expunge, by means of purifying, the elements that from their perspective are harmful, materialised in individuals of a certain type: such a mystifying representation of the real remains extremely timely today. From another perspective, it is noteworthy that Sartre proposes examining the status of the Jew not on the basis of an idea of human nature, but rather from the element of the situation:

> [W]e do not believe in "human nature"; we cannot conceive of society as a sum of isolated molecules … To be in a situation, as we see it, is to choose oneself in a situation, and men differ from one another in their situations and also in the choices they themselves make of themselves. What men have in common is not a "nature" but a condition, that is, an ensemble of limits and restrictions.[53] [If] all of them deserve the name of Jew, it is

---

50   Sartre 1948, p. 8. Cf. Judaken 2006, particularly pp. 123–46: 'In Sartre's account "the Jew" is always defined by the Other … "The Jew" thus becomes the quintessential example of the human being condemned to be what he is not and not to be what he is (p. 135)'. For a critical perspective, rooted in the idea that there is a sort of void in Sartre towards Auschwitz, see Traverso 2002, especially pp. 70–1: 'For Bataille, every reflection on the "Jewish question" in the aftermath of the war can only arise from the enormous and ineluctable fact of extermination … In 1945, Sartre is one of the rare intellectuals to turn their gaze on the solitude of the Jews; he did not realise that behind this solitude, as discrete as it was profound, there was a break in the twentieth century and in history'.

51   Sartre 1948, p. 14.

52   Sartre 1948, pp. 30–1.

53   Sartre 1948, p. 42.

because they have in common the situation of a Jew, that is, they live in a community which takes them for Jews.[54] That Jewish community which is based neither on nation, land, religion ... nor materialist interest, but only on the identity of situation.[55]

Several distinctive signs of Sartre's itinerary return here. In particular, we find a claim that is in some ways essentialist but is also continuously interwoven with a phenomenological approach of the priority of existence over essence. In this sense, there remains operative a critique of any formulation founded on abstract essence, incapable of giving account of the concreteness of human experience. Further, the notion of situation is crucial here. It has a strategic function in Sartre's thought and which, in the postwar period, is increasingly bent further away from the risk of absolutising freedom, which remained present in earlier texts. The reference to situation allows for the freedom of man and the set of conditions, constraints, limits to be held together, on the basis of an articulation in which the practico-inert constitutes an element that is not easily circumvented. The interpretation of the Jew thus can only be found at the intersection of the dimensions indicated, and in that sense solidarity among Jews must be framed by starting from a specific situation.

This formulation leads to a reading that is not ahistoric or abstract, by inscribing the figure of the Jew within a determinate history and a determinate society:

> [The Jew] is a social man par excellence, because his torment is social. It is society, not the decree of God, that has made him a Jew.[56] Jewish authenticity consists in choosing oneself as Jew – that is, in realizing one's Jewish condition. The authentic Jew abandons the myth of the universal man; he knows himself and wills himself into history as a historic and damned creature.[57]

The political decision to which the Jew must arrive does not appear obvious. Two possibilities are opened, both of which are dangerous for the Jew. One consists in claiming his own role, with his own rights, within French society. The other consists in creating an autonomous Jewish nation. In each case, the rights of the Jew do not derive from an abstract human nature, but from his participa-

54   Sartre 1948, p. 48.
55   Sartre 1948, p. 61.
56   Sartre 1948, p. 97.
57   Sartre 1948, p. 98.

tion in social life: 'This means, then, that the Jews – and likewise the Arabs and Negroes – from the moment that they are participants in the national enterprise, have a right in that enterprise; they are citizens. But they have these rights by virtue of being Jews, Negroes, Arabs – that is, as concrete persons'.[58]

It remains necessary to take up the initial question of Sartre's essay, namely the idea that the Jew is 'created' by the anti-Semite: 'The Jewish problem is born of anti-Semitism; thus it is anti-Semitism that we must suppress in order to resolve the problem'.[59] The scope thus consists in combatting antisemitism, understood as conforming to capitalist society: 'This means that anti-Semitism is a mythical, bourgeois representation of the class struggle, and that it could not exist in a classless society'.[60] Every logic of ownership does not necessarily lead to antisemitism, but antisemitism has such a logic at its base, and thus is configured as a bourgeois phenomenon. If antisemitism flows into National Socialism, 'socialist revolution is necessary to and sufficient for the suppression of the anti-Semite. It is for the Jews *also* that we shall make the revolution'.[61] It is clear that Sartre's critique of antisemitism is not articulated in abstract terms but rather immersed within a critical analysis of capitalist society. Already from the references we have examined, the connection (but also the difference) between antisemitism and racism can emerge.

Sartre soon began to examine the latter, as represented in an important text 'Black Orpheus', which appeared as an introduction to a poetry collection edited by Senegalese poet Léopold Senghor, *Anthologie nouvelle poésie nègre et malgache*.[62] Sartre establishes a weave between poetry and politics: African poetry uses the French language in order to destroy it and create a revolution even at the level of the means of expression. The key notion of the discourse is Négritude, an element that on the one hand can be inserted into class relations, and on the other, continuously exceeds them.

---

58   Sartre 1948, p. 105. Translation modified.
59   Sartre 1948, p. 106.
60   Sartre 1948, p. 108.
61   Sartre 1948, p. 109.
62   Cf. Urbanik-Rizk 2006, pp. 57–8: 'The poetry of Négritude offers the model of a new perception of the world ... More than a political lesson ..., the poetry of Négritude is first of all, for Sartre, a poetic lesson'; Barnes 1974, pp. 106–10. For the valorisation of this text which goes in the direction of recognising an 'African philosophy', see Mudimbe 1988, pp. 127–32, here p. 129: 'It could be said of Black Orpheus that while correcting the potential theoretical excesses of negritude, it did so in a high-handed manner, thwarting other possible orientations of the movement. At the same time, it subjugated the militants' generosity of heart and mind to the fervour of a political philosophy ... Nevertheless, Black Orpheus is a major ideological moment, perhaps one of the most important. It displays both the potentialities of Marxist revolution and the negation of colonialism and racism'.

[S]ubjectivity [*subjectivité*] reappears: the relation of the self with the self; the source of all poetry, the very poetry from which the worker had to disengage himself. The black man who asks his colored brothers to "find themselves" is going to try to present to them an exemplary image of their Negritude and will look into his own soul to grasp it. He wants to be both a beacon and a mirror; the first revolutionary will be the harbinger of the black soul, the herald – half prophet and half follower – who will tear Blackness out of himself in order to offer it to the world; in brief, he will be a poet in the literal sense of "vates."[63]

If the relation between 'black' and 'white' had been usually interpreted in Manichean terms as a juxtaposition between Evil and Good, Sartre overturns this Manicheanism in some way by valorising the 'negative' subjectivity of the Black. In this way there remains operative the Hegelian reference, mediated through French readings of the *Phenomenology of Spirit* (particularly Kojève and Hyppolite), to the 'labour' of the negative (and moreover, the question of negativity was already crucial with *Being and Nothingness*), but there are also present Dionysian elements derived from Nietzsche, as well as a series of poetic suggestions. In such an approach what rings out is the power of black freedom:

> Black faces – these night memories which haunt our days – embody the dark work of Negativity which patiently gnaws at concepts ... Freedom is the color of night ... Negritude – like freedom – is a point of departure and an ultimate goal: it is a matter of making negritude pass from the imme-diate to the mediate, a matter of *thematicising* it. The black man must therefore find death in white culture in order to be reborn with a black soul, like the Platonic philosopher whose body embraces death in order to be reborn in truth.[64]

The emphasis on 'black faces' is a point of contact between racism and anti-semitism. Here it is productive to recall Fanon's *Black Skin, White Masks*: by tak-ing up some elements of Sartre's *Anti-Semite and Jew* (and instead criticising, as will emerge later, his 'Black Orpheus'), Fanon emphasises that antisemitism is also racist, 'negrophobic', and conversely, it is the racist (like the antisemite) who creates the 'inferiorised' and not vice versa.[65] At the same time, we also

---

63   Sartre 1964–1965, p. 20.
64   Sartre 1964–1965, pp. 28–9. Translation modified.
65   Cf. Fanon 2008. On the relevance of Sartre's thematisation, above all in *Réflexions sur la*

find a difference between racism and antisemitism: in the former the essentialist element, in the negative, remains clearer with the physical reference to skin color.

For Sartre, the notion of Négritude on the one hand leads to the extreme consequences of 'Western' surrealism, and on the other, displaces Western categories and political practices. In valorising this notion, a decisive figure is Aimé Césaire:

> A poem by Césaire ... bursts and wheels around like a rocket; suns turning and exploding into new suns come out of it; it is a perpetual going-beyond ... What Césaire destroys is not all culture, but rather white culture; what he brings to light is not desire for everything but rather the revolutionary aspirations of the oppressed negro ... The white surrealist finds within himself the trigger; Césaire finds within himself the fixed inflexibility of demands and feeling.[66] In Césaire, the great surrealist tradition is realized, it takes on its definitive meaning and is destroyed: surrealism – that European movement – is taken from the Europeans by a Black man who turns it against them ... Césaire's words do not describe Négritude, they do not designate it, they do not copy it from the outside like a painter with a model: they create it.[67]

According to Sartre, Négritude contains a tragic nature that can only be understood through poetry: 'Thus the Black man attests to a natural Eros; he reveals and incarnates it ... To the absurd utilitarian agitation of the white man, the black man opposes the authenticity gained from his suffering'.[68] Sartre's representation does not lack elements of 'Dionysian' praise for the Black, risking

---

question juive, for Fanon, cf. Cheyette 2005–2006, who insists above all on the reprisal of Sartre's approach (also with elements that are critical) in *Black Skin, White Masks*: '[Fanon's] detailed analysis of *Réflexions* ... is a way of resolving the question, often unsolvable, of the impossible integration of the colonial subject in contemporary France' (pp. 163–4). 'The process of elaboration through which Fanon associates antisemitism and negrophobia ... culminates in the simplicity of the final conclusion: the antisemite is necessarily negrophobic' (p. 165). '[F]or Fanon ... the nucleus of the difference between Jews and Blacks consists in the fact that it remains possible for the former, strong in their "white" essence, to be integrated or go unnoticed within European society, while it is impossible for the latter to do the same, given their "black" essence'. (pp. 169–70).

66   Sartre 1964–1965, pp. 32–3.
67   Sartre 1964–1965, pp. 34–5.
68   Sartre 1964–1965, p. 41.

an 'Africanism' inevitably affected by a series of Western stereotypes, despite the intention of valorising this reality. From this perspective, as well as in light of the work in Subaltern Studies in recent decades,[69] there are surely problematic elements to Sartre's argument in 'Black Orpheus', which seems to provide an aestheticising approach to the question posed, and lacks an adequate historical and social reading, with essentialist traces. In this sense, we find the risk of an exotic, 'Westernist' image of the Black man. Fanon strongly criticises Sartre's representation, noting that negativity must be lived historically, and that the Black man must maintain a skepticism towards the idea of Négritude:

> *Black Orpheus* marks a date in the intellectualization of black *existence* ...
> I am not a potentiality of something; I am fully what I am. I do not have
> to look for the universal. There's no room for probability inside me. My
> black consciousness does not claim to be a loss. It is. It merges with itself
> ... [T]he black experience is ambiguous, for there is not one Negro – there
> are many black men.[70]

It can be argued that the very category of Négritude is problematic, but it is necessary to specify that Césaire's treatment (with his 'singular' lived experience, in moving between Paris and Martinique) is more complex in this regard. If we examine one of his most important texts, *Discourse on Colonialism* (1955), it emerges that Négritude cannot be reduced to a sort of ahistoric essentialism.[71] Instead, Sartre's reading tends to establish a representation that is partly stereotypical, on the basis of a difficulty in creating a political articulation of the problem. The limits do not detract from two noteworthy aspects. First, Sartre's comments do demonstrate a courageous *prise de parole* by a French intellectual in support of blacks. Second, there are some Marxian elements

---

69   Cf. Guha and Spivak 1988.

70   Fanon 2008, pp. 113–15. Cf. Visentin 2013, especially pp. 81–3.

71   Césaire 2000. Cf. Mellino in Césaire 2014, pp. 7–47: '*Discourse on Colonialism* is Césaire's text that was significantly influenced by existentialism and humanist Marxism of its time' (p. 13). 'However, Césaire's Négritude, despite its universalist vocation, and diverging from Sartre's opinion as well as several contemporary postcolonial critics such as Edward Said ... does not represent a "nakedness without color", it does not lie behind the white trappings simply to "destroy itself" ... It is clear, then, that it is precisely this *continuous* reference by Césaire to the *historical* experience of the middle passage and slavery as its main *constitutive* feature which prohibits any simplistic association between its concept and the promotion of a presumed, essential, (pure) essential pre-colonial African identity or a real return by ex-slaves to their place of origin' (p. 27 and n. 16).

here, as Sartre had only just begun to generically interact with Marxism in this period. In this way Sartre's interpretation of Négritude does not lack a Marxist substrate, attempting to create a reasoning founded on a weave between critiques of classist and racist dynamics:

> [I]t is certainly not just by accident that the most ardent cantors of Negritude are also militant Marxists. Nevertheless, the notion of race does not mix with the notion of class: the former is concrete and particular; the latter, universal and abstract ... Thus Negritude is for destroying itself, it is a "crossing to" and not an "arrival at."[72]

> [T]he definition of class is objective; it sums up only the conditions of the white worker's alienation; whereas it is in the bottom of his heart that the negro finds race, and he must wear it on his heart.[73]

The proletarian struggle and the black struggle, albeit based on complex coordinates and not immediately joinable, seem to overlap, here still in terms that are somewhat indefinite, but nevertheless on the basis of a first attempt at politicising the question.[74] The theme of the critique of colonialism will become more complex and articulated in Sartre's writings in the 1950s and early 1960s, gathered in *Situations v* under the title *Colonialisme et néo-colonialisme*.

The essay 'Colonialism is a System' (1956) is particularly important and emblematic. Distancing himself from Camus's position, Sartre describes colonialism as a system, and not a mere set of accidental givens nor a statistical result of individual cases, on the basis of a process that began in the nineteenth century, and at the same time identifies the Algerian situation as a particularly important *exemplum* of such a social structure:

> Algeria ... is, alas, the clearest and most legible example of the colonial system. ... For it is not true that there are some good *colons* and others who are wicked. There are colons and that is it. When we have understood that, we will understand why the Algerians are right to attack, first of all politically, this economic, social and political system and why

---

72 Sartre 1964–1965, pp. 48–9.
73 Sartre 1964–1965, p. 51.
74 In the theoretico-political path I have followed in this section, I have constantly kept in mind the generative analysis of Balibar and Wallerstein (who, however, never refer to Sartre's treatment) regarding the interweaving between the classist and racist dimensions. See Balibar and Wallerstein 2011. See also Basso 2008, especially pp. 112–15.

their liberation [*libération*], and also that of France, can only be achieved through the shattering of colonization.[75]

In this way, French colonialism in Algeria constitutes the point of departure of the argument.

> [W]hen we talk of the "colonial system", we must be clear about what we mean. It is not an abstract mechanism. The system exists, it functions, the infernal cycle of colonialism is a reality. But this reality is embodied in a million colonists, children and grandchildren of colonists, who have been shaped by colonialism and who think, speak and act according to the very principles of the colonial system ... French institutions ... include the right to vote, to free association and the freedom of the press. But the *colon*, whose interests are directly contrary to those of the Algerians ... can only accept these rights *for himself* to enjoy *in France*, among the French. To this extent he detests the token universality of French institutions ... One of the functions of racism is to compensate the latent universalism of bourgeois liberalism: since all human beings have the same rights, the Algerian will be made a subhuman [*sous-homme*].[76]

In 'Portrait du colonisé' Sartre emphasises that

> [C]olonialism denies *human rights* to people it has subjugated by violence, and whom it keeps in poverty and ignorance by force, therefore, as Marx would say, in a state of "subhumanity" ... Racism is *already there*, carried by the praxis of colonialism, engendered at every instant by the colonial apparatus.[77]

> The colonist can absolve himself only by systematically pursuing the "dehumanization" of the colonized, that is by identifying a little more each day with the colonial apparatus.[78]

Two important and connected aspects emerge from the passages we have examined. The first concerns the necessity of problematising the category of universalism: we do not find a critique of such an element, which Sartre takes

---

75   Sartre 2001, p. 10.
76   Sartre 2001, pp. 17–18.
77   Sartre 2001, p. 21.
78   Sartre 2001, p. 22.

up, but rather a highlighting of its internal limits, within a precise historical and social context. Racism constitutes the 'other face', so to speak, of 'the latent universalism of bourgeois liberalism'. Further, the history of universalism is also a history of the exclusion of subjects, and during the French Revolution we observe a framework of *égaliberté*, which applies to French citizens but excludes the colonised. We can think of the 1791 slave revolt, led by Toussaint Louverture in the French colony of Haiti, which led to the declaration of Haiti's independence in 1804.[79] From this point of view, a continuous exclusion of the 'black spectre' throughout the overall scenario is clarified, an exclusion which dramatically discloses the contradictions of universalism connected to the specific characteristics of bourgeois liberalism. One could carry out a sort of 'counter-history' of modern bourgeois ideology, aimed precisely at highlighting racism as more or less its constitutive element. The second important aspect, connected to the first, consists in the deconstruction of the logic of the Rights of Man, functional to bourgeois liberalism, regarding how it came to be determined, by excluding, at least until a historically determinant moment, those *sous-hommes* that instead are deprived of any guarantee. We observe a 'dehumanisation of the colonised', which is able to constitute a sort of 'other face' of bourgeois humanism, testifying to the fact that Sartre's position on humanism is more varied and complex than often represented.

Such an interpretation of racism gives rise to both lines of fracture and continuity with the classist dynamic. The former stand out from the reasoning we have just noted, and thus from the identification of an inferior humanity, which does not even have formal rights (even if mystification is inherent to them), finding itself in a condition of absolute inferiority. '[A] necessary aspect of the colonial system is that it attempts to bar the colonized people from the road of history ... [The French Republic] creates *masses* but prevents them from becoming a conscious proletariat by mystifying them with the caricature of their own ideology'.[80] At the same time, however, as emerges from 'Portrait of the Colonised', a weave remains between the classist and racist dynamic: 'The secret of the proletariat, Marx once said, is that it carries within itself the destruction of bourgeois society. We must be thankful to Memmi for reminding us that the colonized also have their secret, and that we are witnessing the awful death throes of colonialism'.[81] The question of the anticolonialist struggle, which also presents an anticlassist substrate, does not appear

---

79   Cf. James 1963 [1938].
80   Sartre 2001, p. 16.
81   Sartre 2001, p. 23.

as abstractly theoretico-political, but political *sans phrases*, and the Algerian event makes such an element emerge in a disruptive way:

> It is as a reaction to segregation and in the daily struggle that the Algerian personality has discovered itself and has been forged.[82] It is ... a question of our constructing with the Algerians new relations between a free France and a liberated Algeria ... The only thing that we can and ought to attempt – but it is the essential thing today – is to fight alongside them to deliver *both* the Algerians *and* the French from colonial tyranny.[83]

We are at the gates of Sartre's Preface to Fanon's *The Wretched of the Earth*, where the politicisation of the question stands out with particular force:

> Colonial violence not only aims at keeping these enslaved men at a respectful distance, it also seeks to dehumanize them. No effort is spared to demolish their traditions, to substitute our language for theirs, and to destroy their culture without giving them ours. We exhaust them into a mindless state.[84] [T]here is nothing more congruent with us than a racist humanism [*humanisme*], since the only way the European could make himself man was by fabricating slaves and monsters.[85]

We return to the question of racism as the 'other face' of bourgeois humanism, testified to by the fact that Sartre's position is much less unproblematically 'humanist' than generally represented. Moreover, I have emphasised several times throughout the book that, without negating the distance between Sartre and Althusser, the hypostatisation of the two categories humanism and antihumanism risks leading into a *cul de sac*, creating an unproductive perspective theoretically and politically. In any case, for Sartre the critique of the social, political, and ideological structure of racism does not remain on an abstractly theoretical level, but is connected to the anticolonial struggles, with their destabilising scope:

> Fanon hides nothing. In order to wage the struggle against us, the former colony must wage a struggle against itself ... The unity of the Third World,

---

82   Sartre 2001, p. 19.
83   Ibid.
84   Fanon 2004, p. l. Cf. Cormann 2015.
85   Fanon 2004, p. lviii. Translation modified. Translator's note: The English translation omits the phrase 'un humanisme raciste' from the passage.

therefore, is not complete: it is a work in progress that begins with all the colonized in every pre- or post-independent country, united under the leadership of the peasant class. This is what Fanon explains to his brothers in Africa, Asia, and Latin America: we shall achieve revolutionary socialism everywhere and all together or we shall be beaten one by one by our former tyrants.[86]

Sartre forcefully reiterates the interweaving between the critique of colonialism and the critique of the classist horizon. The struggle in the countries of the so-called Third World is not, in fact, socially undifferentiated and in the name of a generic reference to human rights, but appears inserted within a socialist movement, with its expansive character.

> [Fanon] has shown the way: as spokesman for the fighters, he has called for union, the unity of the African continent against every discord and every idiosyncrasy. He has achieved his purpose. If he had wanted to describe fully the historical phenomenon of colonization, he would have had to talk about us – which was certainly not his intention ... A new moment in violence, therefore, occurs, and this time it involves us.[87]

> [Y]ou condemn this war but you don't dare declare your support for the Algerian fighters; have no fear, you can count on the colonists and mercenaries to help you make up your mind. Perhaps, then, with your back to the wall, you will finally unleash this new violence aroused in you by old, rehashed crimes. But, as they say, that is another story. The history of man. The time is coming, I am convinced, when we shall join the ranks of those who are making it.[88]

Here the role of violence returns, on which Sartre's position appears ambivalent and complex, in its extraneity both to a sort of overall valorisation of violence and to the exclusion of its relevance, for example, in the case in question, when it questions the roots of the colonial system.

In the text 'The Political Thought of Patrice Lumumba', Sartre proposes an interesting juxtaposition between Fanon and Lumumba:

> Lumumba and Fanon: these two great dead men represent Africa. Not only their nations: all of their continent. Reading their writings and de-

---

86   Fanon 2004, pp. xlvi–vii.
87   Fanon 2004, p. lvii.
88   Fanon 2004, p. lxii.

ciphering their lives, one might take them to be implacable enemies ...
The differences and the friendship between these two men symbolize
both the contradictions that are ravaging Africa and the common need
to transcend them in pan-African unity.[89]

Lumumba understands, with radicality, that

> the Congo's problems were those of the whole of Africa; better still, his
> country would only find the strength to survive independence in the
> framework of a free Africa.[90]

> [F]or Vietnam and for Algeria – whatever their present difficulties may be
> – unity and centralization preceded independence and were its guaran-
> tee. In the Congo, what happened was the opposite.[91]

The ideal connection that Sartre establishes between Fanon and Lumumba
does not appear obviously disjoined from a strong differentiation between
Algeria and the Congo, due to the political processes in which they were
determined. He describes Lumumba as a sort of 'black Robespierre', within a
context however that had nothing revolutionary about it, and which thus posed
clear limits to the efficacy of his action:

> [Lumumba's] intelligence and his deep commitment to the African cause
> made him a black Robespierre. His project was limited – politics first, the
> rest would come in time – and universal.[92] Lumumba was a revolutionary
> without a revolution. His inflexible Jacobinism brought him into radical
> conflict with the hypocritical improvements to colonialism which the Bel-
> gian government was attempting without dexterity to make.[93]

Several times within Sartre's analysis of the Congolese situation and evaluation of Lumumba, there are present explicit and specific references to socialist
experiences, among which the Cuban experience is particular important:

---

89 Sartre 2001, pp. 87–8. Cf. McBride 1991, pp. 175–6.
90 Sartre 2001, p. 97.
91 Sartre 2001, p. 103.
92 Sartre 2001, p. 98. Cf. Gomez-Muller 2006, who interprets Sartre's engagement with colo-
    nialism under the banner of a sort of concrete universality, founded on the 'praxis of men
    and women who find themselves in a situation of oppression' (p. 119).
93 Sartre 2001, p. 104.

Though painful convulsions were the price they had to pay, newcomers in the USSR, China, Vietnam and Cuba took up controlling positions, governing, inspecting and making decisions during the day, learning and reading at night.[94] That means that every social group is required to sacrifice its interests to the common interest. Nothing better provided that the common interest exists. After the tumultuous few months which followed his taking of power, Castro forced the workers' unions to end their strikes and take their industrial grievances to arbitration ... [B]y demanding sacrifices from everyone, he invited the rural and urban workers to recognize their real unity and their common interest, which was the free exploitation of the island by all for the benefit of all. Put another way, centralism can only equate national unity with the common interest if the revolution from which it has emerged is a socialist one. There was as yet no class struggle proper between the *évolués* who were taking power in the Congo and the unskilled workers or the agricultural labourers ... Thus, owing to the absence of a mass movement, an armed struggle and a socialist programme, centralism, as a unifying *praxis*, seemed arbitrary to everyone.[95]

Analogously to Algeria, in Cuba also all of the difficulties emerge which are inherent to a centralism lacking a socialist platform, and thus a practice of class struggle. Lumumba can be juxtaposed, despite the profound difference of historical and geographical contexts, with Robespierre:

Robespierre and Lumumba died too soon to effect the synthesis which would have made them invincible. And in the France of 1789 as in the Congo of 1961, the masses were still mainly rural ... In neither case did the real victims of exploitation have representatives or an apparatus which could appeal to the politicians to seek unity in the struggle against exploitation ... Lumumba's failure was that of pan-Africanism.[96] And let us make no mistake: Castro's victory was due precisely to the fact that he took the leadership of a socialist revolution [*révolution socialiste*]: the failure of this Congolese, the title "communist" with which people imagined they were blackening him, is all simply due to the fact that he did not want to commit himself to reworking the infrastructure of the country ... His death – I remember that Fanon in Rome was devastated by it – was a cry

---

94   Sartre 2001, p. 104.
95   Sartre 2001, p. 107.
96   Sartre 2001, pp. 111–12.

of alarm ... The Congo has lost only a battle ... The Cubans, however, honour the memory of Martí who died at the end of the last century without seeing Cuba's victory over Spain or the subjugation of the island to American imperialism. If in a few years' time, the Congolese Castro wishes to teach his own people that unity must be won, he will remind them of its first martyr, Lumumba.[97]

A number of aspects which have emerged in our present discussion flow together here, particularly the juxtaposition (despite the profound differences) between Lumumba and Fanon, and the constitutive reference to Cuba, whose experience plays a crucial function in the development of Sartre's political thought. The latter, above all in the 1960s, is supported by the relation between socialism and the critique of colonialism, on the basis of a biunivocal correspondence, though not always in linear terms, between these two elements: on the one hand, rethinking socialism, starting from an immanent critique of the Soviet Union, which can only lead to traversing the colonial question in its centrality, and on the other hand, the anticolonial struggle is not neutral with respect to the social relations of the operative classes. It follows that the theme of colonialism profoundly permeates Sartre's categories, and is also configured, on the one hand, as a presupposition of the *Critique*, and on the other, as its outcome, or at least a possible one, despite a series of internal problems with respect to the *inachevé* character of the text.

In the first part of the *Critique*, in a section that almost constitutes a 'hinge' with the second part (wherein moreover the discussion is not developed further), the critical analysis of colonisation, and the racism at its foundation, plays a decision role. There remains an overall reference to the 'system of colonialism', which refers to what was carried out in the texts of the 1950s, and which finds at its own basis, on the one hand, a confrontation with the present colonial experiences, and on the other, an attempt to rethink Marxism beyond any deterministic reading.[98] In any case, in the *Critique* the Algerian situation is presented as an exemplification of this question:

---

97   Sartre 2001, pp. 113–14.
98   For an interpretation aimed on the one hand at linking the Critique and the writings on colonialism in the 1950s and 1960s, and on the other at giving rise to several particularly important elements of the *Critique*, see Oulc'hen 2015, p. 34: 'As opposed to some texts gathered in Situations V, which seem to refuse Westerners the possibility of 'taking charge, on the theoretical as well as practical level' of the opposition to colonialism, the *Critique* offers its reader, Western or not, the possibility of appropriating, at least from a theoretical point of view, the science for itself acquired by the colonised ... [In the *Critique*] ... Sartre is

[R]acism is not a mere "psychological defense" of the colonist, created for the needs of the cause, to justify colonisation to the metropolitan power and to himself; it is in fact *Other-Thought* produced objectively by the colonial system and by super-exploitation [*surexploitation*] ... Racist thinking is simply an activity which realises in alterity [*alterité*] a practical truth inscribed in worked matter and in the system which results from it ... The racism which occurs to an Algerian colonist was imposed and produced by the conquest of Algeria, and is constantly recreated and reactualised by everyday practice [*pratique quotidienne*] through serial alterity. Of course, the conquest of Algeria in itself can only be taken as a complex process dependent on a certain political and social situation *in France* as well as on the real relations between capitalist France and agricultural, feudal Algeria. Nevertheless, the colonial wars of the nineteenth century *realised* an original situation of violence for the colonialists as their fundamental relation to the natives.[99]

It is clear how the element of alterity, which Sartre has deployed since *Being and Nothingness*, returns here, although rearticulated from that reference, and on the basis of its inscription in the specific situation of Algeria. Within this dynamic, the notion of violence plays a decisive role, which we have seen the entire framework of the *Critique* grasp:

The evolution of violence is clearly expressed here: first a structure of alienation in the *practico-inert*, it is actualised as praxis in colonisation; and its (temporary) victory presents itself as the objectification of the practical ensemble (army, capitalists, commodity merchants, colonialists) in a *practico-inert* system where it represents the fundamental structure of reciprocity between the colonialists and the colonised ... This means, in the first place, that it becomes its own idea in the form of *racism* ... [C]olonist and colonised are a couple, produced by an antagonistic situation [*situation antagonistique*] and by one another ... The colonialist wants the *status quo* because any change in the system ... can only hasten the end of colonisation.[100]

---

not satisfied with this dual colonist/colonised, science for itself/science in itself schema, which is present above all, moreover, in *Situations V*, and in an even stronger way in his preface to Fanon. Further, in the *Critique* he proposes a very rich analysis of the concrete effects of decentring the ideas of the colonists'.

99   Sartre 2004a, p. 714.
100   Sartre 2001, pp. 720–1. Translation modified.

We thus find a reciprocity endowed with an antagonistic character. For Sartre, history is founded, in a Marxian manner, on conflict, in which classist and racist dimensions are strongly interwoven: on the one hand, in Algeria a class struggle unfolds, while on the other, in the relation between colonialist and coloniser there emerges something further, at the level of brutality, than the capitalist–worker dialectic.

> [S]uper-exploitation as a practico-inert process is nothing but oppression as a historical *praxis* realising itself, determining itself and controlling itself in the milieu of passive activity.[101] This conflict [*conflit*], this complex *praxis*, the manifestation of class interest, of the interest of all classes of colonialists is concretised in *groups of violence* at the slightest provocation. And by this I do not mean groups which *realise* real violence ... so much as practical communities [*communautés pratiques*] whose role is to perpetuate the climate of violence by making themselves *violence incarnate*.[102]

In such a process violence and incarnation are connected, another extraordinarily dense element within the analysis of the *Critique*.

Faced with colonial violence or 'super-exploitation', thinking one can react in a non-violent way would be an index of a subordinate attitude. But Sartre was criticised in this regard, from the perspective of abstract and moralistic arguments: from Machiavelli to Marx, the 'Machiavelli of the proletariat' spoken of by Antonio Labriola, Sartre carried out in a generative way the consciousness of the necessity of violence (differently that someone such as Albert Camus), not on the basis of an aestheticising valorisation of violence, but rather of an investigation of its material foundations.[103]

> The only possible way out was to confront total negation with total negation, violence with equal violence, to negate disperal and atomisation by an initially negative unity whose content would be defined in struggle: the Algerian nation. Thus the Algerian rebellion, through being desperate violence, was simply an adoption of the despair in which the colonialists maintained the colonised.[104]

---

101   Sartre 2001, p. 729.
102   Sartre 2001, pp. 726–7.
103   On violence in Marx, starting from Balibar's interpretation, see Basso 2009.
104   Sartre 2001, p. 733. Translation modified.

The objective is to transform such violence 'of desperation' in searching to articulate a socialist scenario, capable of going beyond the interweaving of classism and racism present in the colonial system. In that sense the Algerian struggle, with the production of subjectivity that distinguished it, assumes a particularly emblematic role.

If the distinctive features of the analysis of colonialism interact with Sartre's overall reflection, as Pierre Macherey has acutely emphasised, there emerges a remarkable capacity to graph the processes of subjectivation that develop in the context of an experience such as that of the 'wretched of the earth'.[105] More generally, the attempt consists in restoring lived experience, for example linked to the fact of being black (or being Jewish, to take up the reflections in *Anti-Semite and Jew*), a characteristic that does not exist in the abstract but always in situation, on the basis of a complex set of relations, and also domination, and within a copenetration of freedom and necessity. In this sense, to adopt Macherey's words, 'being black is not only being subject, but being subject with something more (or less), that can be noted as such, i.e., "recognised", "fixed", only in the specific context of the situation, that, in the case of colonialism, is a relation of domination'.[106] We find a process of subjectivation that carries out its action within the specific conditions imposed by the situation. Such a dynamic unfolds with particular force in the anticolonial struggles, but is not reducible to them. The attempt to rethink socialism after the immanent critique of the Soviet Union, on the basis of an interweaving between the reference to other socialist experiences and the increasingly greater cruciality of anticolonial practices, together with other events both in the French context and the international scene, focuses on the key year of 1968.

---

105   Cf. Macherey 2014, especially pp. 75–6, who insists on the relevance of Sartre's conception for Fanon: 'According to Fanon, Sartre's analyses of the question of knowing what "being Jewish" means, or being perceived and recognised as Jewish, can be transposed onto the question of knowing the meaning of "being black" ... In the first place, Fanon was strongly impressed by Sartre's exceptional capacity to restore, as if from the inside, the concrete lived aspect [*vecù*] of an experience'.

106   Macherey 2014, p. 80. In this sense, Macherey brings out the productivity of Sartre's delineation of processes of subjectivation, and conversely, remarks on the difficulties inherent to the Althusserian approach: 'the process of subjectivation carries out its action globally, in the conditions imposed by the situation, and not for every subject taken in isolation, as Althusser seems to figure' (p. 84).

3   'Autour De 68'

Although today it is often reduced to a caricature and banal simplification, 1968, and the *prise de parole* contained within it, plays a very important role in both Sartre's political thought and commitment. This is testified to by the fact that volume VIII of *Situations* is dedicated to 1968: *Autour de 68*. 'Autor' can take a meaning that is both literal and metaphorical. Indeed, in the first place the works that are gathered in this volume, which have a diversified and complex character and are often posed closely in relation to determinate conjunctures, are not only from 1968, but worked out between 1965 and 1970. Secondly, not all of the texts directly regard 1968, but many are connected in a broad sense. I will begin the present discussion specifically with a reference to 1968 as a crucial event on the global level, in which various theoretico-political points developed throughout the 1950s and above all the 1960s intersect. With this in place, I will then focus on a specific analysis of the French May and its impact on Sartre's thought.

The path taken throughout this chapter finds a sort of 'condensation' in 1968. It is enough to think of the manner with which Sartre conceives the confrontation with Marxism starting in 1956, with *Search for a Method*: it is not only a matter of its critique or its 'relaunching' on new theoretical bases, beginning from the rejection of any deterministic approach, as well as from the attempt to make Marxism and existentialism reciprocally interact, arriving at a valorisation of the 'singular universal' and the notion of freedom as liberation that sustains it. The question also takes on a practical character, on the basis of a continuous confrontation with the events of the time. 1956 was a decisive year, particularly in relation to the Hungarian situation (as well as for Khrushchev's denunciation of Stalin's crimes). Further, the entire *Critique of Dialectical Reason* is inscribed in this context, establishing itself as an immanent critique of the Soviet Union on which I have focused at length. By making the advances of the *Critique* interact with other texts of a more contingent character, what emerges is Sartre's interest in other socialisms than the Soviet Union in Eastern Europe, such as Yugoslavia and above all Czechoslovakia, and, still more, his interest in a decisive country such as China, as well as the Cuban situation. Another distinctive sign of the discourse is represented by the critique of antisemitism and racism: in such a framework there is inscribed the position taken in favour of anticolonial struggles, with particular reference to Algeria. From the elements indicated here, and thus the attempt to think socialism on new bases, the reference to 1968 should forcefully stand out.[107]

---

107   For other perspective than what I have outlined, see Birchall 2004, pp. 211–19. See also Hulliung 2013, pp. 117–18.

To understand this historical and political context, in addition to the factors just recalled it is necessary to remark on the importance of the critique of the Vietnam War. A substantial part of *Situations VIII* is dedicated to writings on Vietnam, also in connection with Sartre's commitment as president of the Russell Tribunal, and thus also on the present implications at the level of international law and the specific role played by the United States.[108]

> [The United States government] is guilty of continuing and intensifying the war, although each of its members understands more clearly each day, from the reports of the military chiefs, that the only means of winning is to "liberate" Vietnam from all of the Vietnamese ... In this way the Vietnamese are fighting for all men, and the Americans against all men.[109]

> [The United States'] hegemony is in fact founded on its imperialist positions maintained in South America and elsewhere in the world. What it is obligated to do today in order to save these positions – in Vietnam, in Santo Domingo – forces it to unmask itself and we see a phenomenon that has not been produced for decades: the awakening of American intellectuals, who rise up against the politics of their government.[110]

The critique of the imperialist politics of the United States focuses on a *prise de parole* for the 'wretched of the earth':

> No discussion is possible if one does not first accept – a position that the majority of American leftists are not ready to take – questioning the set of American imperialist politics, not only in Vietnam but in South America, Korea, in all of the Third World.[111]

> Solidarity must be demonstrated with all the Vietnamese, Cubans, Africans, all of the friends of the Third World who accept existence and freedom.[112]

---

108   Cf. Sartre 1968c. *Situations VIII* is divided into four parts, which thus correspond to important nuclei in Sartre's interpretation of 1968: 'I. Vietnam: Le tribunal Russell' (pp. 7–124), 'II. La France' (pp. 125–332), 'III. Israël – Le monde arabe' (pp. 333–70), 'IV. Les intellectuels' (pp. 371–476).
109   Sartre 2008c, pp. 82–3.
110   Sartre 1972a, p. 165.
111   Sartre 1972a, p. 12.
112   Sartre 1972a, p. 19.

Beyond several aspects of Sartre's analysis in this regard, in part reducible to a
sort of Third Worldism, it is necessary to emphasise that the reference to war
in Vietnam remains crucial for the interpretation of 1968. Sartre expresses himself in explicit terms, for example, in the interview with Rossana Rossanda and
il manifesto in 1969:

> The element which unified the struggle was something which, in my opin-
> ion, came from afar; it was an idea which came to us from Vietnam and
> which the students expressed in the formula: *"L'imagination au pouvoir."*
> In other words, the area of the possible is much more vast than the domin-
> ant classes have accustomed us to believe. Who would have thought that
> fourteen million peasants would be able to resist the greatest industrial
> and military power in the world? And yet, this is what happened. Vietnam
> taught us that the area of the possible is immense, and that one need not
> be resigned. It is this which was the lever of the students' revolt, and the
> workers understood it. In the united demonstration of the 13th of May,
> this idea suddenly became dominant.[113]

It is necessary to remark on the centrality of the Vietnam War for understanding that complex of demands, concessions, and practices which intersect in
1968. In this regard the reference to Algeria is particularly important, presented many times in writings dedicated to the question of Vietnam, as we noted
earlier.[114]

If the theme of the Vietnam War is inserted within a more overall critique,
anticolonial struggle and support for the Cuban Revolution play a decisive role.
Indeed, the analysis of colonialism as a system returns in these texts:

> In point of fact colonization is not a matter of mere conquest … Coloni-
> alism is, in fact, a system: the Colony sells raw materials and foodstuffs at
> preferential rates to the colonizing power which, in turn, sells the Colony
> industrial goods at the price current on the world market. This curious
> system of exchange can be established only if work is imposed on a colo-
> nial sub-proletariat for starvation wages.[115]

Outside of Europe, a crucial reference such as Cuba remains operative within
the writings on the 'climate' of '68, although with some emphasis that it is

---

113   Sartre 2008c, pp. 125–6.
114   See for example Sartre 1972a, pp. 14–15, 30, 34–7, 181.
115   Sartre 2008c, p. 70.

necessary to problematise. 'What is admirable in Castro's case is that theory arose from experience, instead of preceding it ... It is in the war, in contact with the peasants, that Castro's revolutionary doctrine is formed'.[116] Cuba and China are brought together as those countries 'in which one begins to understand what true socialism [*vrai socialisme*] is'.[117]

We thus arrive at Sartre's reference to the Chinese Cultural Revolution, which is crucial for a reflection on 1968, as well as the French '68. Sartre specifies that there cannot be a cultural revolution without an earlier political revolution, but it remains extremely prudent for carrying out an overall analysis of the Chinese scenario:

> [T]o the fact that the Vietnam War was at the origin of May ... The essential effect that this war has caused for militant Europeans or Americans is that it broadened the field of the possible. Earlier it seemed impossible that the Vietnamese would be able to resist the formidable American military machine and win ... [The French students] understood that there were possibilities which remained unknown.

> I consider myself to be informed in a very incomplete way about the cultural Revolution. The phenomenon unfolds on ideological, cultural, political levels, namely at the level of the superstructures that represent the superior degrees of the whole dialectical scale ... Personally, I must confess that could not understand the causes of the phenomenon in its totality. The idea of a permanent apocalypse is clearly very seductive, but I am convinced that it is not this at all, and that it is necessary to look in the infrastructure for the causes of the cultural Revolution.[118]

It is clear however that it remains very difficult, on the basis of the argumentation in the *Critique*, to eliminate the problems inherent to bureaucracy, once the fused group has become an organisation, and then finally an institution.

> [O]nly a cultural revolution against the new order can impede the degeneration [of bureaucratisation]. What is being produced today in China is not a mild reform: it is a violent destruction of the entire system of

---

116   Sartre 1972a, p. 200. See also Sartre 1972a, 127–45.
117   Sartre 1972a, p. 199.
118   Sartre 1972b, p. 125. Cf. Sartre 1976b, p. 194: 'I have great respect for Mao, at least until a few years ago. I have not understood the "cultural revolution" very well ..., and I think that it is not clear [what this means] in practice'.

privileges. However, we do not know anything about what the future of China will be. If revolution triumphed in any Western country, the risk of bureaucratic deterioisation would be very large and constantly present.[119]

But Sartre's attention is turned above all on the French situation, as emerges from the text 'Les maos en France': 'The classic parties of the left remained in the nineteenth century, in the age of competitive capitalism. But the *maos*, with their antiauthoritarian praxis, seem to be the only revolutionary force – still in their beginning – capable of adapting themselves to the new forms of class struggle, in the period of organised capitalism'.[120] Beyond Sartre's approach to the French Maoists (not lacking in questionable aspects) and beyond the doubts about their role in 1968, it is clear how neo-Maoism is conceived as adequate to the modalities of present conflicts, within a capitalist context that has profoundly changed since the nineteenth century. In this sense, there seem to emerge some points of contact with Marcuse's analysis in *One Dimensional Man*, a text that played an important role within 1968, precisely on the basis of a necessity of rearticulating the forms of subjectivisation by starting from a consideration of the metamorphoses of capitalism.

From all of these elements, with critical reference to the Vietnam War, racism (Martin Luther King Jr. was killed in 1968), and colonialism along with the valorisation of the Chinese Revolution, the international dimension of 1968 emerges with great clarity. Another decisive reference is the Czechoslovakian '68: the line running from 1956–1968, relative to the events of 'real socialism', remains crucial for understanding Sartre's political thought. 'The machine turns on itself and the individual finds his place rigorously fixed by the abstract requirements of a 'plan' for him that he has not contributed to establishing. In Czechoslovakia, for example, there is a revolt against the dehumanising system of production for the sake of production that is focused in this moment on a claim to freedom'.[121] Here again the *conatus* towards freedom returns, a constitutive tension of Sartre's discourse from its beginnings, which finds one of its condensations in '68. Such practice explodes in the Czechoslovakian revolt, which constituted precisely a search for liberation from seriality established in the institutionalisation of the group, and thus from the sclerotisation of the party.

---

119   Sartre 1972a, p. 129. See also Sartre 1972b, p. 126.
120   Sartre 1976b, p. 47.
121   Sartre 1972a, pp. 219–20.

But in 1968, after twenty years of Stalinism, the situation was very different for Czech and Slovak workers ... To start with, they too had been sated
with lies, though just how sick of them they had been they were only now
becoming fully aware ... workers and intellectuals constantly radicalized
each other.[122] No press or radio has ever been freer than in Czechoslovakia
during the spring of 1968.[123]

The attempt consists in making the demands of workers and intellectuals
reciprocally interact. Indeed, the former perfectly grasped the importance of
freedom of expression, understood in its materiality and tension towards the
search for another horizon beyond the present state of things. Sartre's valorisation of several socialist experiences in Eastern Europe results from the critique
of the French Communist Party, with its doctrinal rigidity and neutralisation of
every revolutionary thrust:

> Third point of communist argumentation: the student movement is
> anarchic because it represents a bourgeois revolt. Excellent! How to ex-
> plain, then, the revolt of the Czechoslovakian and Yugoslavian students,
> who were born in a socialist regime and of which more than half are
> children of workers and peasants? What do these children of labourers
> claim? The same thing, approximately, that the French students claim,
> namely the freedom of critique and self-determination.[124] It is against this
> dehumanisation [*déshumanisation*] that the Polish, Czech, Yugoslavian,
> French, German students and young workers – who live in very different
> regimes – revolt.[125]

The Czechoslovakian situation is not considered in purely 'endogenous' terms,
but by starting from the attempt to grasp within it the importance in relation
to the revolts in Western countries. Sartre concludes the essay 'Czechoslovakia: The Socialism That Came in from the Cold' precisely with the attempt
to rethink socialism from this basis:

> After the month of August 1968, it is necessary to forsake the comforts of
> moralism and to abandon reformist illusions about this type of regime.
> The machine cannot be repaired; the peoples of Eastern Europe must

---

122   Sartre 2008c, pp. 114–15.
123   Sartre 2008c, p. 113.
124   Sartre 1972a, p. 201.
125   Sartre 1972a, p. 204.

seize hold of it and destroy it. The revolutionary forces of the West now have only one way of helping Czechoslovakia effectively in the long-term. That is, listen to the voices that speak to us of its fate ... The duty of the Left in Western Europe is to profit from this analysis, to rethink, without preconceptions or prejudices.[126]

The aspects that we have outlined, which allow several distinctive features of 1968 to emerge in its overall significance, constitute a satisfactory outcome of Sartre's trajectory in the 1960s, which had found its more 'systematic' articulation in the *Critique of Dialectical Reason*. It is necessary to add two important factors at the national level (to which, moreover, a large part of *Situations VIII* is dedicated) to these international events: the critique of Gaullism and the positioning with respect to the French Communist Party. I will not dwell on the former,[127] but the second question necessitates a further observation. If Sartre's critique of the PCF is constant, despite some oscillations, starting from '56, viewed from '68 such problems emerge with particular force. It is a party that is not revolutionary, and not even really reformist, insufficiently critical of de Gaulle and ambiguous towards the events of the Algerian struggle: it constitutes 'a brake on any revolutionary movement in France. Everything which does not emanate from it alone the party either rejects or suppresses'.[128] Contrary to what is often maintained, Sartre was not a fellow traveller of the PCF, and even if he was (which remains at least controversial), it was only in the early 1950s.[129] Insofar as Sartre was not completely extraneous to communist political organisations, as philosophers such as Deleuze and Foucault were, in his texts (and the public positions he took), starting from 1956, his radical dystonia with the PCF is clear, with regard to both French events and the international situation. The aspects he criticised are in several ways similar to various Western communist parties, but surely the PCF had characteristics which were so narrow that Sartre was led, in opposition to it, to an idealisation of the PCI in the early 1960s, as evident for example through his rather problematic praise

---

126   Sartre 2008c, p. 117.
127   Cf. Sartre 1972a, p. 226: 'just as there does not exist an evil Gaullism, so also does there not exist a good Gaullism; there is Gaullism, and it is entirely here: this means that the regime is, in its structure, the expression of the dominant class that battles; in our bourgeois society ... the state apparatuses are necessarily found in the hands of the enemy'. See also, for example, Sartre 1972a, pp. 153, 36 ff., 142–3.
128   Sartre 2008c, p. 127.
129   Cf. Traverso 2014, p. 35: 'Sartre always denounced anticommunism – his aphorism "an anticommunist is a dog" remained famous, and this posture is at the origin of an incurable rupture with Aron – but his relations with the PCF were always conflictual'.

of Palmiro Togliatti.[130] Further, after his contact with the climate of '68, Sartre turned away from the PCI and drew closer to the communist expelled from the PCI who had founded *il manifesto*.

It is necessary to understand, in more specific and 'localised' terms, Sartre's attitude towards the French May. Sartre is undoubtedly an intellectual who can be associated in an immediate way with 1968, and for the French students, he came to be considered in that moment (from a number of viewpoints) as a point of reference, but the relationship is more complex than it seems *prima facie*. Actually, as Sartre himself admitted, he understood the meaning of '68 later, at least a year after. In the 1970s, in interviews gathered together in *On a raison de se révolter*, the question is clearly expressed:

> I was with the students' movement. I wrote articles ... I went to speak with those who occupied the Sorbonne. But fundamentally I did not understand them ... what escaped me first of all was the true (global) significance of this movement, and above all the striking workers that followed ... It took me all of '69 in order to understand something ... until that moment ... no one [among intellectuals] questioned the status of intellectuals, much less themselves. In '68 this was not the main characteristic of the movement, but for the intellectuals it was the point of departure for understanding it: the classic intellectual was profoundly contested ... You see, there were two facts: on the one hand May '68 showed to intellectuals such as me that now there was a strong potential, still uncertain but destined to develop, to the left of the PCF ... But the other aspect of the phenomenon was that this force of the left could not accept us for what we were.[131] I then forgot my first impression and found in '69 that their movement was directly against me ... Against the intellectual, the unhappy consciousness that gets its merits and virtues from this unhappiness.[132]

---

130   Cf. Sartre 1972b, 137–51.

131   Sartre 1974, pp. 63–4.

132   Sartre 1974, p. 68. There is a similar emphasis in Sartre 1977, pp. 126–7: 'the intellectual becomes ... – the classic intellectual, a great denouncer. This was how I saw the intellectual before May. Starting in May, something very particular happened ... in relation to the student contestation, there was something wrong with the intellectual. There was this, if you link, that was seen in the professors: a technician of practical knowledge, professor in a university, and the holder of a certain knowledge that bourgeois society had given him ... I think that in a socialist society as one might dream it, there would no longer be intellectuals because such a contradiction would not exist at all'. On the critique of the intellectual-professor who was not willing to be questioned, with particular reference

For better or worse, Sartre's idea of the intellectual as 'someone who meddles in what is not his business'[133] has become paradigmatic. Such a conception rightly asserts the necessity of a critical function of the intellectual, with a characterisation that is not at all neutral and equidistant, albeit with the problem of the petty-bourgeois social origin of such a figure. But Sartre's positions – for example drawing near the French Maoists, the editorship of *La cause du peuple*, and, particularly in the 1970s, the choice to partner with Benny Lévy – can leave much to be perplexed about. The role of the intellectual *engagé* in Sartre, beyond the caricatures structurally established by adversaries, risks presenting itself in terms that are a bit 'priestly', as a sort of non-institution institution. The universal, classic intellectual of Sartre is posed in very different terms with respect to the later situated, specific intellectual of Foucault, but it was tested precisely by 1968, and it is interesting to note that around 1968, there is an important interaction between the two philosophers, who had earlier polemicised vigorously among themselves.[134] It is after May that there is a *rapprochement*, in the common consideration of the fact that the student days had constituted a new beginning of social struggles.

What is to be questioned is a system of hierarchical knowledge, founded on fixed and static roles, in which the intellectual-professor takes on a 'vertical' function. Moreover, the entire trajectory of education in France (but not only there) had a clearly elitist connotation. A contemporary question is constituted by the fact that the intellectual can articulate radical positions on the social level, in favor of the workers, and against colonialism, but at the same time maintains a hierarchical role toward the students, remaining completely functional, in their own place of work, to the disciplinary apparatus of the state, and the logic of production-reproduction of the existing mechanism. '[Some intellectuals] felt the movement was contesting *them* in their capacity as *intellectuals*, whereas until then the intellectual had always been there to help others, to be available – the natural person to provide the theories, the ideas'.[135] This problem appears difficult to overcome, because the

---

to Raymond Aron, see Sartre 1972a, pp. 187–8: 'The only way of learning consists in contesting ... The University is made in order to form men who contest'. On the Sartre-Aron conflict regarding the question of engagement, see Sirinelli 1995, pp. 376–81, which maintains a completely different claim than what I argue here, and is completely 'crushed' by the Aronian approach.

133   Sartre 2008c, p. 230.
134   Cf. D'Alessandro 2010, particularly pp. 33–7.
135   Sartre 2008c, p. 289.

intellectuel engagé (who, leaving aside the miserable political parable of various intellectuals in the French '68, cannot absolutely be identified with the Leninist professional revolutionary, nor even with the Gramscian organic intellectual) also does not constitute a revolutionary vanguard, but, if anything, arrives after the event, more or less destabilising, has taken place, and takes the position *ex post* in order to maintain it. After '68 Sartre himself, who was of course not a university professor, deemed it necessary to problematise his position in this regard. 'It is necessary that teachers give themselves the task not of finding among the mass of their students those that seem worthy of integration to an elite, but rather of giving the full mass access to the culture. But this clearly supposes the adoption of new methods of teaching'.[136] In Sartre there is an oscillation between bourgeois individuation, conforming to the 'present state of things' of the university, which can only produce 'one dimensional' individuals, and the search for critical spaces within the existing university, in order to try and introduce elements of fracture, on the basis of a sort of 'revolutionary reformism', to adopt a formula from André Gorz.[137]

The stakes of the argument are represented by the alliance between workers and students, an alliance which in 1968 there was an attempt to foster (not without difficulty). The students understood the revolt, albeit with contradictions, as unrelated to the university insofar as it is separate from the rest of society. Indeed, earlier I emphasised that the 'spring' was constituted by the critique of the Vietnam War, and the questioning of racism and the class relations interwoven with the critique of the university system, as the demonstrations themselves showed.[138] The *prise de parole* of the French May, however, leaves a series of questions open: 'The students' revolt is a typical expression of the difficulties of a counter-culture'.[139] Beyond of course the capacity of articulating new spaces of action against authoritative structures, critical knowledge and the 'counter-culture' present the risk of eluding the theme of transformation,

---

136   Sartre 1972a, p. 191. On the necessity of creating new methods of teaching, trying to 'politicise the courses', see Sartre 1972a, p. 248. On Sartre's rethinking of intellectual identity, see Verstraeten 1972, p. 376: 'what emerged after May was the failure of the classic intellectual ... and the discovery that the first form of fidelity to the universal of his function, the univocal modality of revolutionary action, passed through the liquidation of one's own privilege, through self-liquidation ... it is no longer a matter of naming the universal, designating it, testifying to it, but *becoming it*'.

137   Sartre 1972a, pp. 195–7.

138   Sartre 1972a, p. 184.

139   Sartre 1972a, p. 184.

in the sense of a real destitution of the existing social relations. Sartre observes, referring to the reprisal (and caricature) of the Chinese Cultural Revolution, that, in the French (and European) context, such subversion was not preceded by a social and political revolution, with all the difficulties that derive from it.[140] It is not a matter of interpreting the succession of preconstituted phases in linear terms, but rather of highlighting the presence of an impasse, the index of a problem in articulating the relation with power. It is one thing to realistically consider the non-repeatable aspect of the October Revolution, but this must not be confused with a kind of anarchistic refuge-taking in a position that does not fully confront the problem of the 'disciplinary apparatuses of the state'.

This does not mean that I disagree with a position like Michel de Certeau's on the French May as a 'symbolic revolution'. Certeau's position has important elements, as he understood a series of historical and political changes that were underway:

> A symbolic revolution ... either because it signifies more than it effectuates, or because of the fact that it contests given social and historical relations in order to create authentic ones.[141] Last May speech was taken the way, in 1789, the Bastille was taken. The stronghold that was assailed is a knowledge held by the dispensers of culture, a knowledge meant to integrate or enclose student workers and wage earners in a system of assigned duties. From the taking of the Bastille to the taking of the Sorbonne, between these two essential symbols, an essential differences characterizes the event of May 13, 1968: today, it is imprisoned speech that was freed.[142]

Henri Lefebvre, who valorised the contestation of Nanterre,[143] provides another important perspective on the French '68. The entire treatment of 'everyday life' can be understood precisely from the libertarian demands, which found a condensation in '68, on the basis of the attempt to rethink revolution, understanding it not as the seizure of power, but in its capacity to transform the lives of subjects in their concreteness. Without extensively comparing these positions, which are not fully interlocking, and Sartre's own view, it is necessary to emphasise that although there are several points of contact, Sartre's

---

140   Cf. Poster 1975, pp. 390–5.
141   Certeau 1997, p. 5.
142   Certeau 1997, p. 11.
143   Lefebvre 1968b.

perspective distinguishes itself in a much more marked way due to the search to have the French May interact with the workers' struggles. Further, '68 is found at the origin of a new season of social conflicts, albeit according to different modalities among various European countries. Until now I have highlighted several characteristics of the student revolt, which are irreducible to a university platform in its self-referentiality. It is necessary to linger on the role played by the workers, and on the scope of fostering a strong interaction among students and workers, with the potentialities as well as difficulties present in this attempt.

> [A]ctually the students were not alone. Ten million striking workers followed them. Certainly not from the first day and not until the end. But soon enough and far enough because the workers themselves were amazed.[144] With that said, the exchanges were very difficult at the level of discussion: people who are not from the same environment never have anything to say – they can only do things together. For this reason, the only positive relations that could be established between students and workers in the month of May were those of the 'committees of revolutionary action' created almost everywhere ... Actually, the striking workers were terminated and there was no longer possibility of a general link between the general movement and the workers. However, I do not consider all that was initiated, so to speak, in the month of May to be a failure, because the links that were formed in the action committees did not fail.[145] May 1968 was not a flame without future; this insurrection, betrayed but not won, left traces in the workers and above all in the youth.[146]

We find here a complex and articulated analysis, one that is perhaps unfinished, but supported by the attempt to examine the question posed with its lights and shadows, with its spaces that were opened as well as its unresolved problems. Although it is done in retrospect, Sartre's valorisation of '68 does not appear disjointed from an emphasis on its internal limits. Despite the investigation of the latter, Sartre's gaze tends to emphasise the potentialities inherent to the subjective practices, even where it seems everything is lost: 'the links that were formed ... did not fail'.

---

144   Sartre 1972a, p. 215.
145   Sartre 1972a, pp. 168–9.
146   Sartre 1972a, p. 312.

To understand such stakes, it is necessary to grasp, avoiding a dogmatic and ahistoric approach, the changes with respect to competitive capitalism of the nineteenth century. At the centre of the discourse is so-called 'neo-capitalism', in which the role played by not-immediately productive subjects appears increasingly important. In truth, Sartre adopts the category with a certain prudence, also underlining certain limits, and moreover not establishing an analytical examination on the level of social processes. Despite this, it came to have a certain weight within the texts of the 'autour de '68':

> [T]oday the students and workers are closer than was the case in their parents' generation ... Today the class average has transformed ... to be in the foreground, the problem is no longer that of property ... but power [*potere*].[147] It is also necessary to adapt the struggle to the new techniques of modern capitalism, to the human engineering that alienates the individual first in the universe of "organisation" by giving them the illusion of contact with the managers of the company.[148]

> [I]t is necessary to find new forms of struggle and look for what the organisation of revolutionary power can be in the neo-capitalist society of so-called "consumers".[149]

I will take up this question later, but it would seem to present some similarities with the advances of the Frankfurt School. Actually Sartre, despite knowing very little of the Frankfurt authors, articulates a perspective that, with much difficulty, can be brought together with Adorno's approach.[150] If anything, there emerge several points of contact with the Marcuse of *One Dimensional Man*. In any case, the Sartrean outlook is irreducible to either an 'apocalyptic' register of Frankfurt derivation, or an immediately expansive reading of the processes of neo-capitalism.

> [T]he movement of May expressed a radical contestation of the values codified in the university and society as well as a will to consider them as if they were already dead ... I was always convinced that the Vietnam

---

147   Sartre 1972a, p. 203.
148   Sartre 1972a, p. 153.
149   Sartre 1972a, p. 212.
150   Cf. Sherman 2007, who confronts this relation however without really considering Sartre's political thought, mainly relying on *Being and Nothingness*.

War is found at the origins of May ... The essential effect that this war had
on the European or American militants is that it widened the field of the
possible ... They understood that there were possibilities which remained
unknown.[151] The concept of revolution is not directly found in reality: a
reality exists and revolution consists in changing it ... I think that revolution, if it can be done, can only be peoples' access to freedom and I believe
that in a certain sense all revolutions have had the same sense, even for
Lenin.[152]

After some years of distance, the movement of '68 is led back to that practice of
freedom that constituted one of the distinctive aspects of Sartre's path. Actually, there are elements of continuity in the revolutionary event described in the
passage above, but also elements of discontinuity, for example in reference to
the interpretation of '68 as a 'symbolic revolution' and not the taking of power,
which de Certeau provides. In the final chapter I will return to the problems
left open by such a framework, particularly in relation to the political underes-
timation of the question of power (insofar as Sartre recognises, on the level of
analysis, the increasing importance of this element) and the risk of outlining
an *anarchisant* approach, which finds its point of departure in the assumption
of freedom as liberation.

The text 'L'idée neuve de Mai 1968' is particularly important, wherein, as
already evident in the title, there is the centrality of the *conatus* towards the
'new', the tension towards a practice of emancipation.

Third point of communist argumentation: the student movement is
anarchic because it represents a bourgeois revolt. Excellent! How to explain, then, the revolt of the Czechoslovakian and Yugoslavian students,
who were born in a socialist regime and of which more than half are children of workers and peasants? What do these children of laborers claim?
The same thing, approximately, that the French students claim, namely
the freedom of critique and self-determination ... To qualify as 'anarchic'
individuals who protest ... is to stick a poisonous label on a movement one
wants to harm because it is new, because it is authentically revolutionary, because it threatens old apparatuses. What the young revolutionaries
claim, bourgeois or not, is not anarchy, but, more precisely, democracy,
a true socialist democracy that has not failed anywhere. Finally, the last

151   Sartre 1972b, pp. 127–8.
152   Sartre 1974, p. 260.

argument: only the workers can make revolution. I respond that there is not one politicised student who has ever said something different.[153]

Sartre answers the PCF's argument (and the intellectuals who maintain it) point-by-point, emphasising the extreme doctrinal rigidity, which is also incapable of grasping the changes underway, and thus the spaces of subjectivation present in the situation. First, it is necessary to reiterate that Sartre's attempt is to rethink socialism beyond the socialism of the Soviet Union, thus valorising socialist experiments in Eastern Europe such as Czechoslovakia. It is interesting to note Sartre's valorisation in another text of the Basque struggles, which are capable of exemplifying '*another* socialism, decentralised and concrete: such is the singular universality [*universalité singulière*] of the Basque, whose E.T.A. justly opposes the abstract centralism of the oppressors'.[154] The stakes of socialism cannot be understood without fully taking on the centrality of the colonial question, as the path outlined in this chapter has emphasised.

I linger on a final point, which reprises the theme of the reciprocal interaction between the student and worker struggles. Indeed, for Sartre 'inventing the new' is supported by this *conatus*, and not at all by the attempt to substitute the working class with the emergence of new subjects, unrelated to the dimension of labour. In *Les bastilles de Raymond Aron*, a reckoning with an old friend, who became increasingly conservative, Sartre draws a balance sheet of classic positions on insurrection, and, naming Blanqui, Lenin, and Rosa Luxemburg, strongly leans in favor of the latter due to her capacity to outline the elements which remain productive for the practices of subjectivation in '68, on the basis of a dynamic relation between movement and organisation, and thus a rejection of a vertical structure.[155] Earlier Sartre also showed harmony with Luxemburg's approach, in a framework that was not distinguished by a full subsumption of class to party. Such an aspect returns in the interview with Rossana Rossanda and *il manifesto* in 1969, supported by the attempt to make the social and political movements interact, not eliminating the role of the party, but outlining a sort of soviet that is rooted in the concreteness of the labour dimension, according to an open relation between class and party.[156] Sartre valorises class not by hypostatisating it in ontological or sociological terms, but rather through a comprehension of its shadow

---

153   Sartre 1972a, pp. 201–2.
154   Sartre 1976b, p. 35.
155   Sartre 1972a, p. 180.
156   Cf. Sartre 2008c, pp. 135–7.

zones, and a connection with the specific practices in which it is realised: 'Consciousness is only born in struggle: class struggle only exists insofar as there exists places where an actual struggle is going on'.[157] We find an expansive dynamic, distinguished by a relation, never determined once and for all, between movement and institution: beyond Sartre's oscillations in this regard, the question of authority is not eliminated, but rather attempted to be considered in its adherence to the conflictual practices in which it is inscribed, on the basis of a *conatus* towards the freedom and equality of the workers' singularity.

Although there exist points of contact with the theorisation in *One Dimensional Man*, starting from the assumption of the element of freedom as liberation at the foundation of the argument (even with the difficulties that are observed, which I will return to in the next chapter), with respect to Marcuse, Sartre wants to specify that all is not lost, subsumed in the society of consumers, in which there unfolds

> a movement in which people have in common, if not an ideology, at least a will to break with the system in which they live, an awareness of the necessity of inventing new forms of struggle and counter-violence. But this also presupposes that this movement has the possibility, at least theoretically, to make revolution ... The weapon of the worker (the only one, but it is the absolute weapon) is the refusal to hand over his own product to society ... They threw themselves into action with an entirely new feeling of freedom, of inventiveness, but without always understanding what was happening.[158]

Such an 'invention of the new' constitutes one of the stakes, not lacking internal problems and contradictions, that would emerge in the following years. The perspective outlined is irreducible to a generically libertarian approach, instead trying to articulate collective freedom as an element that cannot result from the mere summation of individual freedoms, since in acting in common one tends towards a coimplication between the singular and universal dimensions, albeit according to unexpected and open coordinates.

> I think 1968 was a time when they became aware of freedom, only to lose that awareness again afterward. But that time was important and

---

157   Sartre 2008c, p. 123.
158   Sartre 1972a, pp. 214–15. On the relation between Sartre and Marcuse, cf. Fergnani 1978, pp. 257–70, who highlights both points of contact and distance.

beautiful, unreal and true. It was an action [*action*] by which the technicians, the workers, the living forces of the country became aware that collective freedom [*liberté collective*] was something other than the combination of all individual freedoms [*libertés individuelles*]. That was what 1968 amounted to.[159]

---

159   Beauvoir 1984, p. 360.

CHAPTER 7

The Invention Of The 'Singular Universal'

1   Open Problems

The theoretico-political path which Sartre charts out is complex and subject to a continuous conceptual rearticulation, but it always situates itself with a specific confrontation with the events of the time. In particular, the reference to 1968 is crucial: in many ways, the reflection on the dynamics of 1968 brings Sartre's work in the *Critique* and writings that followed, until the mid-70s, to fruition. I will make only cursory references to these latter texts for reasons that will emerge shortly, and will mostly keep a very important text, *The Family Idiot*, outside of my argument. That text is partially dislocated from the red thread of this book, but I will recall it in the final section of this chapter, insofar as it is especially important for understanding the notion of the 'singular universal'. Sartre's 1970s writings on the one hand are in continuity with earlier aspects of his work, while, on the other, seem to introduce new elements and with them a series of problems. In this regard it is necessary to recall two biographical facts. The first is that Sartre became almost totally blind in 1973, in addition to the other physical problems which were increasingly common for him. In this way, during the latter half of the 1970s Sartre found himself in a rather weakened condition, no longer able to study and write autonomously. The second fact is a consequence of this condition, as he worked in close contact with Maoists and ex-Maoists, above all Benny Lévy (also known under the pseudonym of Pierre Victor), who became his personal secretary until his death.

Earlier I made reference to the conversations between Sartre, Pierre Victor, and Philippe Gavi, published with the title *On a raison de se révolter*, which on the one hand are posed in continuity with the reflections of the 1960s, while also marking a distance taken from several aspects developed there, such as, for example, by means of a partial departure from Marxism. With respect to the *Critique*, which presented a critical movement against a 'certain' Marxism, for the sake of relaunching 'another' Marxism, in Sartre's comments here we observe an increasing departure from Marxism, such that the critique of the Soviet Union and the critique of Marxism are 'welded' together. The articulation of a 'true socialism' is further conceived, if not as a fracture, then at least as not fully in continuity with Marxism.

Such an approach, which was already present in *On a raison de se révolter*, will emerge still more clearly in the writings that followed it. Given the conditions, it is very difficult to establish how much this position was Sartre's and how much it was Benny Lévy's, as well as how much an increasingly physically weakened Sartre was strongly influenced by Benny Lévy. Elements of continuity with the earlier work remain, and again the typically Sartrean *conatus* of 'thinking against oneself' returns, not satisfied with the conclusions reached, but always looking to rearticulate the reasoning, even questioning the presuppositions that were accepted until that moment. But something different emerges than this framework, relative to the partnership with Benny Lévy. In my view, the influence of Lévy was deleterious. Earlier a neo-Maoist, Benny Lévy had by then assumed very ambiguous and problematic theoretico-political positions, and strongly connected with a sort of Jewish philosophy, which was also conditioned by Lévinas's thought (in 1997 he moved to Jerusalem, where he founded, together with Alain Finkielkraut and Bernard-Henri Lévy, the *Institut d'études lévinassiennes*). Unfortunately, partially due to his own errors and partially due a bit of a 'priestly' character he embodied in his role as an intellectual (with several blunders in the practical writings, but also some important initiatives: it is enough to think of the foundation of the newspaper *Libération* in 1973, for example), and partially due to growing physical problems, he attributed too much importance to Benny Lévy and trusted him too much.[1] In this regard, Simone de Beauvoir's judgment in *Adieux: A Farewell to Sartre* is quite interesting:

> Victor had changed a great deal since Sartre first met him. Like many other former Maoists he had turned toward God – the God of Israel, since he was a Jew. His view of the world had become spiritualistic and even religious. Sartre jibbed at this change of direction … Sartre had always thought it

---

1   For Sartre's judgment on Benny Lévy/Pierre Victor, see Sartre 1976b, p. 211: 'Pierre represented at the same time the radical theoretical activity and autonomy – independent from every indication of the party – and the political militant linked to mass concrete action. Now, you would tell me – and you would be right – that Pierre was a leader and that, for this reason, contradicted what I think we need to arrive at, namely a full equality between the members of a group – and beyond this – a society. Pierre … was the head of the *Gauche prolétarienne* and … exercised considerable authority over the group. An authority which he ended up realising was harmful. It is precisely one of the reasons why the ex-*Gauche prolétarienne* dissolved itself. We have had many discussions in this regard – as seen in *On a raison de se révolter* – and Pierre gradually came to my ideas, particularly about freedom and the rejection of hierarchies, all hierarchies, and the refusal of the notion itself of the leader'. Gaudeaux (2006, pp. 385–94, here p. 394) rightly emphasises the misleading interpretation of Sartre that Benny Lévy provides: 'While Pierre Victor certainly read Sartre, he did not understand him, because otherwise he would have changed and not used this language'. For an overall analysis of the relation between the two, see Repaire 2013 and Hanus 2013.

right to think against himself, but he never did so in order to sink into mere facility. This vague, yielding philosophy that Victor attributed to him did not suit Sartre at all ... He therefore turned to a substitute – Victor, a militant and a philosopher, would be the "new intellectual" of whom Sartre dreamed and whom he would have helped to bring into existence ... Sartre could no longer read. He could no longer reread what he had written. This, I believe, was very important. I am incapable of judging a text that I have not read myself. Sartre was like me.[2]

It is difficult to establish the contours of Sartre's thought in his final years, additionally because, with his blindness, he did not work or write autonomously. In this sense, it is necessary to trace two considerations on different levels. The first, which is philological, is that in these years it is indeed complicated to establish what belongs to Sartre and what does not, and thus what the borders are between Sartre and Benny Lévy. The second is whether the overall articulation, even with its opacity, is convincing, or if, rather, it creates more problems to resolve. To return to the first question, if it is admitted that there was not a coincidence between the two positions, the impression is that Benny Lévy tried to fully appropriate Sartre's thought, with a curious inversion of relations of force between the importance of Sartre's perspective and the instead rather irrelevant position of Benny Lévy, if not for the understanding of a certain intellectual climate, and a pathetic parable that involved some French ex-Maoists (namely Alain Finkielkraut and Bernard-Henri Lévy)[3] in the decades that followed.

One problem which underlies the strong distance between the two concerns Jewish philosophy. There is no doubt that the critique of antisemitism is constitutive of Sartre's discourse, and that *Anti-Semite and Jew* is a quite important text (despite having a series of limits, even with a still not really completed reelaboration of the rupture of Auschwitz), and also crucial for the sake of understanding the mechanisms of racism and colonialism. This element also returns in the *Critique* with reference to Stalin's antisemitism. Further, I highlighted earlier how this text constituted a guide-text for Fanon to articulate his own position. After this, Sartre valorised Israel, and took a position that was in many ways pro-Israel in the Israeli-Palestinian conflict. Or rather, on several occasions he claimed a sort of equidistance between the two nationalisms operative there, but, although taking account of the asymmetries between

---

2   Beauvoir 1984, pp. 119–20. See also Todd 1981.
3   Cf. Lévy 2000, which interprets Sartre's trajectory with a completely different approach than the one I have adopted in this book.

the two situations, in which one, Palestine, was (and is) deprived of a state, he nevertheless came to situate himself, in a rather problematic way, in closer proximity to Israel. One part of *Situations VIII, Autour de 68* is dedicated to the conflict in the Middle East.[4] This dedication finds its *ratio existendi* in the temporal proximity with the decisive events for the Middle Eastern conflict of 1967, but also in the fact that one of the reasons Sartre was critiqued by students in '68, who sympathised with Palestine, was because of his own position on Israel. This choice, which does not constitute the natural consequence of *Anti-Semite and Jew*, remains unchanged throughout his entire thematisation in the 1960s and 1970s.

But neither the critique of antisemitism nor the substantially supportive position towards Israel (even though these two elements are not immediately compatible) led Sartre to the articulation of a political messianism, and even less to a sort of overarching Jewish philosophy. The entire treatment lacks such elements. In this way the valorisation of messianism, within several writings – or better, conversations – during the final months of his life (such as, for example, *L'espoir maintenant*) that were elaborated together with Benny Lévy or mainly by him, appears substantially extraneous to Sartre.[5] Not only messianism, but any form of political Judaism remains far from Sartre's perspective. Indeed, the outline of a Jewish philosophy constitutes a radical negation of the central thesis of *Anti-Semite and Jew*, according to which it is antisemitism that makes the Jew: every 'essentialisation' of the Jew is completely dismissed. It is necessary however to focus on two other relevant theoretico-political knots addressed in Sartre's final years.

One key element is provided by the question of fraternity, which also finds its root in a valorisation of the ethical dimension that was operative earlier in his work without receiving systematic presentation.[6] In the late Sartre *fratern-*

---

4   Sartre 1972a, pp. 333–70. For example, see p. 335: 'I support a negotiated peace, both for political reasons and because I am a friend of the two parties in struggle … This means, therefore, from my point of view: 1) in one way or another, Israel must restore the territories it occupies; 2) Israel's sovereignty must be recognised; 3) that the problem of the Palestinians must immediately be the object of the next negotiations, since this question is decisive'. See also, several years later, Sartre 1974, p. 298: 'one cannot be pro-Palestinian without also being a bit pro-Israeli, as Victor is, and one cannot be pro-Israeli without being pro-Palestinian, as I am. And this position creates a strange situation'.

5   Cf. Sartre and Lévy 1980, which gathers articles that appeared in the *Le Nouvel Observateur*. On Judaism, see pp. 16–17, 71–81. For a different interpretation than I offer here, see Judaken 2006, pp. 208–39.

6   For a valorisation of ethics (or morality: there is not a clear differentiation between the two dimensions. In this sense Sartre is much different than Hegel), see Sartre 1974, pp. 118–19: 'For the Marxists morality is a superstructure. We must see if we can consider it in this way. For me

ité comes to play a decisive function, but on the basis of an attempt to establish a 'positive' sense, capable of going beyond the 'fusional' moment of insurrection. For example, in the *Critique* the notion of *fraternité* is presented as that element of commonality that allows freedom and equality to be kept together in the moment of common praxis. There is a coimplication between the singular and universal dimension, so that it does not seem that there is 'I' and 'you', and that individual and collective freedom refer reciprocally to one another. At least in the *exemplum* of the French Revolution, by the dynamic internal to such a notion it seems that, once the phase of the fused-group is passed, the only fraternity possible is constituted by the *fraternité-terreur*. It is true that, in the first part of the *Critique*, there is a regressive method, in which one starts from more abstract categories, similar to what Marx outlines in the critique of political economy. The scenario thus cannot be interpreted in terms of a temporal succession, and therefore an inevitable passage to fraternity-terror. But it is also true that the role of the event of the French Revolution is crucial for understanding the *Critique*, and thus the historical dimension in its concreteness is incomprehensible on a purely logico-categorial level. On the one hand, the centrality of fraternity, the 'forgotten' parable of the Revolution, emerges, while on the other we find an impasse at the moment in which we try to conceive it beyond the insurrectional practice, and thus as a concrete modality that 'stably' articulates the relations between individuals: a fraternity beyond fraternity-terror.

In the 1970s this kind of attempt to deconstruct but also reopen the discourse remained operative – an attempt to try and go beyond the approach outlined earlier, as well as to 'think against oneself', if necessary. But the modality with which fraternity is conceived in this period, with a very 'compositive' sense, influenced by Lévinas's notion of the Other, arouses more than a few doubts. In this sense, the element of revolution is subjected, particularly by Benny Lévy, to a critique that is both simplistic and politically ambiguous, reducing it to the domain of the idea of *Sujet-maître*, or rearticulating it on the basis of a sort of political Judaism. In the conversations between Sartre and Benny Lévy collected in *L'espoir maintenant*, the concept of fraternity takes on a key role: 'If ... I take society as being the result of a bond [*lien*] of people that's more basic than politics, then I take it that people should, can, or do entertain a certain primary relationship, which is that of fraternity [*fraternité*]'.[7] We find here the

---

moral systems are superstructures, but concrete, living morality is found at the level of production ... Marx himself has not posed the problem of morality, but in some way continuously speaks of it'.

7   Sartre and Lévy, 1996, p. 86.

risk of a sort of 'naturalism', in which *fraternité* constitutes a presupposition of the discourse, unchained from a historical and political analysis. In this way we return to several problematics (already highlighted at the level of the relation with Judaism) which clearly belong to Benny Lévy and remain at least doubtful as to whether Sartre really shared them. And, even if he really held such a position, it is a matter only of conversations, which, from various perspectives, go in directions at odds with his entire corpus, or that in any case give a reading of this work in extremely problematic terms. To take up the words of Simone de Beauvoir, 'how could [Benny Lévy] so weaken the notion of fraternity, so strong and firm in the *Critique of Dialectical Reason*? I let Sartre know the full extent of my disappointment. It surprised him. He had expected a certain amount of criticism, but not this radical opposition. I told him that the whole *Temps modernes* team was with me'.[8]

There remains another question, which in my view is more important (and to which I will return in the next section), that is synthesised with the title – *Pouvoir et liberté* – of a work that Sartre wanted to work on and which was later developed by Benny Lévy, albeit in a way not only provisional but even schematic, and posthumously published.[9] It is more of a collection of notes than completed text, containing reflections from 1975 through 1980, the fruit of a continuous confrontation between the two. For reasons analogous to what I have just indicated above, this creates more than a few uncertainties concerning the 'positive' articulation provided by the book – or rather, it is interesting on the deconstructive level, as an attempt to escape from an impasse (but in so doing creating another, still more problematic one!). Both of the notions in the title of the work necessitate a rearticulation. In the postwar period, the key element of Sartre's entire intellectual horizon, freedom, had become more focused. If in the earlier texts the risk of a sort of absolutisation of freedom existed, with the *Critique* there emerges the crucial and ineluctable role of the practico-inert, and therefore an objectivity that is run up against, and the collective dimension, with its lights and shadows, is increasingly important, putting any individualistic approach into question. The function of the concept of situation is emblematic from this perspective. Individuals are inserted within

---

8   Beauvoir 1984, p. 119.

9   Cf. Lévy 2007, a text that shows the effect of the conversations between Sartre and Benny Lévy in a period that goes from 1975 to 1980. Here there are present various elements that we also find in *L'espoir maintenant*, and particularly Judaism (also through the mediation of Lévinas) and a valorisation of fraternité connected to it. The political (or unpolitical) articulation of the discourse marks a strict distance from Marxism, including heterodox and 'heretical' Marxisms. In this regard see also Lévy 1984, which retraces Sartre's entire thought from this angle.

a situation and cannot ignore it, according to an inextricable weave between freedom and necessity. At the same time, it is an open problem whether, despite these considerations, there remains an *anarchisant* approach at the root, something in many ways congenial to 1968, namely the idea that freedom as liberation constitutes a sort of *primum* of the discourse.

With respect to freedom, the other side of the coin is represented by power. One risk which follows in many ways from a particular manner of conceiving freedom is that of the rejection of power, on the basis of a juxtaposition of movement with organisation and institution, as if these constituted an inevitable return to seriality. Earlier I emphasised that in the *Critique* the question is posed in more articulated terms. However, the difficulty highlighted here remains open, insofar as sometimes the theme of power seems to be too easily eluded, risking a substantial subordination to the disciplinary apparatuses of the state.[10] But, even after '68, there remains operative an attempt to outline the relation between movement and institution in a more generative way, seeing if it is possible to reactivate what the soviets 'named', despite an awareness that the event of the Bolshevik Revolution is not repeatable. It is a matter of interrogating in what terms the theme of individual and collective political subjects can be thought politically and historically, starting from their being situated.

2   **Beyond the 'Individual–Collective' Dualism: Rethinking Subjectivation**

The question of the 'singular universal' is crucial for the path we have taken, as it attempts to provide an emancipatory political articulation of Sartre's discourse. I will examine (and in several cases, take back up) such elements not so much in relation to the late writings, which were elaborated by Benny Lévy and to which Sartre's contribution is not always clear. Instead, I will look at the texts from the 1960s and early 1970s. The 'singular universal' can be considered a red thread of Sartre's entire conceptualisation. It permeates the entire structure of the *Critique*, distinguished by the attempt to keep two apparently incompatible elements together, namely the universality of history, which can never entirely

---

10   Cf. Fergnani 1978, p. 251: '[In *On a raison de se révolter*] *liberté retrouvée* is the possibility of conceiving a political struggle centered on the *déprise du pouvoir*, on the definitive dismissal of the concept of the militant-soldier ... it is an important, widely accepted analysis ... as a chapter of an increasingly open critique ... of the 'democratist' ideology of the citizen elector; it is less convincingly, instead, if considered from a historico-political angle'.

be understood, and which does not possess a linear character, and singularity, which is relative both to the subject and to the rooting in a conjuncture that is never fully 'subsumable' within a generalising rational schema. Two relatively brief texts are particularly significant in this regard: 'Merleau-Ponty *vivant*' (1961) and 'Kierkegaard: The Singular Universal' (1966).[11]

'Merleau-Ponty *vivant*', a tribute to a friend, with whom he entered into conflict for philosophical but above all political reasons, gives rise to the question of the singular universal in a vivid way.

> Trapped from within, [Merleau-Ponty's] life turned back upon itself to seize the advent of the human in all its singularity [*singularité*] ... Unlike Stendhal, he was not trying to understand the individual he was, but rather, in the manner of Montaigne, to understand the person, the incomparable mix of the particular and the universal.[12]

> To effect being is to consecrate it, which to be sure means to humanize it ... That suffices for man never to be the animal of a species, or the object of a universal concept, but rather, as soon as he appears, to be the explosion of an event ... Man will never think man. He makes him at every instant ... Man will never be the total object of knowledge, for he is the subject of history [*sujet de l'Histoire*].[13]

Various elements which are commented on throughout the text stand out in the distance as well as the proximity between the two philosophers, particularly the crucial nature of the event and the reading of the 'human' on this basis, a 'human' that can never be hypostasised, since it is rooted in concrete conditions, invoking the relation between subject and history.

> Severing our ties with our contemporaries, the bourgeoisie imprisons us within the cocoon of private life and defines us, with snips of the scissors, as individuals [*individus*], which means, as molecules without history who drag themselves from one instant to the next. In Merleau, we discover singularity [*singuliers*] through the contingency of our anchorage in nature and history, that is, through the temporal adventure which we are in the womb of the human adventure. Thus history makes us universal in the exact measure which we make it particular. This is the important gift

---

11   I have modified the translated title of this essay in order to preserve the reference to
      Sartre's expression 'the singular universal'.
12   Sartre 1998, p. 611.
13   Sartre 1998, p. 618.

which Merleau offers us, through his desperate struggle to keep digging in
the same place. Setting out from the well-known universality of the singular, he arrives at the singularity of the universal. It is he who unearthed
the capital contradiction: Every history is all history, when *l'homme-éclair*
is kindled, all is said. Every life, every moment, every era … are incarnations. The word becomes flesh, the universal is only established by the
living singularity which deforms it by singularizing it … But for Merleau,
universality is never universal, except in high-altitude thinking. It is born
along with the flesh, flesh of our flesh. It retains in its most subtle degree
our singularity. Such is the warning that anthropology – psychoanalysis
or Marxism – should never forget; nor, as do the Freudians too often, that
each man is everyman, and that in all men, we must take into account
the *flash of light*, the singular universalization of universality. Nor, should
we forget, as novice dialecticians, that the Soviet Union is not the simple
beginning of universal revolution, but its incarnation as well, and that 1917
gives future socialism its indelible characteristics.[14]

Here the fact emerges that despite the extremely strong polemic between the
two on a political level (above all after *The Communists and Peace*), the entire
treatment of the *Critique* is affected, not without dissonances, by an interaction
with Merleau-Ponty. In this regard we can refer to the critique of the bourgeois individualistic idea and the valorisation of singularity within the 'human
adventure', on the basis of a continuously reciprocal referral between singular and universal: 'the universal is only established by the living singularity'.[15]
Universality as such constitutes an abstraction, and thus must be incarnated
in singular situations. It does not constitute a given object, but rather an open
project.[16] The importance of mediations, in Sartre, manifests in the fact that
the concrete dialectic between universal and singular is only effective in the
specificity of situations, and thus the universal becomes singular through the
mediation of particularity. The entire reasoning on incarnation, as the embodiment of the forces present, plays a crucial function in this regard, and is affected

---

14   Sartre 1998, p. 622. On the close relation, despite strong dissonances, between singular-
      ity in Sartre and Merleau-Ponty, see Caeymaex 2005; Kirchmayr pp. 151–84 in Sartre 1999.
      On the basis of an interpretation marking the radical distance between the two, see Revel
      2015, particularly pp. 113–55.
15   Cf. Barot p. 77 in Sartre 2008b, who highlights the 'impossible realisation of the universal,
      "uni-totality", as universal': 'the universal only exists as singular (as individual, as event,
      etc.)'.
16   For a rearticulation of the question of singularity which does not reference Sartre but has
      much in common with the approach I have taken, see Lordon 2015, pp. 302–3.

by the confrontation-clash with Merleau-Ponty. Such a notion is connected to the modality with which the lived concrete, or the singular universal, can develop the set of totalisations underway or reexteriorise them. The *Critique*, and in particular its second part, would be incomprehensible without the reference to incarnation, constituting the Soviet Union as an incarnation of Marxism, and not one of its mystifications *sic et simpliciter*.

A number of these elements return with force in 'Kierkegaard: The Singular Universal', a text that arose from the attempt, already present in *Search for a Method*, to foster a strange connection between Marx and Kierkegaard, on the basis of a valorisation of the singular as an element that grasps the subject in its irreducibility to a generalising schema (contra Hegel), as well as in relation to the event. I have already taken into consideration this text in relation to the presence of a conception of history as not characterised by a linearity, but rather 'riddled with holes' [*trouée*].[17] The question of subjectivity emerges within such a jagged historical horizon:

> The subjective [*subjectif*] has to be what it is – a singular realization of each singularity ... And subjectivity [*subjectivité*] is temporalization itself: it is *what happens to me*, what cannot be but in happening. It is myself in so far as I can only be a random birth – and, as Merleau-Ponty said, in so far as I must, no matter how short my life, *at least* experience the occurrence of death.[18]

> Kierkegaard testified to a double universality. The revolution consisted in the fact that historical man, by his anchorage, turned this universality into a particular situation and this common necessity into an irreducible contingency. In other words, far from this particular attitude being, as in Hegel, a dialectical incarnation of the universal moment, the anchorage of the individual made this universal into an irreducible singularity [*singularité irréductible*].[19]

Here emerges a perspective that is in many ways harmonious with Kierkegaard and critical of the Hegelian dialectic, due to its 'encaging' of the singular dimension in the universal, and thus its neutralisation. Sartre's critical, open dialectic also distances itself from the Hegelian approach in its attempt to grasp singularity insofar as it is non-knowledge, in its reference to a lived experience

---

17   Sartre 2008c, p. 141. Translation modified.
18   Sartre 2008c, pp. 145–6.
19   Sartre 2008c, p. 156.

irreducible to rational transcription, on the basis of a non-homology between thought and reality. In the preface to *The Family Idiot*, Sartre claims:

> [W]hat, at this point in time, can we know about a man? ... [A] man is never an individual; it would be more fitting to call him a *singular universal*. Summed up and for this reason universalized by his epoch, he in turn resumes it by reproducing himself in it as singularity. Universal by the singular universality of human history, singular by the universalizing singularity of his projects, he requires simultaneous examination from both ends.[20]

The entirety of *The Family Idiot* could be conceived as an analysis of the Flaubert-singularity that universalises itself through the work of the author: Flaubert, conditioned by his familial context and the characteristics of his age, tried to go beyond these conditions, arriving at an impasse. In this sense, one can speak of subjectivation regarding Flaubert, insofar as his trajectory can seem 'nonpolitical', as well as insofar as Sartre criticises him for the fact that such practice concerns the imagination as a place of refuge from the *bêtise* of bourgeois life, to which moreover Flaubert himself is anyway internal.

At the same time, to return to 'Kierkegaard: The Singular Universal', Sartre reactivates Hegel versus Kierkegaard, since he provides a dialectical articulation of history: 'Kierkegaard demonstrated his historicity [*historialité*] but failed to find History [*Histoire*]. Pitting himself against Hegel, he occupied himself over-exclusively with transmitting his instituted contingency to the human adventure and, because of this, he neglected praxis, which is rationality'.[21] Here the movements of *Search for a Method* return, where Kierkegaard is 'used' against Hegel and Hegel against Kierkegaard. Sartre thus distinguishes between *Histoire*, for which Hegel's contribution is important in its comprehension, however unfinished, and *historialité*, which instead fits into a path relative to a singular human adventure, for which Kierkegaard's perspective is decisive. Such an approach resounds within the entire structure of the *Critique*, but also in earlier texts, such as *Truth and Existence*, with respect to the dimension of projectuality of the 'for itself', subject to *historialisation* within a historical trajectory. The attempt to keep the 'historical process', distinguished by 'transcendental necessity', together with 'historialisation' and its 'free immanence', returns here:

---

20   Sartre 1981a, p. xi. Translation modified.
21   Sartre 2008c, p. 168.

Kierkegaard is alive in his death in as much as he affirms the irreducible singularity of every man to the History which nevertheless conditions him rigorously ... Kierkegaard and Marx: these living-dead men condition our anchorage and institute themselves, now vanished, as our future. How can we conceive of History [*Histoire*] and the transhistorical [*transhistorique*] in such a way as to restore to the transcendent necessity of the historical process [*processus historique*] and to the free immanence of a historiciza-tion [*historialisation*] ceaselessly renewed, their full reality and reciprocal interiority, in theory and practice? In short, how can we discover the sin-gularity of the universal and the universalization of the singular, in each conjuncture, as indissolubly linked to each other?[22]

Such a reflection, which finds the 'singular universal' at its base through a weave of two figures apparently distant from each other such as Marx and Kierkegaard, tries to declare the relation between history and politics on the basis of their interweaving, but also by means of a 'gap', of their non-immediate coincidence. Sartre's entire trajectory is distinguished precisely by the presence of two polarities, one constituted by the universality of history, and the other by the singularity of political contingency. The concept of situation has a stra-tegic function in this regard, trying to keep objectivity and subjectivity, freedom and necessity, together, albeit on the basis of an instability, as testified to by the *inachevé* character of the *Critique*.

Within the analysis of the *Critique* and other texts of the 1960s and 1970s, the singular universal, and thus the attempt to think 'the singularity of the uni-versal and the universalisation of the singular', is presented in terms of the relation between exterior and interior, invoking the interiority of exteriority and the exteriority of interiority. There appear to be two polemical referents of the argument. The first is that of the centrality of interiority, which nat-urally finds enormous difficulties in articulating the relation with exteriority, and therefore also with politics: from this perspective, the interaction with any Marxist approach, even a reformulated one, is difficult if not impossible. Such primacy of interiority constitutes a risk that is anything but absent in Sartre, and indeed, in many ways can be imputed to several phases of his itinerary, both those before World War II (moreover, Sartre himself admitted that his interest in history and politics really only manifested with the war and the Res-istance), as well as the late years (which, however, are quite controversial and do not really present texts elaborated by Sartre). In the 'heart' of his political

---

22   Sartre 2008c, pp. 168–9.

thought, from the early 1950s to the late 1970s, in my view this centrality of interiority is, if not eroded, then at least subjected to a strong tension.

The second polemical reference is constituted by the primacy of exteriority, an element that directly regards Marxism, including its more heterodox versions, which according to Sartre contains the risk of not grasping the crucial nature of the relation between interiority and exteriority. Such a problem cannot be resolved by maintaining that the revolutionary act can *ipso facto* change interiority, as the dynamic following revolutions, and the serialising 'solidification' characterising it, testify. According to Sartre, both Lukács's idealism and, in a completely different manner, Lévi-Strauss's structuralism, present great difficulties in conceiving this relation other than in the sense of a 'crushing' of interiority by exteriority. Such dimensions, also considered in their obscure side, are also strongly highlighted by the investigation, not lacking Freudian traces, of *Anti-Semitism and Jew*: the Jew is exteriorly 'created' by the anti-semite, but at the same time, a subtle mechanism is operative, for which the Jew is driven to introject the gaze of the non-Jew onto himself. Sartre tries to articulate the nexus between subjectivity and objectivity by way of a reciprocity between the two elements, yet always starting from an outside: no longer in the sense of a subjectivity that can immediately overcome objectivity, as testified to by the importance of the practico-inert, with its objectivity, and the collective. Moreover, such a relation cannot be investigated abstractly, but rather by starting from a historically conditioned point of view. From the analysis of the *Critique*, what then stands out is the centrality of the totalisation-in-envelopment, connected to the processes of constitution of all temporalisations: it is a matter of a non-linear movement whose realised figures represent historically determinant moments, accounting for the multiplicity of singular totalisations, *rareté*, and the exteriority of matter.

Such a way of interpreting the relation between singularity and universality gives rise to the question of the role of the subject, and subjects, within history and its character of universality (which however can never be completely grasped), but also within the singular events in which it is found at work. In the framework of the *Critique* this problem is articulated through the relations between the constitutive dialectic, which is individual, and the constituted dialectic, which presents the different levels of the group, the social being, and institutions. The nexus between singularity and universality, if it is not conceived abstractly but rather on a level that is both historical and political (with the instability of such elements), cannot elude the theme of the relation between individual subject and collective subject. Sartre's attempts to go beyond the dichotomy between these elements, and therefore beyond the juxtaposition between individualism and organicism (or holism), trying to grasp what is 'between' individuals, intersubjectivity, understanding the latter, however, not in a compositive or harmonic way (which is moreover what he risked doing in his final years). There is no doubt that an echo of Husserl's intersubjectivity is present here, but, within Sartre's framework, which hinges on the notion of situation, the question takes on a substantially different meaning, since in Husserl the relational dimension risks being presented as a mere *petitio principii*. Thesis VI of the *Theses on Feuerbach* can also be reactivated, which conceives *Gattungswesen* by starting from the relation between individuals. Étienne Balibar declares the Marxian problem here in terms of transindividuality.[23] In my view, although this category is absent from Sartre's lexicon, it is adequate for noting the crucial nature of intersubjectivity in his political thought. But a further step needs to be taken. If one wishes to examine the concrete praxis of individuals beyond the dualism between individual and collective subject, through the overall historical process on the one hand, and in a singular conjuncture on the other, then the question of the relation between subjects and groups is decisive.

Among other things, it is noteworthy that Sartre's theorisation of the group is not really taken into consideration in the contemporary debate, insofar as it provides various important theoretical nuclei. I will limit myself to remarking on the importance of the phenomenological representation of the group, which is not a substance, nor a superorganism: the reference to this element has the task of describing political experiences, above all revolutionary and postrevolutionary ones. The group does not eliminate the plurality and concrete alterity of subjects: it is a matter of a sort of intersubjectivity that is totalised. Each subjectivity is made 'third' by the others, totalising their link. Each 'third' is posed between the group and the singular individual: there are many of us to carry out the totalisation through which the group is formed. In the hot phase of the 'fusion' the parts are not there prior to the whole. The revolutionary group does not *sic et simpliciter* constitute the natural outcome of the spontaneous belief of the proletariat. Its praxis is irreducible to either

---

23   Cf. Balibar 2007, which, by using thesis six of the *Theses on Feuerbach* that identifies human essence with the ensemble [*ensemble*] of human relations, valorises the Marxian 'ontology of relations': 'The words Marx uses reject *both* the individualist point of view ... *and* the organicist point of view ... Perhaps things would be clearer formally (though not in their content) if we, in our turn, added a word to the text ... The word does in fact exist, but is to be found in twentieth-century thinkers (Kojève, Simondon, Lacan): we have, in fact, to think humanity as a *transindividual* reality and, ultimately, to think transindividuality as such. Not what is ideally "in" each individual (as a form or substance), or what would serve, from outside, to classify that individual, but what exists *between individuals* by dint of their multiple interactions' (pp. 30–2).

Hegelian totality or structuralist totality. In order to rethink subjectivation it is necessary to always keep in mind that the group is a totalisation underway, always open, but at the same time in need of its 'condensation' that provides the presence of forms of authority, which are however not founded on a fixed hierarchy. Further, such an element can always dissolve itself into seriality: there is not a temporal succession between series and group, since the former never completely disappears.

Describing and rearticulating this Sartrean movement, André Gorz claims in *Le socialisme difficile* that

> groups are the constituent dialectical moments of the social (and not the constituted); they are specifically organised for social and historical action; they are the recovery of the necessity of freedom ... it must be possible ... that the unity of multiplicity, instead of being exterior and *undergone*, is interiorised and *produced* in all by each and in each by all through the production of a common object, a common action, in short of the necessity of freedom ... Each becomes the path of all towards all, and all the path of each towards themselves. The *necessity of freedom* is thus the praxis of the common individual that is reflected and recognised in the common praxis and common object, and that carries out the total-isation underway, and at the same time, felt as *required by this totalisation* carried out around him.[24]

In its connection with class, the group cannot be hypostatised from a sociological perspective, as it is rooted in the practical dimension. Common action, the fruit of common individuals (a possible reformulation of the Marxian social individuals), is presenting as an 'inventing the new', but also as a reactivation of several elements of the past, by means of a sort of 'invention and repetition', as emerges from the conference at the Gramsci Institute in 1961:

> [I]t is necessary that there is a constant aspect of subjectivity, and this aspect is repetition. It retotalises without stopping, therefore it is repeated without stopping ... Thus subjectivity appears here as a being of repeti-tion, but, at the same time, it is a being of invention ... The material of invention – if it can be put in this way – is subjectivity. We will never find, we will never discover human invention if it is considered as a pure praxis founded on a clear consciousness ... The repetition-invention in a given,

---

24   Gorz 1967, pp. 282–3

immediate relation which transcends being in exteriority is called projection. In other words, what is essential of subjectivity is knowing itself only from the outside of its own invention, and never within.[25]

This sense of invention permeates the subject, not moving at all in a 'consciousistic' direction by way of a unilateral valorisation of interiority: beyond any essentialism, the subject is given in the open, and unforeseen, dynamic of action. The element of class consciousness (also of Lukácsian derivation) is affected by this development: 'class consciousness has its own limits, which are the limits of the situation'.[26] 'So we see that, in the course of struggle, the subjective moment, as a mode of being internal to the objective moment, is absolutely indispensable to the dialectical development of social life and the historical process'.[27] The question of Sartre's humanism would be problematised from this point of view. This is not a matter of maintaining, with a gesture of provocation, that Sartre is instead an antihumanist, but rather of reiterating that such a pursuit can only be designated in part with the term 'humanism', and a specification of the characteristics of this often equivocal notion, or that it can be interpreted only by going beyond the dichotomy of 'humanism-antihumanism', at least in how it is often posed. Although there are oscillations before and after the text, in the *Critique* the question appears extremely controversial, as there is a radical critique of bourgeois humanism, and subjectivation has nothing essentialistic about it. In this regard Alain Badiou's observations in *The Century* are helpful. These comments are aimed at identifying points of distance but also, paradoxically, points of context between Sartre's radical humanism and Foucault's radical antihumanism. The question becomes particularly complex if it is interpreted in relation to the historically situated dimension of revolutionary practice:

> We could thus say: a certain twentieth century lets itself be identified, at its midpoint, around the fifties and sixties, by the confrontation between radical humanism and radical anti-humanism. As is the wont of the dialectical thinking of contradictions, there is a unity of the two conflicting orientations. That is because both of them treat this question: What becomes of man without God. And they are both programmatic ... Radical humanism and radical anti-humanism agree on the theme of Godless man as opening, possibility, programme of thought. That is why the

---

25   Sartre 2013, pp. 63–4.
26   Sartre 2013, p. 71.
27   Sartre 2013, p. 72.

two orientations will intersect in a number of situations, in particular in all the revolutionary episodes. In a certain sense the politics of the century, or revolutionary politics more generally, creates situations that are subjectively undecidable between radical humanism and radical anti-humanism.[28]

If we wanted to articulate a contemporary discourse on political subjects, avoiding both subjectivism and an objectivistic, deterministic closure of subjectivity, both a humanist and an antihumanist framework appear insufficient. Sartre does not understand subjectivity in opposition to objectivity. Moreover, subject and object, taken separately, do not have any sense. He attempts to grasp the objectivity of subjectivity, thus conceiving the subjective dimension by starting from objective elements. In the *Critique*, subjects appear as 'quasi-objects', acted on by events, against any 'Promethean' idea of subjectivity. In this sense, subjectivist existentialism, utilised (also by Sartre) as a kind of trademark, is actually, already with *Search for a Method*, conceived as a sort of ideology, subordinated in some way to Marxism. These observations support the idea that humanism and existentialism are not absent in Sartre, but such elements need to be problematised with respect to the simplified representation provided (and which Sartre himself contributed to spreading by publishing 'Existentialism is a Humanism', except perhaps insofar as he later regretted it). In any case, their role within Sartre's thought was greatly overestimated by interpreters.

Further, it helpful here to reinvoke Pierre Macherey's observations in *Le sujet des normes*, which we cited earlier. On the one hand, Macherey highlights the limits of the Althusserian conception of subjectivity, and on the other, by valorising Sartre's perspective, in referencing the analysis of colonialism, he emphasises that being black signifies nothing more (or less) than simply being subject: such a situation can only be understood in the context of the situation, with the dynamic of domination immanent to it.[29] According to Macherey, Sartre's ability to pose the question of subjectivation by starting from the concrete conditions of the situation (and not from an abstract subject) forcefully stands out, as he tries to restore the lived nature of an experience. Such elements, while not configured in objectivistic terms, derive from a determinate situation, insofar as it is a complex set of relations wherein subjectivity is grasped through objective factors. Although sometimes there remains in Sartre the risk of assuming

---

28   Badiou 2007, pp. 172–3.
29   Cf. Macherey 2014, pp. 80–1, as well as 105–6, 223–4.

human freedom as a sort of unfounded presupposition of the discourse, the notion of situation tries to keep freedom and necessity together on the basis of a weave in which necessity is certainly not downgraded to a subordinate role.

It is necessary to take back up the question of groups in their connection with the element of subjectivity. We find a sort of phenomenology of groups, on the basis of the attempt to hold open the reference to the plurality of situations and subjects, adhering to the material mechanisms of labour, and thus working out a continuous interaction with class dynamics. But such a position does not end up as a sort of pluralism. Moreover, one of Sartre's political critiques of Merleau-Ponty is precisely that of being pluralist, without grasping (or without wanting to grasp) that every plurality can only inevitably be traced back to a unity. Further, totalisation indicates precisely a movement of unification and dispersion together, in which the dimension of unity thus remains constitutive, but, precisely because it is totalisation, and not totality (and even less so totalitarianism), unity is never fully achieved, being crossed with centrifugal thrusts: from this perspective, there also emerges an element of differentiation. This perspective cannot be traced back to the Hobbesian domination of political unity, nor to a sort of valorisation of plurality versus unity. When reference is made to the group, often it is limited to the fused group, and therefore to the moment of insurrection, whose *exemplum* is the storming of the Bastille: 'fusion', however, does not represent the only figure of political action.[30] I do not intend to question here the fact that the common action of the fused group remains of central importance for the interpretation of Sartre's entire political thought. Despite its apparently abstract, categorial dimension (above all in part one), the *Critique* cannot be understood without two decisive historical events: the French Revolution and the Russian Revolution. Sartre's discourse is not aimed at a demolition (inevitably reactionary) of those two extraordinary practices of emancipation, despite their internal limits and the problems that derive from them, irreducible to misleading deviations. We find a critique of institutionalisation, which risks also becoming an 'ossification', with the return to a new seriality.

Two aspects of problematisation seem particularly important. The first is given by the idea of the non-repeatability of the model of revolution as the taking of power and in any case the dislocation of the revolutionary dynamic, in the twentieth century, with respect to the French Revolution, in many ways the 'mother of all revolutions' (as it was for Marx), and the Russian Revolution. The events examined in the last chapter are emblematic from this per-

---

30   Cf. Bourgault 2001, p. 225.

spective: beginning from the revolutionary situation outside of Europe, with particular reference to the Cuban Revolution, to the anticolonial struggles of the 'wretched of the earth', *in primis* in Algeria. 1968 constitutes a paradigmatic year in that sense, in the confluence of a multiplicity of subjects and practices, but on the basis of a rearticulation with respect to the idea of revolution as the taking of power and as an attempt to declare an emancipation that is not only linked to the revolutionary event but that tries to rethink everyday life and the social relations between subjects. We find a subjectivation founded on the 'interiority of exteriority' and the 'exteriority of interiority', always starting from an 'outside', with the lights and shadows of such a scenario, with the advancements on the level of workers' struggles, anticolonial struggles, students' struggles, but also with a series of limits and problems, among them the difficulty of creating a critique of power adequate to the constitution of organisational and institutional forms that 'condense' the practices of the fused group. We thus arrive at the second (and final) open problem.

With respect to the developments of the French Revolution and the Russian Revolution, the attempt is to declare politically the group in a way such that the institution is not configured under the banner of seriality. Within the *Critique*, Sartre highlights the necessity for the organised group to reorganise itself. The acting in common of the group, through the pledge, tries to produce a unity without negating the differentiation. The pledge is the culminating moment of revolution, with the constituent power that is at its base.[31] A crucial question is how to make the revolution last: for the group it is a matter of exorcising the relapse into inertia by conforming to an inertia created by itself, so to speak, of making it inert through acting on the inert. In the 1970s, the reference to the question of duration, while not finding a systematic treatment, comes into view with a certain frequency in Sartre's texts. The interesting aspect is provided by the attempt to open the space of revolutionary duration, trying to articulate a notion of institution in which the common element to singularities can find a political condensation. The difficulty is connected to the fact that, in the late reflections, the attempt at conceiving *fraternité* beyond the *fraternité-terreur* (for example) risks moving in a compositive and 'naturalistic' direction, presupposing a sort of originary fraternity-reciprocity. Beyond the *inachevé* character of the *Critique* and the impasse of Sartre's discourse in the final years, this problem remains open in today's situation, in the sense that the defeat of the Soviet Union and real socialism, despite the structural problems immanent to them, leaves open, and in many ways leaves outstanding,

---

31   Cf. Jameson 2004, p. 30.

such a *conatus* of emancipation. Moreover, it is interesting to note that in Marx the question of emancipation took on an extraordinary importance, as an element that is connected to the revolutionary event, as a capacity to sediment a different modality of conceiving social relations with respect to the present in the scenario subjected to critique: from the 'human emancipation' of 'On the Jewish Question' to the 'realm of freedom' in *Capital* Volume 3, such a tension towards the realisation of each and all continuously returns.

Sartre tries to establish several political coordinates in this sense. For example, in the interview with Rossana Rossanda and *il manifesto*, he valorises the search for a complex relation between unity and plurality, organisation and movement:

> What seems to me interesting in your schema is the duality of power which it foreshadows. This means an open and irreducible relation between the *unitary* moment, which falls to the political organization of the class, and the moments of self-government, the councils, the fused groups. I insist on that word "irreducible" because there can only be a permanent tension between the two moments. The party will always try, to the degree that it wants to see itself as "in the service" of the movement, to reduce it to its own schema of interpretation and development; while the moments of self-government will always try to project their living partiality upon the contradictory complex of the social tissue.[32]

Albeit with a series of difficulties, Sartre tried to politically articulate the invention of the new several times, even 'thinking against himself'. At the heart of the discourse we find the emancipation of subjects, 'quasi-objects' acted on by the event and aimed, according to different modalities, at giving duration to such common praxis: the question of the interiority of exteriority and the exteriority of interiority returns. Reviving *liberté, égalité, fraternité*, with and beyond the French Revolution, is finalised by opening new political spaces, which are condensed in daily practices, characterised by the attempt to radically change social relations against the 'sad passions' of the status quo. Such an attempt does not imply any 'newism' (the new is not identified with every element of innovation) and is not supported by the idea of a linear path or deprived of shadow zones and points where it does not 'take'. The stakes consist in interpreting the political scenario beyond the dichotomy between movement and institution and starting from the question of incarnation: the universal is real-

---

32   Sartre 2008c, p. 136.

ised under the form of singularity. It is necessary to insist on the fact that actions, both singular and common, with their interweaving of reason and passion, can sediment into customs, habits, and modes of life. In this regard it is generative to reactivate something from the eighteenth century, which vividly unfolded in 1789, on the basis of an 'inventive ambition that restored and instituted at the same time',[33] but also the Marxian tension towards an association distinguished by the coimplication between 'each' and 'all'. In Sartre, the very centrality of the question of totalisation insofar as it is connected to a dynamic condensation of the forces present, unification as well as dispersion, is irreducible both to a logic of totality and to the idea that social relations can unfold in an absolutely spontaneous way without interacting with the institutional dynamic. Such a perspective reveals itself to be complex and composite, while constantly traversed by a *conatus* of transformation both inside and outside of subjects.

---

33   With reference to the eighteenth century, see Starobinski 2006, p. 9.

Bibliography

Althusser, Louis 2003, *The Humanist Controversy and Other Essays, (1966–67)*, translated by G.M. Goshgarian, London: Verso.

Althusser, Louis 2005 [1965], *For Marx*, translated by Ben Brewster, London: Verso.

Althusser, Louis et al. 2015 [1965], *Reading Capital: The Complete Edition*, translated by Ben Brewster and David Fernbach, London, Verso.

Archard, David 1980, *Marxism and Existentialism: The Political Philosophy of Sartre and Merleau-Ponty*, Belfast: Blackstaff Press.

Arendt, Hannah 1951, *The Origins of Totalitarianism*, New York: Harcourt, Brace, and Co.

Aronson, Ronald 1987, *Sartre's Second Critique*, Chicago: University of Chicago Press.

Aronson, Ronald 1992, 'Sartre on Progress', in *The Cambridge Companion to Sartre*, edited by Christina Howells, Cambridge: Cambridge University Press.

Aronson, Ronald 1995, 'Sartre and Marxism', *Sartre Studies International*, 1: 34–44.

Baczko, Bronislaw 1974, *Rousseau. Solitude et communauté*, Paris: École Pratique des Hautes Études.

Baczko, Bronislaw 1999, *Giobbe amico mio: Promesse di felicità e fatalità del male*, translated by Paolo Virno, Rome: manifestolibri.

Badiou, Alain 1998, *Abrége de métapolitique*, Paris: Seuil.

Badiou, Alain 2011, 'Sartre et le marxisme', in *Sartre et la marxisme*, edited by Emmanuel Barot, Paris: La dispute.

Badiou, Alain 2007 [2005], *The Century*, translated by Alberto Toscano, London: Polity.

Balibar, Étienne 1997, *La crainte des masses: Politique et philosophie avant et après Marx*, Paris: Galilée.

Balibar, Étienne 2007 [1994], *The Philosophy of Marx*, translated by Chris Turner, London: Verso.

Balibar, Étienne 2014 [2010], *Equaliberty: Political Essays*, translated by James Ingram, Durham, NC: Duke University Press.

Balibar, Étienne and Immanuel Wallerstein 2011 [1988], *Race, Nation, Class: Ambiguous Identities*, translated by Chris Turner, London: Verso.

Barale, Massimo 1981, *Il tramonto del liberale: Sartre e la crisi della teoria politica*, Naples: Guida.

Barale, Massimo 1977, *Filosofia come esperienza trascendentale. Sartre*, Florence: Le Monnier.

Barnes, Hazel E. 1974 [1973], *Sartre*, London: Quartet Books.

Barnes, Hazel E. 1981, *Sartre & Flaubert*, Chicago: University of Chicago Press.

Barot, Emmanuel 2011, 'Aux racines de l'idéologie', in *Sartre et la marxisme*, edited by Emmanuel Barot, Paris: La Dispute.

Basso, Luca 2008, 'Ambivalenza della governance e dimensioni della soggettività', in *Governance: oltre lo Stato?*, edited by Giovanni Fiaschi, Soveria Mannelli: Rubbettino.

Basso, Luca 2009, 'The Ambivalence of "Gewalt" in Marx and Engels: On Balibar's Interpretation', *Historical Materialism*, 2: 215–36.

Basso, Luca 2012, *Marx and Singularity: From the Early Writings to the* Grundrisse, translated by Arianna Bove, Leiden: Brill.

Basso, Luca 2015, *Marx and the Common: From Capital to the Late Writings*, translated by David Broder, Leiden: Brill.

Basso, Luca 2017, 'Al di là della contrapposizione umanismo-antiumanismo: Soggettività e marxismo fra Sartre e Althusser', in *Sartre e il problema della soggettività. Intorno alla Conferenza di Roma del 1961, Bollettino Studi sartriani*, 11: 161–83.

Basso, Luca 2019, 'Sartre, Marx e il marxismo: A partire da *Questioni di metodo*', in *Sartre/Merleau-Ponty. Un dissidio produttivo*, edited by R. Kirchmayr and E. Lisciani Petrini, *aut aut*, 381: 149–72.

Bastid, Paul 1979 [1939]. *Sieyès et sa pensée*, Paris: Hachette.

Beauvoir, Simone de 1984 [1981], *Adieux: Farewell to Sartre*, translated by Patrick O'Brian, New York: Pantheon Books.

Birchall, Ian 2004, *Sartre Against Stalinism*, New York-Oxford: Berghahn Books.

Bourgault, Jean 2005, 'Repenser le corps politique', *Les Temps modernes*, 632–634: 477–505.

Bourgault, Jean 2011, 'Tours et detours de l'idéologie: Sartre et l'action politique', in *Lectures de Sartre*, edited by Philippe Cabestan and Jean-Pierre Zarader, Paris: Ellipses.

Bourgault, Jean 2011, 'Sartre et le maoïsme', in *Sartre et la marxisme*, edited by Emmanuel Barot, Paris: La dispute.

Bredin, Jean-Denis 1988, *Sieyès: La clé de la Révolution française*, Paris: Fallois.

Cabestan, Philippe 2011, 'Désir, besoin, et rareté', in *Lectures de Sartre*, edited by Philippe Cabestan and Jean-Pierre Zarader, Paris: Ellipses.

Cabestan, Philippe 2015, *Qui suis-je?: Sartre et la question du sujet*, Paris: Hermann.

Caeymaex, Florence 2005a, 'Praxis et inértie: La "Critique de la raison dialectique" au miroir de l'ontologie phénoménologique', in *Sartre: Violence et éthique*, edited by Gérard Wormser, Lyon: Sens publique.

Caeymaex, Florence 2005b, *Sartre, Merleau-Ponty, Bergson: Les phénoménologies existentialistes et leur héritage bergsonien*, Hildesheim-Zürich-New York: Olms.

Carney, John C. 2007, *Rethinking Sartre: A Political Reading*, Lanham-Boulder-New York: University Press of America.

Carpi, Guido 2015, 'Il marxismo russo e sovietico fino a Stalin', in *Storia del marxismo. 1. Socialdemocrazia, revisionismo, rivoluzione (1848–1945)*, edited by Stefano Petrucciani, Rome: Carocci.

Cera, Giovanni 1972, *Sartre tra ideologia e storia*, Rome-Bari: Laterza.

Certeau, Michel de 1997, *The Capture of Speech and Other Political Writings*, translated by Tom Conley, Minneapolis: University of Minnesota Press.

Césaire, Aimé 2000 [1955], *Discourse on Colonialism*, translated by Joan Pinkham, New York: Monthly Review Press.

Césaire, Aimé 2014, *Discorso sul colonialismo*, translated by L. Di Genio and edited by Miguel Mellino, Verona: Ombrecorte.

Charbonnier, Vincent 2011, 'Sartre et Lukács: des marxismes contradictoires?', in *Sartre et la marxisme*, edited by Emmanuel Barot, Paris: La dispute.

Cheyette, Bryan 2006, 'Fanon et Sartre: Noirs et Juifs', *Les Temps modernes*, 635–636: 159–74.

Chignola, Sandro and Giuseppe Duso 2008, *Storia dei concetti e filosofia politica*, Milan: Franco Angeli.

Chiodi, Pietro 1973 [1965], *Sartre e il marxismo*, Milan: Feltrinelli.

Contat, Michel 2008, *Pour Sartre*, Paris: Presses universitaires de France.

Contat, Michel and Michel Rybalka 1970, *Les écrits de Sartre*, Paris: Gallimard.

Coombes, Sam 2008, *The Early Sartre and Marxism*, Bern: Peter Lang.

Coorebyter, Vincent de 2001, 'Les boxeurs contre la cuisine anglaise: sens et totalisation dans la "Critique de la Raison dialectique" II', *Ecrits posthumes de Sartre, II*, edited by Juliette Simont, Paris: Vrin.

Cormann, Grégory 2015, 'Se récapituler au futur: Sartre et Fanon, l'enjeu d'une Préface', *Les Temps modernes*, 686: 105–34.

Dahlmann, Manfred 2013, *Freiheit und Souveränität: Kritik der Existenzphilosophie Jean-Paul Sartres*, Freiburg: Ça Ira.

Dardot, Pierre and Christian Laval 2012, *Marx, prénom: Karl*, Paris: Gallimard.

Darnell, Todd and Dennis Rohatyn 1992, 'Sartre's Debt to Rousseau', *Bulletin de la Société Américaine de Philosophie de Langue Française*, 4: 244–63.

D'Alessandro, Ruggero 2010, *La teoria e l'immaginazione: Sartre, Foucault, Deleuze e l'impegno politico 1968–1978*, Rome: Manifestolibri.

Delacampagne, Christian 2005, 'L'une des dernières philosophies de l'histoire', *Cités*, 22: 111–20.

Deleuze, Gilles 2004, *Desert Islands and Other Texts, 1953–1974*, translated by Mike Taormina and edited by David Lapoujade, New York: Semiotext(e).

Deleuze, Gilles and Félix Guattari 1983 [1972], *Anti-Oedipus: Capitalism and Schizophrenia*, translated by Robert Hurley, Mark Seem, and Helen R. Lane, Minneapolis: University of Minnesota Press.

Della Volpe, Galvano, 1964 [1956], *Rousseau e Marx e altri saggi di critica materialistica*, Rome: Riuniti.

Desan, Wilfrid 1965, *The Marxism of Jean-Paul Sartre*, New York: Anchor Books.

Di Leo, Rita. 2012, *L'esperimento profano: Dal capitalismo al socialismo e viceversa*, Rome: Ediesse.

Dobson, Andrew 1993, *Jean-Paul Sartre and the Politics of Reason*, Cambridge: Cambridge University Press.

Ducange, Jean-Numa 2011, 'Sartre et Guérin: débats et controverses sur la Révolution française', in *Sartre et la marxisme*, edited by Emmanuel Barot, Paris: La dispute.

Eksen, Gaye Cankaya 2017, *Spinoza et Sartre: De la politique des singularités à l'éthique de générosité*, Paris: Classiques Garnier.

Fanon, Frantz 2004 [1961], *The Wretched of the Earth*, translated by Richard Philcox, New York: Grove Press.

Fanon, Frantz 2008 [1952], *Black Skin, White Masks*, translated by Richard Philcox, New York: Grove Press.

Fergnani, Franco 1978, *La cosa umana: Esistenza e dialettica nella filosofia di Sartre*, Milan: Feltrinelli.

Fetscher, Iring 1988, 'Sartre und der Marxismus', in *Sartre: Ein Kongress*, edited by Traugott König, Hamburg: Rowohlt.

Fischbach, Franck 2011, 'L'aliénation comme réification', in *Sartre et la marxisme*, edited by Emmanuel Barot, Paris: La dispute.

Flynn, Thomas R. 1984, *Sartre and Marxist Existentialism: The Test Case of Collective Responsibility*, Chicago: University of Chicago Press.

Flynn, Thomas R. 2006, 'Marxisme existentialiste ou existentialisme marxiste?', in *Sartre: le philosophe, l'intellectuel et la politique*, edited by Arno Münster and Jean-William Wallet, Paris: L'Harmattan.

Flynn, Thomas R. 2014, *Sartre: A Philosophical Biography*, Cambridge: Cambridge University Press.

Gaudeaux, Jean-François 2005, 'Sartre et la violence', in *Sartre. Violence et éthique*, edited by Gérard Wormser, Lyon: Sens publique.

Gaudeaux, Jean-François 2006, *Sartre, l'aventure de l'engagement*, Paris: L'Harmattan.

Goldschmidt, Victor 1983, *Anthropologie et politique: Les principes du système de Rousseau*, Paris: Vrin.

Gomez-Muller, Alfredo 2006, 'Sartre et le colonialisme: la critique de l'universalité abstraite', in *Sartre et la culture de l'autre*, edited by Alfredo Gomez-Muller, Paris: L'Harmattan.

Gorz, André 1960, *La morale della storia*, translated by Jone Graziani, Milan: il Saggiatore.

Gorz, André 1967, *Le socialisme difficile*, Paris: Seuil.

Gorz, André 1977, *Fondements pour une morale*, Paris: Galilée.

Gray, Kevin W. 2006, 'The Influence of the Hungarian Revolution on the "Critique of Dialectical Reason"', in *Sartre: le philosophe, l'intellectuel et la politique*, edited by Arno Münster and Jean-William Wallet, Paris: L'Harmattan.

Guha, Ranajit and Gayatri Chakravorty Spivak 1988 (eds.), *Selected Subaltern Studies*, Oxford: Oxford University Press.

Guigot, André 2001, *L'ontologie politique de Jean-Paul Sartre*, Lille: Presses universitaires du Septentrion.

Guigot, André, 2007, *Sartre. Liberté et histoire*, Paris: Vrin.

Hanus, Gilles 2013, *Penser à deux? Sartre et Benny Lévy face à face*, Lausanne-Paris: L'Âge d'homme.

Hartmann, Klaus 1966, *Sartre's Sozialphilosophie*, Berlin: de Gruyter.

Haug, Wolfgang Fritz 1976, *Kritik des Absurdismus*, Köln: Pahl-Rugenstein Verlag.

Hegel, G.W.F. 1977 [1807], *Phenomenology of Spirit*, translated by A.V. Miller, Oxford: Oxford University Press.

Heidegger, Martin 2008 [1977]. *Basic Writings*, translated and edited by David Ferrell Krell, New York: HarperCollins.

Heller, Agnes 2018 [1974], *The Theory of Need in Marx*, translated by Stephen Bodington and Ken Coates, London: Verso.

Hobsbawm, Eric 1995 [1994], *The Age of Extremes: The Short Twentieth Century 1914–1991*, London: Abacus.

Holz, Hans Heinz 1951, *Jean-Paul Sartre: Darstellung und Kritik seiner Philosophie*, Meisenheim/Glan: Westkulturverlag.

Howells, Christina, 1988, *Sartre: The Necessity of Freedom*, Cambridge: Cambridge University Press.

Hulliung, Mark 2013, *Sartre and Clio: Encounters with History*, Boulder-London: Paradigm Publishers.

Husson, Laurent 2011, 'Sartre et Lefebvre: aliénation et quotidienneté', in *Sartre et la marxisme*, edited by Emmanuel Barot, Paris: La dispute.

Ireland, John 2009, ' "Ouragan sur le sucre": Sartre, Castro et la révolution cubaine', *Les Temps modernes*, 656: 9–37.

James, C.L.R. 1963 [1938], *The Black Jacobins: Toussaint L'Ouverture and the San Domingo Revolution*, New York: Vintage Books.

Jameson, Frederic 1971, *Marxism and Form*, Princeton: Princeton University Press.

Jameson, Frederic 2004, 'Entre structure et évenement: le groupe', in *Sartre, Lukács, Althusser*, edited by Stathis Kouvélakis and Vincent Charbonnier, Paris: Presses universitaires de France.

Jameson, Frederic 2014, 'Sartre's Actuality', *New Left Review*, 88: 113–19.

Jay, Martin 1984, *Marxism and Totality: The Adventures of a Concept from Lukács to Habermas*, Berkeley, CA: University of California Press.

Jeanson, Francis 1947, *Le problème morale et la pensée de Sartre*, Paris: Le Seuil.

Judaken, Jonathan 2006, *Jean-Paul Sartre and the Jewish Question: Anti-antisemitism and the Politics of the French Intellectual*, Lincoln: University of Nebraska Press.

Kelly, Michael 1999, 'Towards a Heuristic Method: Sartre and Lefebvre', *Sartre Studies International*, 1: 1–15.

Kirchmayr, Raoul 2005, 'L'enveloppement: Sartre et la pensée de la singularité dans la

"Critique de la raison dialectique" II', in *Sartre. Violence et éthique*, edited by Gérard Wormser, Lyon: Sens publique.

Knee, Philip 1983, 'Solitude et sociabilité: Rousseau et Sartre', *Dialogue*, 26: 419–36.

Koch-Oehmen, Reinhard 1988, *Lukács und Sartre: Zum Verhältnis von Bürgerlicher Gesellschaft und Sozialphilosophie des westlichen Marxismus*, Hamburg: Argument.

Koselleck, Reinhardt 2004 [1979], *Futures Past: On the Semantics of Historical Time*, translated by Keith Tribe, New York: Columbia University Press.

Krieger, Leonard 2005, 'Histoire et existentialisme chez Sartre', *Cités*, 22: 155–82.

Lawler, James 1976, *The Existentialist Marxism of Jean-Paul Sartre*, Amsterdam: B.R. Grüner.

Lefebvre, Henri 1968a, *La droit à la ville*, Paris: Anthropos.

Lefebvre, Henri 1968b, *L'irruption de Nanterre au sommet*, Paris: Anthropos.

Leguil, Clotilde 2012. *Sartre avec Lacan: Corrélation antinomique, liason dangereuse*, Paris: Navarin-Le Champ Freudien.

Lévi-Strauss, Claude 1966 [1962], *The Savage Mind*, Chicago: University of Chicago Press.

Lévy, Benny 1984, *Le nom de l'homme. Dialogue avec Sartre*, Lagrasse: Verdier.

Lévy, Benny 2007, *Pouvoir et liberté*, edited by Gilles Hanus, Lagrasse: Verdier.

Louette, Jean-François 2009, *Traces de Sartre*, Grenoble: Ellug.

Macherey, Pierre 2014, *Le sujet des normes*, Paris: Éditions Amsterdam.

Marx, Karl 1964 [1850], *Class Struggles in France, 1848–1850*, New York: International Publishers.

Marx, Karl 1978 [1972], *The Marx-Engels Reader*, edited by Robert C. Tucker, New York: W.W. Norton & Company.

Marx, Karl 1990 [1867], *Capital: A Critique of Political Economy Volume 1*, translated by Ben Fowkes, London: Penguin.

Marx, Karl 1993 [1939], *Grundrisse: Foundations of the Critique of Political Economy (Rough Draft)*, translated by Martin Nicolaus, London: Penguin.

Mayer, Matthias 2006, *Ohnmächtige Ethik. Psychoanalyse und Marxismus bei Jean-Paul Sartre*, Göttingen: Cuvillier.

Mazauric, Claude 2010, 'Sartre et l'histoire de la Révolution française', *Études sartriennes*, 14: 99–123.

McBride, William 1991, *Sartre's Political Theory*, Bloomington: Indiana University Press.

Merleau-Ponty, Maurice 1955, *Les aventures de la dialectique*, Paris: Gallimard.

Merleau-Ponty, Maurice 1969 [1947], *Humanism and Terror: An Essay on the Communist Problem*, translated by John O'Neill, Boston: Beacon Press.

Mészàros, Ivan 1979, *The Work of Sartre: Search for Freedom*, Brighton: Harvester Press.

Moravia, Sergio 2004 [1973], *Introduzione a Sartre*, Rome-Bari: Laterza.

Mudimbe, Valentin Y. 1988, *The Invention of Africa: Gnosis, Philosophy, and the Order of Knowledge*, Bloomington: Indiana University Press.

Münster, Arno 2007, *Sartre et la morale*, Paris: L'Harmattan.

Münster, Arno 2005, *Sartre et la praxis: Ontologie de la liberté et praxis dans la pensée de Jean-Paul Sartre*, Paris: L'Harmattan

Murdoch, Iris 1987 [1953], *Sartre, Romantic Rationalist*, New Haven: Yale University Press.

Murphy, Jay 1996, 'Sartre on Cuba Revisited', *Sartre Studies International*, 2: 27–48.

Nancy, Jean-Luc 1993 [1988], *The Experience of Freedom*, translated by Bridget McDonald, Stanford: Stanford University Press.

Negri, Antonio 1999 [1992], *Insurgencies: Constituent Power and the Modern State*, translated by Maurizia Boscagli, Minneapolis: University of Minnesota Press.

Neudeck, Rupert 1975, *Die politische Ethik bei Jean-Paul Sartre und Albert Camus*, Bonn: Bouvier.

Noudelmann, François 1993, 'Sartre et l'inhumain', *Les Temps modernes*, 565–566: 48–65.

Noudelmann, François 1996, *Sartre: L'incarnation imaginaire*, Paris: L'Harmattan.

O'Donohoe, Benedict 2013, 'Roquentin and the Autodidact: The Critique of Humanism in "La nausé"', in *Severally Seeking Sartre*, edited by Benedict O'Donohoe, Newcastle upon Tyne: Cambridge Scholars Publishing.

Oulc'hen, Hervé 2014, *Sartre et le colonialisme: La critique d'un système*, Paris: La Digitale.

Paci, Enzo 1988 [1950], *Il nulla e il problema dell'uomo*, Milan: Bompiani.

Philonenko, Alexis 1981, 'Liberté et mauvaise foi chez Sartre', *Revue de Métaphysique et de Morale*, 86, 2: 145–63

Polin, Raymond 1971, *La politique de la solitude: Essai sur J.-J. Rousseau*, Paris: Sirey.

Poster, Mark 1975, *Existential Marxism in Postwar France: From Sartre to Althusser*, Princeton: Princeton University Press.

Rademacher, Lee M. 2002, *Structuralism vs. Humanism in the Formation of the Political Self: The Philosophy of Politics of Jean-Paul Sartre and Louis Althusser*, Lewiston: Edwin Mellen Press.

Raimondi, Fabio 2011, *Il custode del vuoto: Contingenza e ideologia nel materialismo radicale di Louis Althusser*, Verona: Ombrecorte.

Rametta, Gaetano 2009, 'Sartre e l'interpretazione dialettica della rivoluzione', *Etica & Politica*, 2: 371–98.

Rancière, Jacques 2001 [1974], *Althusser's Lesson*, translated by Emiliano Battista, London: Continuum.

Renaut, Alain 1993, *Sartre, le dernie philosophe*, Paris: Grasset.

Repaire, Sébastien 2013, *Sartre et Benny Lévy: Une amitié intellectuelle, du maoïsme triomphant au crépuscle de la révolution*, Paris: L'Harmattan.

Revel, Judith 2015, *Foucault avec Merleau-Ponty: Ontologie politique, présentisme et histoire*, Paris: Vrin.

Richter, Mathias 2011, *Freiheit und Macht: Perspektiven kritischer Gesellschaftstheorie – der Humanismusstreit zwischen Sartre und Foucault*, Bielefeld: Transcript.

Rizk, Hadi 2006, 'La Révolution française das la "Critique de la Raison Dialectique"', *Études sartriennes*, 11: 169–83.

Rizk, Hadi 2011, *Comprendre Sartre*, Paris: Armand Colin.

Rizk, Hadi 2014, *Individus et multiplicités: Essai sur les ensembles pratiques dans la "Critique de la Raison Dialectique"*, Paris: Kimé.

Roth, Karl Heinz 1974, *Die "andere" Arbeiterbewegung und die Entwicklung der kapitalistischen Repression von 1880 bis zur Gegenwart*, München: Trikont.

Rousseau, Jean-Jacques 1979 [1762], *Emile, or On Education*, translated by Allan Bloom, New York: Basic Books.

Rousseau, Jean-Jacques 1997 [1761], *Julie, or the new Heloise*, translated by Philip Stewart and Jean Vaché, Dartmouth, NH: Dartmouth College Press.

Rousseau, Jean-Jacques 2002 [1762], *The Social Contract and The First and Second Discourses*, edited by Susan Dunn, New Haven: Yale University Press.

Rovatti, Pier Aldo 1969, *Che cosa ha veramente detto Sartre*, Rome: Ubaldini.

Sartre, Jean-Paul 1946, 'Materialisme et revolution', in *Situations, II* [new ed.], Paris: Gallimard.

Sartre, Jean-Paul 1947 [1945], 'La liberté cartésienne', in *Situations, I*, Paris: Gallimard.

Sartre, Jean-Paul 1948 [1946], *Anti-Semite and Jew*, translated by George J. Becker, New York: Schocken Books.

Sartre, Jean-Paul 1950 [1964], 'Faux savants ou faux lièvres', in *Situations, VI: Problèmes du marxisme, 1*, Paris: Gallimard.

Sartre, Jean-Paul 1955, *Literary and Philosophical Essays*, translated by Annette Michelson, New York: Criterion Books.

Sartre, Jean-Paul 1960a, *The Devil & the Good Lord and Two Other Plays*, translated by Kitty Black, New York: Vintage Books.

Sartre, Jean-Paul 1960b, 'Ideología y revolución', in *Sartre visita a Cuba*, La Habana: Ediciones Revolución.

Sartre, Jean-Paul 1960c, 'M. Jean-Paul Sartre dresse un parallèle entre Cuba et l'Algérie', *La Monde*, 1 September 1960.

Sartre, Jean-Paul 1963 [1957], *Search for a Method*, translated by Hazel E. Barnes, New York: Alfred A. Knopf.

Sartre, Jean-Paul 1964, *Situations, IV: Portraits*, Paris: Gallimard.

Sartre, Jean-Paul 1964–1965 [1948], 'Black Orpheus', translated by John MacCombie, *The Massachusetts Review*, 6, 1: 13–52.

Sartre, Jean-Paul 1966, *Morale e società: Atti del Convegno di Roma Organizzato dall'Istituto Gramsci*, Rome: Riuniti.

Sartre, Jean-Paul 1968a [1952–1954], *The Communists and Peace with A Reply to Claude Lefort*, translated by Martha H. Fletcher and John R. Kleinschmidt, New York: George Braziller.

Sartre, Jean-Paul 1968b [1956–1957], *The Ghost of Stalin*, translated by Martha H. Fletcher and John R. Kleinschmidt, New York: George Braziller.

Sartre, Jean-Paul 1972a, *Situations, VIII: Autour de 68*, Paris: Gallimard.

Sartre, Jean-Paul 1972b, *Situations, IX: Mélanges*, Paris: Gallimard.

Sartre, Jean-Paul 1973 [1961], 'Soggettività e marxismo,' *aut aut*, 136–137: 131–51.

Sartre, Jean-Paul 1973b [1949], *Troubled Sleep*, translated by Gerard Hopkins, New York: Vintage Books.

Sartre, Jean-Paul 1974, *On a raison de se révolter: Discussions*, Paris: Gallimard.

Sartre, Jean-Paul 1976a, *No Exit and Three Other Plays*, translated by Stuart Gilbert, New York: Vintage International.

Sartre, Jean-Paul 1976b, *Situations, X: Politique et autobiographie*, Paris: Gallimard.

Sartre, Jean-Paul 1977, *Sartre: Un film réalisé par Alexandre Astruc et Michel Contat*, Paris: Gallimard.

Sartre, Jean-Paul 1981a [1971], *The Family Idiot: Gustave Flaubert 1821–1857 Volume 1*, translated by Carol Cosman, Chicago: University of Chicago Press.

Sartre, Jean-Paul 1981b, *Oeuvres romanesques*, Paris: Gallimard.

Sartre, Jean-Paul 1988 [1948], *"What is Literature?" and Other Essays*, Cambridge. MA: Harvard University Press.

Sartre, Jean-Paul 1991a [1985], *Critique of Dialectical Reason Volume 2: The Intelligibility of History*, translated by Quintin Hoare and edited by Arlette Elkaïm-Sartre, London: Verso.

Sartre, Jean-Paul 1991b, *Esistenzialismo e marxismo: La conferenza di Araquara*, translated by Nicola Badaloni, Catanzaro: Abramo.

Sartre, Jean-Paul 1992a [1943], *Being and Nothingness: A Phenomenological Essay on Ontology*, translated by Hazel E. Barnes, New York: Washington Square Press.

Sartre, Jean-Paul 1992b [1983], *Notebooks for an Ethics*, translated by David Pellauer, Chicago: University of Chicago Press.

Sartre, Jean-Paul 1992c [1989], *Truth and Existence*, translated by Adrian van den Hoven and edited by Ronald Aronson, Chicago: University of Chicago Press.

Sartre, Jean-Paul 1993, 'La Conférence de Rome, 1961: Marxisme et subjectivité', *Les Temps modernes*, 560: 11–39.

Sartre, Jean-Paul 1998, 'Merleau-Ponty *vivant*', translated by Benita Eisher, in *The Debate Between Sartre and Merleau-Ponty*, edited by Jon Stewart, Evanston, IL: Northwestern University Press.

Sartre, Jean-Paul 1999, *Merleau-Ponty*, edited by Raoul Kirchmayr, Milan: Raffaello Cortina.

Sartre, Jean-Paul 2001 [1964], *Colonialism and Neocolonialism*, translated by Azzedine Haddour, Steve Brewer, and Terry McWilliams, London: Routledge.

Sartre, Jean-Paul 2004a [1960], *Critique of Dialectical Reason Volume 1: Theory of Practical Ensembles*, translated by Alan Sheridan-Smith, London: Verso.

Sartre, Jean-Paul 2004b [1936], *The Transcendence of the Ego: A Sketch for a Phenomen-ological Description*, translated by Andrew Brown, London: Routledge.

Sartre, Jean-Paul 2005a, 'Morale et Histoire (1964–1965)', *Les Temps modernes*, 632–633–634: 268–414.

Sartre, Jean-Paul 2005b [1961], *Visita a Cuba: Reportage sulla Rivoluzione cubana e sull'incontro con Che Guevara*, Bolsena: Massari.

Sartre, Jean-Paul 2006 [1985], *L'intelligibilità della storia: Critica della Ragione dialettica II*, translated and edited by Florinda Cambria, Milan: Marinotti.

Sartre, Jean-Paul 2007 [1946], *Existentialism is a Humanism*, translated by Carol Macomber, New Haven: Yale University Press.

Sartre, Jean-Paul 2008a [1951–1952], 'Liberté-Égalité: Manuscrit sur la genèse de l'idéo-logie bourgeoise', *Études sartriennes*, 12: 165–256.

Sartre, Jean-Paul 2008b [1950–1951], 'Mai-juin 1789: Manuscrit sur la naissance de l'Assemblée nationale', *Études sartriennes*, 12: 19–154.

Sartre, Jean-Paul 2008c [1974], *Between Existentialism and Marxism*, translated by John Matthews, London: Verso.

Sartre, Jean-Paul 2009, *L'universale singolare: Saggi filosofici e politici 1965–1973*, trans-lated by Raoul Kirchmayr, Milan-Udine: Mimesis.

Sartre, Jean-Paul 2012 [1952], *Saint Genet: Actor and Martyr*, translated by Bernard Frechtman, Minneapolis: University of Minnesota Press.

Sartre, Jean-Paul 2013, 'Marxisme et subjectivité (1961)', in *Qu'est-ce que la subjectivité?*, edited by Michel Kail and Raoul Kirchmayr, Paris: Les Prairies ordinaires.

Sartre, Jean-Paul 2013b [1938], *Nausea*, translated by Richard Howard, New York: New Directions Books.

Sartre, Jean-Paul 2013c, *We Have Only This Life to Live: The Selected Essays of Jean-Paul Sartre, 1939–1975*, edited by Ronald Aronson and Adrian van den Hoven, New York: The New York Review of Books.

Sartre, Jean-Paul 2015a, 'Les racines de l'éthique: Conférence à l'Institut Gramsci, mai 1964', *Études sartriennes*, 19: 11–118.

Sartre, Jean-Paul 2015b, *Marxismo e soggettività. La conferenza di Roma del 1961*, edited by Raoul Kirchmayr, Milan: Marinotti.

Sartre, Jean-Paul 2016 [2013], *What is Subjectivity?*, translated by David Broder and Trista Selous, London: Verso.

Sartre, Jean-Paul and Benny Lévy 1991 [1980], *L'espoir maintenant: Les entriens de 1980*, Lagrasse: Verdier.

Sartre, Jean-Paul and Benny Lévy 1996, *Hope Now: The 1980 Interviews*, translated by Adrian van den Hoven, Chicago: University of Chicago Press.

Scanzio, Fabrizio 2000, *Sartre et la morale: La réflexion sartrienne sur la morale de 1939 à 1952*, Naples: Vivarium.

Schaff, Adam 1965, *Marx oder Sartre?: Versuch einer Philosophie des Menschen*, Berlin: VEB Deutscher Verlag der Wissenschaften.

Schwarz, Theodor 1976, *Jean-Paul Sartre et le marxisme*, Lausanne: L'Age d'homme.

Scuccimarra, Luca 2002, *La sciabola di Sieyès: le giornate di brumaio e la genesi del regime bonapartista*, Bologna: il Mulino.

Sherman, David 2007, *Sartre and Adorno: The Dialectics of Subjectivity*, New York: State University of New York Press.

Sieyès, Emmanuel Joseph 1993 [1789], 'Qu'est-ce que le Tiers Etat', in *Opere e testimonianze politiche Tomo 1, Scritti editi*, translated by Giovanna Troisi Spagnoli and edited by Roberto Zapperi, Milan: Giuffré.

Silbertin-Blanc, Guillaume 2009, 'L'effet anti-humaniste de l'existentialisme dans le marxisme', *Études sartriennes*, 13: 55–92.

Simont, Juliette 1998, *Jean-Paul Sartre: Un demi-siècle de liberté*, Paris: De Boeck Université.

Simont, Juliette 2001, 'Sartre et la question de l'historicité: Réflexions au-delà d'un procès', *Les Temps modernes*, 613: 109–30.

Sirinelli, Jean-François 1995, *Deux intellectuels dans le siècle, Sartre et Aron*, Paris: Fayard.

Starobinski, Jean 1971 [1957], *Jean-Jacques Rousseau: la transparence et l'obstacle: Suivi de sept essais sur Rousseau*, Paris: Gallimard.

Starobinski, Jean 2006 [1964], *L'invention de la liberté: 1700–1789*. Paris: Gallimard.

Todd, Olivier 1981, *Un fils rebelle*, Paris: Grasset.

Traverso, Enzo 2002, 'Il genocidio invisibile: Le "Réflexions sur la question juive" de Jean-Paul Sartre', in *Bataille-Sartre: un dialogo incompiuto*, edited by Jacqueline Risset, Rome: Artemide.

Traverso, Enzo 2014, *Che fine hanno fatto gli intellettuali?*, translated by G. Morosato, Verona: Ombrecorte.

Tronti, Mario 2015, *Dello spirito libero. Frammenti di vita e di pensiero*, Milan: Il Saggiatore.

Valentini, Francesco 1959, 'Sartre e il marxismo', *Aut Aut*, 51: 189–94.

Vassallo, Sara 2003, *Sartre et Lacan: Le verbe être, entre concept et fantasme*, Paris: L'Harmattan.

Védrine, Hélène 2005, 'Paradoxes et difficultés d'une théorie de l'histoire chez Sartre', in *Sartre. Violence et éthique*, edited by Gérard Wormser, Lyon: Sens publique.

Verstraeten, Pierre 1972, *Violence et éthique: Esquisse d'une critique de la morale dialectique à partir du théâtre politique de Sartre*, Paris: Gallimard.

Verstraeten, Pierre 2008, *L'Anti-Aron*, Paris: Éditions de la Différence.

Virno, Paolo 1999, *Il ricordo del presente: Saggio sul tempo storico*, Turin: Bollati Boringhieri.

Visentin, Stefano 2013, 'Trasformazioni della "Verwandlung"', in *Fanon postcoloniale: I dannati della terra oggi*, edited by Miguel Mellino, Verona: Ombrecorte.

Webber, Jonathan 2009, *The Existentialism of Jean-Paul Sartre*, London: Routledge.

Weismüller, Christoph 2004, *Zwischen analytischer und dialektischer Vernunft: Eine Metakritik zu Jean-Paul Sartres "Kritik der dialektischen Vernunft"*, Würzburg: Königshausen & Neumann.

Wolin, Richard 1990, 'Sartre, Heidegger, et l'intelligibilité de l'histoire', *Le Temps modernes*, 531–533: 413–35.

Zervos, Sophie 2009, *Sartre zwischen Freud und Marx: Subjektivität und Identität in Theorie und Literatur*, Hamburg: Dr. Kova.

Index of Names